CHILDREN IN THE HOLOCAUST AND ITS AFTERMATH

CHILDREN IN THE HOLOCAUST AND ITS AFTERMATH

Historical and Psychological Studies of the Kestenberg Archive

Edited by
Sharon Kangisser Cohen, Eva Fogelman, and Dalia Ofer

berghahn
NEW YORK · OXFORD
www.berghahnbooks.com

First published in 2017 by
Berghahn Books
www.berghahnbooks.com

© 2017, 2019 Sharon Kangisser Cohen, Eva Fogelman, and Dalia Ofer
First paperback edition published in 2019

All rights reserved. Except for the quotation of short passages for the purposes of criticism and review, no part of this book may be reproduced in any form or by any means, electronic or mechanical, including photocopying, recording, or any information storage and retrieval system now known or to be invented, without written permission of the publisher.

Library of Congress Cataloging-in-Publication Data

Names: Cohen, Sharon Kangisser, editor. | Fogelman, Eva, editor. | Ofer, Dalia, editor.
Title: Children in the Holocaust and its aftermath : historical and psychological studies of the Kestenberg Archive / edited by Eva Fogelman, Sharon Kangisser Cohen, and Dalia Ofer.
Description: New York : Berghahn Books, [2017] | Includes bibliographical references and index. Identifiers: LCCN 2016053249 (print) | LCCN 2016054798 (ebook) | ISBN 9781785334382 (hardback : alk. paper) | ISBN 9781785334399 (eBook)
Subjects: LCSH: Hebrew University. Kestenberg Archive. | Jewish children in the Holocaust--Interviews. | World War, 1939-1945—Children—Interviews. Classification: LCC D804.48 .C553 2017 (print) | LCC D804.48 (ebook) | DDC 940.53/1809253--dc23
LC record available at https://lccn.loc.gov/2016053249

British Library Cataloguing in Publication Data

A catalogue record for this book is available from the British Library

ISBN 978-1-78533-438-2 hardback
ISBN 978-1-78920-080-5 paperback
ISBN 978-1-78533-439-9 ebook

We would like to dedicate this book to Leah Fogelman, a child survivor of the Holocaust; and to Professor Yehuda Bauer, an inspirational teacher to us all, who believes in the centrality of oral history for Holocaust studies and research.

 # Contents

	Acknowledgments	ix
Introduction		1
	Sharon Kangisser Cohen, Eva Fogelman and Dalia Ofer	

PART ONE: METHODOLOGY

Chapter 1	Age, Circumstance, and Outcome in Child Survivors of the Holocaust: Considerations of the Literature and a Report of a Study Using Narrative Content Analysis	15
	Gila Sandler Saban, K. Mark Sossin, and Anastasia Yasik	

PART TWO: IMMEDIATE POSTWAR PERIOD

Chapter 2	A Child's View: Children's Depositions of the Central Jewish Historical Commission (Poland)	43
	Sharon Kangisser Cohen	
Chapter 3	Starting Over: Reconstituted Families after the Holocaust	62
	Beth B. Cohen	
Chapter 4	"Both Valuable and Difficult": A Meeting Point between Historical and Psychological Interviews	81
	Rita Horváth and Katalin Zana	

PART THREE: POSTWAR MEMORY, COPING MECHANISMS, AND ADJUSTMENT

Chapter 5	Performative Memory-Making and the Future of the Kestenberg Archive	99
	Stephenie Young	

Chapter 6	Shadows of Memory and Intergenerational Legacies in Child Survivors' Testimonies from the Kestenberg Archive *Dana Mihăilescu*	122
Chapter 7	Symbolic Revenge in Holocaust Child Survivors *Nancy Isserman*	150
Chapter 8	Resilience in Child Survivors: History and Application of Coding of the International Study of Organized Persecution of Children *Helene Bass-Wichelhaus*	170

PART FOUR: NON-JEWISH VICTIMS OF WAR AND NAZISM

Chapter 9	"They Were Jews, but They Were Very Kind People": Polish Language Testimonies in the Kestenberg Child Survivor Archive *Katarzyna Person*	187
Chapter 10	War Children in Nazi Germany and World War II *Ilka Quindeau, Katrin Einert, and Nadine Teuber*	200
Chapter 11	Insights into the German Interviews of the Kestenberg Archive: Children of Perpetrators and How They Dealt with Their Parents' Actions *Christina Isabel Brüning*	224

PART FIVE: PERSONAL REFLECTIONS

| Chapter 12 | Always Moving Forward
Andrew Griffel | 249 |

| | Index | 261 |

Acknowledgments

This volume was written as a direct result of the initiative taken by Dr. Eva Fogelman to donate the oral history interviews of the International Study of Organized Persecution of Children founded in 1981 by Judith and Milton Kestenberg to the Oral History Division of the Avraham Harman Institute of Contemporary Jewry at the Hebrew University of Jerusalem. Under the direction of Sharon Kangisser-Cohen 1,500 interviews with Holocaust child survivors and war children from different countries under German occupation and Germany during the third Reich have been digitized and catalogued and preserved making it possible to be used in scholarly research. The archive now known as the Kestenberg Holocaust Child Survivor Archive is continuously adding to its collection follow-up interviews as well as other collections of Holocaust child survivors, including the Kindertransport interviews donated by Melisa Hacker. The digitization of the archive and its catalogue was funded by the Conference on Jewish Material Claims Against Germany and the Fondation pour la Mémoire de la Shoah and Child Development Research.

The publication of this volume was supported by the Dushkin Fund of the Institute of Contemporary Jewry at the Hebrew University of Jerusalem. The editors would also like to thank Janet Kestenberg Amighi for her continued encouragement and financial support to continue to make the world aware of persecution of children and prevention of future genocides. We are thankful to Chris Chappell, senior editor, Jessica Murphy, and Rebecca Rom-Frank at Berghahn Books for believing in this project and for bringing it to fruition. We would also like to thank Ms. Nikki Littman, the language editor for her excellent work. A special thanks goes to Ms. Dalia Sagi, the administrator at the Institute of Contemporary Jewry for all of her work to facilitate the project.

We appreciate the ongoing support we receive from our spouses Udi Cohen, Jerome Chanes and Gur Ofer to continue our commitment to Holocaust scholarship.

Introduction

Sharon Kangisser Cohen, Eva Fogelman, and Dalia Ofer

Reading the testimonies of child survivors of the Holocaust is an emotionally and intellectually challenging exercise that demands listening to disparate narratives simultaneously. In their interviews the survivors recall their suffering as children who were persecuted without mercy, while also remembering, as adults, their tragic past and their lives ever since. They revisit the landscape of their suffering and loss and communicate the ways in which the trauma of their past has continued to impact their lives. Thus, these interviews not only provide a window into the past but also give researchers a way to understand how individuals live with their traumatic past. A child survivor of the Holocaust is defined as any Jewish child, thirteen or under at the start of persecution in their country, who survived in German-occupied Europe by whatever means, whether in hiding, as a partisan, in the ghettos, on the run, or in the camps. Thus, the suffering for some began in Germany in 1933, while for others it started in 1944 in Hungary. The war children are non-Jews who lived in Germany during the Third Reich from 1933 to 1945 or in Poland from the time of the German invasion in 1939 until liberation.

For child survivors to volunteer to speak about their ordeals was antithetical to how most engaged in their post-liberation world. Researchers[1] have argued that for the most part, child survivors of the Holocaust did not speak about their wartime experiences in the postwar years. For many, "not remembering" was key to coping with pain and trauma. Unlike adult survivors, child survivors did not necessarily relate to themselves as survivors in the years immediately following the war. Instead, they tried to adapt themselves to their new environments and to integrate as quickly as possible into their new home environment. This reaction stemmed from a strong need to belong. During the first few decades following the war, child survivors were, therefore, consumed with rebuilding their lives. Despite their silence, they carried their painful memories with them. However, as they began to age, many began to express a willingness and even a need to talk about their past experiences. In their later years, many began to look back at their past and reclaim parts of themselves that were from the foundations of their lives. This phenomenon parallels the development in historiography of the Holocaust in which researchers began to examine the specific experience of children during the Holocaust. For example, an examination of the unique experience of hidden children in Holland was conducted by historian Debórah Dwork in her work *Children with a Star: Jewish Youth in Nazi Europe*.[2] A growing interest in their stories, propelled by historical research and a validation of their pain and suffering, gave child survivors the confidence to speak about their past.

Child Survivor Testimony

Despite the decision of many child survivors not to record their experiences, there were child survivors who were interviewed as part of testimony projects that began immediately after liberation.[3] While some child survivors were interviewed as part of these early projects, it was not until 1979 that historian Yaffa Eliach devoted her audiotape oral history project at Brooklyn College specifically to those who survived the Holocaust as children.[4] The largest collection of child survivor testimony was created in 1981. The Kestenberg Archive of Testimonies of Child Holocaust Survivors (originally the Jerome Riker International Study of Organized Persecution of Children) was initiated by psychoanalyst Judith Kestenberg and attorney Milton Kestenberg. Kestenberg was an attorney who represented Holocaust survivors who applied to the German government for reparations. He assisted survivors in preparing documents on the lasting effects of their ordeals under the Third Reich on their daily functioning and provided emotional support in the face of a German legal system that was denying the physical and psychological damage that they had inflicted on the Jews. Since child survivors could not remember a sequential narrative of their experiences, they were rarely compensated for their traumatization. Milton Kestenberg was instrumental in guiding them to reconstruct a narrative of their years of persecution. Parenthetically, some parents were reluctant for their children to apply for reparations because they did not want to subject them to the memories of their horrific past.

In the meantime, Judith Kestenberg had a few child survivors as psychoanalytic patients in her practice and would discuss her cases with her husband, Milton Kestenberg, who shed light on their traumas. Together they started the Jerome Riker International Study of Organized Persecution of Children in 1981, which mushroomed in 1984 after the American Gathering of Jewish Holocaust Survivors in Philadelphia. The Kestenbergs set up a table at the gathering to register child survivors who were willing to be interviewed. Many of the child survivors believed that they had no story and were reluctant to participate; if their parents had survived, they tended to see themselves as the second generation rather than as survivors per se. Nonetheless, a group showed up to a meeting at the gathering and a new identity—Holocaust child survivors—began to emerge.

The Kestenbergs along with Eva Fogelman organized monthly meetings in New York, similar to the Vietnam veteran rap groups.[5] Each session was an entity into itself with no prearranged topic. There was a core group, initially survivors of ghettos or concentration camps, who attended regularly, and new participants arrived monthly. Members were encouraged to be interviewed. Soon, those who found the interview process a transformative experience encouraged others to be interviewed. There are, however, those who are, to this day, reluctant to be interviewed for fear of breaking down, because they say they do not remember much about the war, or because they live with shame and guilt that they do not want exposed.

What is unique about the Kestenberg interviews is that, first, many of the child survivors were speaking for the first time. Second, the interviews were conducted by mental health professionals. The interviewers were knowledgeable about the historical facts of Europe before World War II, the war years, and post-liberation, but they were also attuned to the psychological ramifications of the child's life both during and after the Holocaust. The team of interviewers learned Judith Kestenberg's kinesthetic techniques of recalling events using all five senses.[6] This was particularly important for enabling the preverbal child survivors to develop a narrative of what they had experienced: for example, trying to imagine who had carried them or how they had been carried in the train to Terezin, or trying to recall the last time they had seen their parent by visualizing the clothes that the parent had worn. Imaginings of what might have happened to the child was another technique that added to the narrative.[7] The Kestenberg interviews were audiotaped and not videotaped and were not shared with family members unless requested. This anonymity enabled interviewees to be more open about their emotions, current lives, and relationships.

The protocol for the Kestenberg interviews evolved over time. Those who were themselves child survivors had to be interviewed before they were allowed to conduct interviews. The Kestenbergs and Eva Fogelman organized training sessions in New York for interviewers. A core committee met on a regular basis to review the questions. The interview was semistructured in nature, meaning that the interviewee was told to speak about his or her life before, during, and after the Holocaust, and the interviewer followed the flow with the ultimate goal of guiding the interviewee to achieve a sense of integration. A fragmented life developed coherence as the interviewer led the survivor to express a sequential narrative.

The best explanation of a semi-structured interview was offered by Rachel Auerbach who conducted interviews with survivors at Yad Vashem in the 1950s and 1960s:

> We must let the witness speak freely and follow the thread of his reconstructed individual narrative in as natural a manner as possible. We must guide him, but without needlessly interrupting the flow of his speech, except very gently and discreetly, without detracting from the vein of inspiration and air of confession we have stimulated. We must not forget that, from a certain perspective, the testimony is the witness's autobiographical account, whose focal point is the witness himself—what he saw and what happened to him—and that only on this basis can his story serve as the basis for historical research. This does not mean that the witness is the subject of the testimony. The subject of the testimony is the event, the phenomenon, the fate of the individual as an instance of the fates of many people, which reflects the situation of a society and a people—a picture of an era.[8]

Many of the child survivors were interviewed at least twice. In the second interview survivors often discussed experiences that they may not have been ready to speak about initially. The interviewers were also able to review the first interview and assess what was missing in their life story. The second interview was also an opportunity to ask more-specific questions about aging, identity, memory, and childhood games, among other more idiosyncratic subjects.

Although many of the earlier oral history collections focused on the experience of the war, collections created in the late 1980s and 1990s moved toward a life story approach, mirroring the dominant trend in oral history as a whole. The questionnaires were developed by psychologists, and the aim of the project was to record life both before, during, and after the Holocaust, thus illustrating how the war affected the individual's life and fortitude.

Similar to other oral history projects, the Kestenberg collection's rationale changed and developed over time. After conducting a number of interviews, it became clear that an additional rationale was the therapeutic value for conducting interviews with survivors of the Holocaust. The interviewees were seen to benefit from having a listening ear and having their suffering, pain, and losses validated. Interviewing a traumatized person about life before, during, and after the dehumanization, persecution, and multiple losses facilitates the integration of self. A survivor values being perceived as a total human being and not just a victim. It is popularly assumed that an individual who underwent trauma must inevitably suffer from posttraumatic stress disorder (PTSD). The various analyses of these interviews, however, allow us to move beyond the typical PTSD stereotype of historical trauma victims. Researchers are able to explore the interaction between socialization, personal characteristics, the trauma, and all the situational factors, past and present. Thus, coping behavior, attitudes, and feelings are neither monolithic nor static. Furthermore, the interview facilitated the integration of the self that had been fragmented with a self from before and after the persecution. The very process of the interview motivated some child survivors to search for meaning rather than to connect to the past and losses through survivor guilt or identification with the victimization. Writing memoirs, attending commemorations, educating young people, speaking to adult audiences, returning to one's home or the place of persecution, working in the helping professions, or speaking up for other traumatized groups have all been proved to be channels for healing.

Unlike other projects, the Kestenberg collection includes all groups of children who the Kestenbergs defined as "victims of war." While the majority are Jewish survivors, they are not the only interviewees. The suffering of other groups, particularly Polish non-Jewish children, is also documented and recorded, revealing the extent of the criminality of National Socialist (or Nazi) racial policy: while singling out the Jews, the Nazis also persecuted those they considered "racially inferior" or "undesirable" population groups, including even Germans. By incorporating interviews conducted with non-Jewish children who lived through World War II, this collection gives voice to the suffering of children who lived under Nazi occupation and whose lives were invariably affected and irrevocably changed. It includes interviews with individuals whose parents were Nazi perpetrators. The project thus makes a bold statement about children who are victimized as a result of their parents' actions and choices and who suffer the repercussions of this throughout their lives.

Children in the Holocaust and Its Aftermath is an interdisciplinary study by researchers who examined the Kestenberg archive. This archive comprises more than 1,500 testimonies of child survivors worldwide, of war children from Germany and Poland, and of some caretakers. It also includes immediate post-liberation depositions taken by the Central Jewish Historical Commission (CJHC) in Poland. Due to both its geographical and experiential scope, the archive provides scholars with an invaluable and ongoing resource that the researchers of this volume have examined from different scholarly positions in their diverse fields.

Three of the chapters in this volume examine the testimonies of non-Jews who were children during World War II. Katarzyna Person discusses and compares the testimonies of Polish Jewish and Polish non-Jewish survivors; Christina Brüning describes how the children of perpetrators dealt with their parents' actions; and Ilka Quindeau, Katrin Einert, and Nadine Teuber, who conducted their own interviews with children who grew up during the Third Reich that are to be included in the Kestenberg archive, examine accounts of these children's experiences during the war and how these experiences impacted their postwar lives. In addition, their analysis of the oral histories of war children reveals that some experienced PTSD symptoms as a result both of living through the terror of war and of the nature of the parent–child relationship.

In their interviews the child survivors did not only convey their wartime experiences, but also depicted the early postwar period during which they struggled to reestablish their lives. In her chapter, Beth Cohen uses interviews from the Kestenberg archive to describe the reconstruction of Jewish families in the wake of the Shoah. Her chapter contributes to our understanding of the immediate postwar years and the challenges faced by survivors in rebuilding their lives. Dana Mihăilescu examines the survivors' postwar experiences, particularly the impact of family structure on the children's memory and personality development. Helene Bass-Wichelhaus discusses the attribute of resilience among child survivors, while Nancy Isserman's study is a psychological work on the attitudes of survivors toward the perpetrators, and, in particular, on their expressions of revenge.

The specific geographical location during and after the Holocaust has an added dimension that sheds light on the impact of trauma on the coping mechanisms and identities of child survivors. The postwar context also contributes to the coping of child survivors. In their chapter, Rita Horváth and Katalin Zana discuss the specific characteristics of the Holocaust in Hungary and how they have impacted the way survivors and their children have interpreted and reacted to their postwar lives. There are very few works with a comparative analysis of the postwar context of survivor communities, a context that invariably affected how these individuals related to their past. This collection of chapters therefore fills this gap and presents the reader with the beginning of a comparative account.

The use of qualitative interviews is a research tool used in many disciplines as a way of understanding the complexity of the individual experience. The fact that the interview is used in areas as disparate as the humanities, social sciences, legal studies, and medicine attests to its richness and to the opportunities it presents for furthering our grasp on human behavior and experience. Due to its plurality, there is, of course, no one theoretical and methodological approach in this collection, and this is the source of its richness. In a chapter on the long-term effects of the Holocaust on child survivors, Gila Saban, Mark Sossin, and Anastasia Yasik raise methodological questions relating to qualitative research by employing both qualitative and quantitative research designs to study their narratives. Using a narrative content analysis, they demonstrate that parental competence and maternal adjustment have the greatest impact on the child's functioning in later life.

The use of the interview as the basis of research also represents a shift in the politics or positioning of the research subject. Interviewees are not the objects but rather the subjects of research, a point that is discussed in Sharon Kangisser Cohen's chapter examining early reports given by child survivors of the Holocaust to the CJHC in Poland. Although the interviews collected by the CJHC were written up by the interviewers and not the interviewees, thereby affecting the construction of their personal narratives, the memories that the survivors articulate gives them more authority in determining what children remember from the war years. This trend of research exemplifies what historians have defined as the democratization of history or history from the bottom up, which puts the voice of individuals at the center of the historical narrative and proves the significance of oral history interviews to historical inquiry. Interviews are used by historians to reconstruct a historical period and to experience and introduce "new evidence from the underside . . . by bringing recognition to substantial groups of people who have been ignored."[9] Through the interview, the historian is able to trace both individual and collective consciousness that is, according to Paul Thompson, "part and parcel of that very past."[10]

Testimony is particularly important in terms of the history of the Shoah. From its inception, Yad Vashem recognized the importance of collecting oral testimonies from survivors, because verbal testimony that is given by survivors constitutes virtually the only material regarding the fate of the victims. Yehuda Bauer further points out, "Because the documentation is largely one-sided, that is German, survivors' testimonies are crucial to understanding the events of the period. They become extremely useful and reliable when cross-checked with and borne out by many other testimonies. They are then, I would argue, at least as reliable as a written document of the time."[11] However, the use of oral history or qualitative interviews is seen by some scholars as problematic for scholarly inquiry or the investigation of the past. Memory is a never-ending topic in examining oral histories. Some claim that memory is an unreliable source: accuracy diminishes with time and is vulnerable to a broad range of interfering stimuli. The vividness of remote memories depends heavily on rehearsal (i.e., thinking and talking about them), and yet studies have shown that the more frequently they are reproduced, the less accurate they become. Unpleasant facts may be forgotten or repressed. New information can interfere with memory, modifying and distorting it. Once incorporated into the original memory, the memory cannot be distinguished from what is actually reconstructed, especially after much time has elapsed.[12] Furthermore, scholars have debated whether the earlier testimonies are more authentic historically than later testimonies. Dalia Ofer has concluded that

> the assertion that earlier accounts are fuller, more authentic, and more accurate is not necessarily true. The most important areas in which later testimony has added to our store of knowledge are associated with daily life in the ghettos and labor camps, problems of human relations, the world of the individual, and relations between the individual and the community. When they retold their stories a generation later, the survivors assigned more importance to the family and home and to their childhood experiences before and during the Holocaust. This is especially noticeable among those who were children during the war: at the remove of decades they frequently include friends and teachers in their life stories.[13]

She further emphasized that historiography of the Holocaust has evolved. Thus, "the belated testimonies, with the information they contain, can offer fresh information and insights, a new understanding and reevaluation of society and the individual during the Holocaust. Historians read them critically, drawing on other disciplines in order to appreciate the various elements that shape the testimonies and to learn how to read them as history."[14]

Yet, scholars who use qualitative interviews in their research view memory as a vehicle through which the past is not reproduced but rather reconstructed and conveyed and through which the individuals impart their sense of the past and their identity. Life stories or narrative interviews uncover more than just the historical circumstances of the individuals' lives; they are also, as Jerome Bruner pointed out, testimonies on the "meaning of experience."[15] While acknowledging that memory changes over time, this approach views these transitions or changes as something that enhances understanding of the individuals. As Alessandro Portelli explained: "the discrepancies and the errors are themselves events, clues for the work of desire and pain over time, for the painful search for meaning."[16] In Stephenie Young's chapter she studies the Kestenberg interviews in order to understand how the individual's memory is influenced by the incorporation of public memory; how the post-Holocaust context has influenced the individuals' testimony.

The last chapter in the volume was written by Andrew Griffel, a child survivor who was himself recently interviewed for the Kestenberg collection. Griffel's chapter is not his testimony but rather a self-exploration and reflection of his experience and its effect on his life. It represents an individual in dialogue with himself and his memories, a constant reinterpretation and renegotiation of the events he has lived through in light of subsequent life events. It is an important reminder that when we use testimony as the basis of scholarly research we are writing about peoples' lives in which self-representation and understanding are often dynamic. Furthermore, his chapter highlights that while researchers often use certain aspects of the individuals' testimony to discuss a particular theme or issue, the individual is larger and more complex than any of the features we might be trying to understand.

Authors

Eva Fogelman is a social psychologist, psychotherapist, and filmmaker. She is the codirector of the International Study of Organized Persecution of Children, a project of Child Development Research. She pioneered awareness groups for the children of Holocaust survivors and intergenerational groups. She is also the founding codirector of Generations of the Holocaust and Related Traumas, and the Training Institute of Mental Health, as well as the founding director of the Jewish Foundation for Christian Rescuers, now the Jewish Foundation for the Righteous. She is the author of the Pulitzer Prize–nominated *Conscience and Courage: Rescuers of Jews During the Holocaust*, coeditor of *Children During the Nazi Reign: Psychological Perspective of the Interview Process*, and writer and coproducer of the award-winning documentary *Breaking the Silence: The Generation After the Holocaust*. She is, in addition, an adviser to the United States Holocaust Memorial Museum.

Sharon Kangisser Cohen is the Director of the Diane and Eli Zborowski Centre for the Study of the Holocaust and Its Aftermath and the Deportation Project at The International Institute for Holocaust Research, Yad Vashem. She is, in addition, a lecturer at Haifa University and the Rothberg School for international students at the Hebrew University of Jerusalem. She holds a PhD from the Hebrew University in the field of Holocaust studies, and has published numerous articles relating to the postwar lives of survivors of the Holocaust. Her most recent book, *Testimony and Time: Survivors of the Holocaust Remember*, was published in 2015 by Yad Vashem.

Dalia Ofer is the Max and Rita Haber Professor of Holocaust and East European Studies at the Hebrew University of Jerusalem (emerita). She was head of the Avraham Harman Institute of Contemporary Jewry (2003–2007) and of the Vidal Sassoon International Research Center for the Study of Antisemitism (1995–2002). Her book *Escaping the Holocaust: Illegal Immigration to the Land of Israel* (Oxford University Press, 1990) received the Ben Zvi award and the 1992 National Jewish Book Award. Her coedited volume, *Women in the Holocaust* (Yale University Press, 1999), was also a finalist for two National Jewish Book Awards. She is the coeditor of *Jewish Women: A Comprehensive Historical Encyclopedia* (Shalvi Publishing, 2007) and more recently of *Holocaust Survivors: Resettlement, Memories, Identities* (Berghahn, 2012), as well as the editor of *Israel in the Eyes of the Survivors* (Hebrew; Yad Vashem, 2014).

Notes

1. For more on this issue see Kestenberg and Fogelman, *Children during the Nazi Reign;* Kangisser Cohen, *Child Survivors;* Kestenberg and Brenner, *The Last Witness;* Krell, "Child Survivors of the Holocaust: 40 Years Later, Introduction"; Moskovitz and Krell, "Child Survivors of the Holocaust."
2. Dwork, *Children with a Star.*
3. In Lublin as early as 1944, the Central Jewish Historical Commission in Poland interviewed Holocaust survivors in order to get an account of their wartime experiences. This interview project expanded to other European communities, such as the Wiener Library in London, the Centre of Contemporary Jewish Documentation in Paris, and the Jewish Historical Institute in Warsaw. Between 1945 and 1946 the staff of the National Committee for Attending Deportees in Hungary (DEGOB), recorded the personal stories of approximately 5,000 Hungarian Holocaust survivors. The first to record survivor testimonies electronically and thus provide audio testimonies was American psychologist David Boder. Boder used a wire recorder for his 1946 project and gathered more than one hundred testimonies. Electronic recording of survivor testimonies did not, however, become general practice until a decade later, in the 1950s, when museums and memorials throughout the world began developing their own collections with survivors. The earliest of these collections was established at Yad Vashem, which began collecting testimonies in the late 1950s and 1960s.
4. The Yaffa Eliach child survivor interviews are now housed at the Museum of Jewish Heritage, New York City.
5. Lifton, *Home from the War*, 75–95.
6. Kestenberg, "Overview of the Effect of Psychological Research Interviews on Child Survivors" 5–13.

7. Ibid.; Kestenberg, "Overview of the Effect of Interviews, 63.
8. Auerbach, "A guide for collecting testimony", 6
9. Thompson, *Voice of the Past,* 8.
10. Ibid., 172.
11. Bauer, *Rethinking the Holocaust,* 25.
12. Niewyk, *Fresh Wounds,* 2. For more on this issue refer to Browning, *Collected Memories.*
13. Ofer, "The Community and the Individual," 532.
14. Ibid., 535.
15. Bruner, "Narrative and Paradigmatic Modes of Thought," 97.
16. Portelli, *The Order Has Been Carried Out,* 16.

References

Auerbach, Rachel. "Mekorot ve drakhim hadashim li-gviyat 'eduyot'" (A guide for collecting testimony). *Yedi'ot Yad* Vashem 2 (July 29, 1954). Bauer, Yehuda. *Rethinking the Holocaust.* Yale University Press, 2002.
Browning, Christopher. *Collected Memories Holocaust History and Postwar Testimony.* Madison: University of Wisconsin Press, 2003.
Bruner, Jerome. "Narrative and Paradigmatic Modes of Thought." In *Learning and Teaching the Ways of Knowing: 84th Yearbook of the National Society for the Study of Education,* edited by E. Eisner, 97–115. Chicago: University of Chicago Press, 1985.
Dwork, Debórah. *Children with a Star: Jewish Youth in Nazi Europe.* New Haven, CT: Yale University Press, 1991.
Kangisser Cohen, S. *Child Survivors of the Holocaust in Israel: Finding their Voice. Social Dynamics and Postwar Experiences.* Portland, Oregon and Brighton: Sussex Academic Press, 2005.
Kestenberg, Judith S. "Overview of the Effect of Psychological Research Interviews on Child Survivors." In *Children during the Nazi Reign: Psychological Perspective in the Interview Process,* edited by Judith S. Kestenberg and Eva Fogelman, 27–28. Westport, CT: Praeger, 1994.
Kestenberg, Judith S., and Ira Brenner. *The Last Witness: The Child Survivor of the Holocaust.* Washington: American Psychiatric Association, 1996
Kestenberg, J., and E. Fogelman (eds.). "Overview of the Effect of Psychological Research Interviews on Child Survivors." In *Children during the Nazi Reign: Psychological Perspective on the Interview Process.* Westport, CT: Praeger: 1994.
Kestenberg, M. "The Effect of Interviews on Child Survivors—Child Survivors Revisited. In *Children During the Nazi Reign: Psychological Perspective on the Interview Process.* edited by Judith S. Kestenberg and Eva Fogelman, *57–71.* Westport, CT: Praeger, 1994.
Krell, Robert. "Child Survivors of the Holocaust: 40 Years Later Introduction." *Journal of the American Academy of Child Psychiatry* 24, no. 4 (1985): 378–380.
Lifton, R.J. *Home from the War: Vietnam Veteran Neither Victims nor Executioners.* New York: Simon and Schuster, 1973.

Moskovitz, Sarah, and Robert Krell. "Child Survivors of the Holocaust: Psychological Adaptations to Survival." *Israel Journal of Psychiatry and Related Sciences* 27, no. 2, (1990): 81–91.
Niewyk, Donald L. *Fresh Wounds: Early Narratives of Holocaust Survival.* Chapel Hill: University of North Carolina Press, 1988.
Ofer, D. "The Community and the Individual: The Different Narratives of Early and Late Testimonies and their Significance for Historians." In *Holocaust Historiography*, edited by David Bankier, 519–535. Jerusalem: Yad Vashem, 2009.
Portelli, Alessandro. *The Order Has Been Carried Out: History, Memory and Meaning of a Nazi Massacre in Rome.* New York: Palgrave Macmillan, 2004.
Thompson, Paul. *The Voice of the Past: Oral History.* Oxford: Oxford University Press, 1998.

PART ONE

METHODOLOGY

 1

AGE, CIRCUMSTANCE, AND OUTCOME IN CHILD SURVIVORS OF THE HOLOCAUST

Considerations of the Literature and a Report of a Study Using Narrative Content Analysis

Gila Sandler Saban, K. Mark Sossin, and Anastasia Yasik

Introduction and Overview

Narratives elicited in interviews of child Holocaust survivors provide historical testimony as well as emotive and heartrending descriptions of subjective experience of exposure to trauma. Each survivor's distinctive story of life before, during, and after the Holocaust is woven into his or her own autobiographical memory. Their stories incorporate elements that are explicitly recalled, often elaborated semantically, and consciously retained. Procedural and unconscious facets of memory also contribute to the way the story is remembered and told, though these are generally more embodied and sensorimotor. Interview narratives, as conducted and considered within the framework of the International Study of Organized Persecution of Children (ISOPC) Child Development Research (CDR),[1] underscore each survivor's uniqueness while contributing to more-generalized conclusions about children's psychological processing of their encounters with atrocity, brutality, loss, separation, fear, encampment, hiding, and more.

As the ISOPC archive has grown, we have sought to expand what we know about children and findings regarding lasting psychological effects to more-recent state-sponsored persecutions and genocides. Methodologically, interviews have been valuably viewed individually, comparatively, and inductively, often informed within a psychoanalytic frame. We may further examine elements of the narratives themselves because they may index mental and emotional states. The application of narrative coding analysis and the highlighting of various categories and dimensions of experience may offer further knowledge about interviewees' states of mind. Formalizing a priori narrative analytic methods and mixed-method designs (looking at both qualitative and quantitative data) can contribute substantively to both exploratory and hypothesis-testing approaches. Herein, we exemplify how one such approach is applied to the ISOPC interviews, using a well-developed method of narrative content analysis.

This study is conducted against the background of an aging and decreasing number of Holocaust survivors, a world in which organized child persecution sadly persists, and within a fast-growing field of trauma psychology. The research looks to benefit the living child survivors of the Holocaust. In addition, be it from the experience or witnessing of abuse,[2] violence,[3] natural disasters,[4] terrorism,[5] or war,[6] children across the world continue to be challenged by the hardship of recovering from trauma. Although progress has been made in framing interventions for children in the immediate wake of trauma and loss, questions still remain regarding the long-term outcome for individuals who have been traumatized by systematized persecution. Factors contributing to symptoms of posttraumatic stress disorder (PTSD), depression, and anxiety, as well as fear of separation and interpersonal difficulties,[7] need further explication. Children suffer from disruption of primary attachments, while also demonstrating vulnerability to intergenerational transmission of stress and distress from their traumatized parents.[8] Assessment of posttraumatic sequelae, analysis of comorbidity and differential diagnosis,[9] and the study of treatment efficacy utilizing various approaches,[10] have all contributed to a substantive literature.

Utilizing a portion of the ISOPC archive, this study examines long-term effects of the Holocaust on child survivors. Both within and outside of this project, child survivors have borne witness, written memoirs, and volunteered and participated in professionally conducted interviews[11] in which they have recounted their stories in great detail. Many narratives have been reviewed qualitatively, while quantitative studies have generally involved survey or target-question responses regarding experiences during and in the aftermath of the war.[12] The narratives themselves are rarely transposed into quantitative data. In the broader psychology literature, the strengths of both qualitative and quantitative approaches are increasingly combined and include narrative coding designs wherein transcribed verbal accounts are organized and systematically analyzed using specific criteria.[13] Formalized narrative coding analysis tools have been developed for use in evaluating themes, content,[14] and process variables. These narrative content research methodologies have been shown to be relevant to psychological and diagnostic variables, lending support for the application of such methods to Holocaust- and persecution-related interviews.

Perspectives Relevant to the Life Trajectories of Child Survivors

Many child survivors of the Holocaust have demonstrated tremendous resilience as they rebuilt their lives, raised families, and engaged in successful careers.[15] Many others have confronted underlying social emotional difficulties in their adult lives due to early traumatic histories.[16] Success in one realm of life did not preclude difficulties in another. Some child survivors have had difficulties forming and maintaining close and intimate relationships,[17] as well as with child bearing,[18] parenting, and, upon death of a loved one, managing grief.[19] Child survivors who were hidden during the time of war have shown ongoing difficulties regarding integration of identity. They endured the loss of their own familial, communal, and religious traditions,[20] while assuming alternative self-characteristics in order to survive.[21] Emotional constriction resulted from the need to repress natural spontaneity by remaining silent, controlling their voices, cries, laughter, and, at times, bodily functions, so as not to draw attention to themselves. Prior research has documented that child survivors have shown vulnerability to a delayed onset of PTSD, as well as features of anxiety[22] and depression.[23]

Factors identified in the literature as heightening risk for long-term adjustment difficulties (as reflected in symptom-development and reduced levels of quality of life in adulthood) include: age at the time of the trauma, implying a host of cognitive, psychodynamic, developmental factors, and the critical nature of the postwar situation. Immediately after the end of the war and liberation, child survivors were confronted with the reality of their losses and had to endure new transitions and adjustments.

Age has been examined from a developmental perspective with regard to attachment and coping with loss and distress. Kestenberg and Brenner noted that adults who were older children and adolescents when under persecution were often later able to hold onto positive prewar memories. By contrast, many adults who were younger children when under persecution had little or fragmented recollections of their parents and their families, and some did not even know their own names. Hence, it has been reported that those who were youngest later struggled to recall and make sense of their own histories, lacking an internalized secure attachment to a parent or caregiver. Those who did not have a close surrogate figure or who were institutionalized during and after the war lacked sufficient attachment representations, further complicating their ability to form meaningful relationships in adulthood.

Developmental psychology finds that while declarative memories are undeveloped and fragmented among those who are quite young, procedural, kinesthetic and olfactory memories are strong. Sensory stimuli that resemble those that were present when memories were encoded will elicit recollections from early childhood. Preverbal procedural memories are critical in attachment and developing mentalization processes. Because children at a young age make sense of their world through their bodies, many of these children were found to express somatic complaints as adults linked to their traumatic experiences. Young survivors often had only fragmented prewar memories, leading some researchers[24] to conclude that age was more critical than the nature of the trauma (e.g., in concentration camp versus in hiding) in determining later outcome for child survivors.

The current study was designed to study the factor of age empirically, while modeling use of narrative analysis, because it has potential for further use in child survivor research.

Method

Findings as Reported in This Chapter

Though sound scientific and statistical methods were employed throughout the data analysis, in the reported findings below the authors have avoided mathematical jargon that is more likely to be found in a professional journal. Most correspondences between constructs were identified using Pearson-r correlations, and inter-rater reliability was tested using intraclass correlations (ICC). Multiple interaction effects among constructs were identified using regression analyses. The following rubric informed the text: (1) All correspondences reported met minimal criteria for significance; in other words, the chance that the relationship reported is genuine, and not random, is 95 percent or greater. Though additional results may, upon further investigation, turn out to be meaningful, a conservative approach was adopted. (2) Consistent with research standards, if the significant result attained a correlation of 0.20 or less it is reported as small, if it is between 0.21 and 0.35 it is reported as medium, and if it is above 0.35 it is reported as large. Of course, precise statistical details are available to readers and researchers who may want them. Study procedures and results will be summarized, followed by a discussion of what was gleaned.

Procedure and Participants

One hundred interviews were randomly selected from ISOPC CDR archive from among four hundred English language–transcribed interviews. Reliability was established between ratings conducted by the current researcher and the original coding[25] that was conducted by the original coders of the Kestenberg Archive of Testimonies of Child Holocaust Survivors across half the sample, as well as between the current researcher and a co-rater across the other half of the sample. Since several of the original *Code Book* items are on a three-point Likert scale, the first author developed and used a modified five-point Likert scale because such an expansion allows for greater precision in defining the range of variables. An evaluation was conducted to determine whether using the five-point scale yields more-reliable coding results and whether this impacts the findings.

Of the hundred interviews included in this study, 57 percent were of women. The majority of the data (58%) was gathered from individuals who were between the ages of 50–59 at the time they were interviewed, followed by 22 percent who were 60–69 years old, 19 percent who were 40–49, and one individual over 70. The mean age of the interviewees at the onset of persecution was 6.58 ($SD = 4.60$), ranging from birth to 14 years of age. Specifically, 15 percent were from birth to 12 months, 17 percent were 1–3 years of age, 15 percent were 4–6 years of age, 28 percent were 7–10 years of age, and 25 percent were 11–14 years of age.

The transcribed interviews were uploaded for coding and scoring by the Psychiatric Content Analysis and Diagnosis (PCAD) 2000 Gottschalk-Gleser Scales[26] on a specified set of constructs. The PCAD computerized narrative analysis brings inherent advantages and disadvantages in comparison to purely qualitative analysis. While the PCAD is not as nuanced, associative, or insight-bearing as a trained clinician, an advantage is that applying the same exact coding and analytic procedures to each interview transcript fosters comparative study and the application of parametric statistics, yielding rich data. In addition, all hundred interviews were read by and coded on items from the original CDR *Code Book*, as well as the revised *Code Book* items.[27]

Measures

Age

Age was measured as a continuous variable according to *Code Book* item #9: "Child's age at start of persecution (in country of origin): years, months."[28] Measuring age at onset of persecution is consistent with prior studies.[29]

Early Memories

Quality of early memories was assessed using Likert scale CDR *Code Book* items and revised items pertaining to quality and intensity of prewar memories. High and sufficient inter-rater reliability was established between the current researcher and the original raters of the data and between the current researcher and the co-rater.

Postwar Situation

Again, CDR *Code Book* items and revisions thereof pertained to postwar physical and mental health, postwar parenting, the competence of parents during the postwar period, and postwar adjustment of parents to daily life and functioning. Varying within high and sufficient ranges, inter-rater reliability was established between the first author and the co-rater, as well as between the first author and the original raters of the data for all variables except for questions regarding paternal adjustment, an item for which reliability was not established. Hence, the original and revised paternal adjustment variables were removed from analysis.

Depression, Anxiety, and Quality of Life

These constructs and subcomponents were measured using the computerized version of the original paper-pencil Gottschalk-Gleser Scales Scales[30] called the PCAD 2000,[31] which is a tool that has been used in a variety of clinical contexts.[32]

The derived codes transcribed verbal data into measurable psychological constructs such as depression, anxiety, and quality of life. As the PCAD 2000 transposes verbal data into measurable psychological constructs, it divides each construct into subcategories that are further operationalized and coded. For example, one subcategory on the Depression Scale, "hostility outward," may be further identified as "overt" exemplified by "self killing, fighting, injuring other individuals or threatening to do so." Each code is assigned a numerical weight based on the level of intensity represented by that category.

Norms and Reliability for This Measure

The Gottschalk-Gleser Scales have been normed on both male and female adults (age 18 and older) and both male and female children (age 17 and younger).[33] Inter-rater reliability was reported to be very high for human scoring, and very high between the computerized and manual versions. Reliability improves with the length of the narrative sample. No upper limit has yet been defined. Studies in other languages and cultures confirmed original normative, reliability, and validity studies.[34]

Results

Notably, no significant associations were found between wartime variables, specifically age at onset of persecution, valence of prewar memories, postwar health, maternal competence, and paternal competence, and mental health and distress difficulties. These adulthood mental health factors included depression, anxiety, and quality of life.

Examination of hypothesized correspondences between postwar parenting on experiences of depression, anxiety, and quality of life in adulthood also found no evidence of consistent concurrence. For example, there was no evidence supporting the model that, viewed as a group, later mental health factors varied as functions of whether the child survivor was parented by others (other relatives, adoptive parents, foster care, group homes, orphanages), by their own parents, or by no identifiable parent figure during the immediate postwar period.

However, age at onset of persecution showed significant and medium-strength correspondences to mutilation anxiety and shame anxiety subtypes of a broader anxiety measure on the Gottschalk scales. Children who were younger when persecution began tended to show greater levels of anxiety related to fear of injury experienced as an adult. The younger the child was at onset of persecution, the higher the level of anxiety related to feelings of inadequacy and humiliation the individual experienced in adulthood.

Both maternal and paternal competences were significantly correlated with separation anxiety in adulthood (demonstrating a high correspondence using the original measure of maternal competence, and a medium correspondence using the revised measure). Findings of correspondence between postwar parenting and anxiety are somewhat more robust than the age-anxiety correlations, highlighting the importance of quality of parenting in the immediate postwar period in cases of parents and children who were reunited. Those who experienced poorer parenting by their parents during the postwar period showed greater degrees of anxiety related to loss and abandonment in adulthood.

Maternal and paternal competences in the immediate postwar period were each found to be highly correlated with separation depression. Age at onset of persecution was found to be a predictor for self-accusation. This medium-level association suggests that the younger the individual was when exposed to persecution, the greater the degree of certain feelings of negative self-regard, specifically guilt, shame, and hostility, each directed inward as experienced in adulthood.

As with anxiety, the quality of postwar parenting was found to have a stronger link than age to depression in adulthood. Specifically, those with poorer parenting in the aftermath of the war showed higher levels of depression related to loss of, and abandonment by, loved ones.

No significant associations were demonstrated between components of the quality of life scale and mental health in adulthood. Furthermore, age at onset of persecution showed no direct correspondence to somatic concerns or health and sickness.

In order to assess how the intensity of prewar memories might influence the relationship between age at the onset of persecution and specific mental health variables such as depression, anxiety, and quality of life, interaction effects were analyzed. The combination of age [the younger the child, the greater the effect] and the intensity [on a scale from low to high, the more negative the memory] serves as a predictor of anxiety, nearly a predictor of depression, and not a predictor of quality of life. Maternal adjustment (derived from the original 1997 CDR *Code Book*) was found to be a predictor for depression in adulthood, meaning that those whose mothers had a poorer postwar adjustment to social and work life showed higher levels of depression later in life. (Notably, Maternal Adjustment-R, the variable revised for the current study to increase reliability, did not show significant results. This discrepancy warrants further exploration.)

Discussion

Findings and Conclusions

Overall, findings punctuate the complexity of predicting and tracking long-term effects of Holocaust trauma experiences. Alongside the findings reported, the lack of support for some generalized effects of age, as well as wartime and postwar parenting variables in relation to later mental health characteristics, reminds us of multifaceted influences on vulnerability and resilience evident in each individual's storied life trajectory. As reflected in the conscientious and highly pondered clinical case studies evident in this text and in the broader Holocaust literature, a host of constitutional, experiential, and nuanced biographic factors become channeled into deeply personal narratives that cannot be substituted for by overarching generalizations. Even significant results must be kept in perspective, because exceptions are to be expected.

Though the current study regarding child Holocaust survivors did not find many direct and consistent effects of the broadest predictor variables—specifically, age, prewar experiences/memories, postwar physical and mental health, postwar parenting circumstances, and postwar parenting competencies—with mental health sequelae in adulthood, more fine-tuned and interactional analyses substantiated the importance of developmental factors in understanding the impact of persecutory trauma. Furthermore, the employment of narrative analysis shows promise for future studies of Holocaust interview data. Further use of the Gottschalk-Gleser Scale appears warranted in this regard, because only a small portion of narrative analytics were directly examined in the current study. The current study finds that age at the onset of persecution appears significantly associated with two out of six Gottschalk-Gleser anxiety subscales and one of seven depression subscales. Specifically, child survivors impacted when relatively older were found to have higher levels of mutilation anxiety, and child survivors impacted when relatively younger were found to have higher levels of shame anxiety and a greater degree of self-accusation. While age at the onset of persecution may not, in a simple and generalizable way, be associated with global mental health in adulthood, specific patterns may emerge that correspond to developmental factors as manifested in their personality traits. Findings suggest that children experiencing persecution when older were more inclined to be haunted by trauma-laden memories of what was witnessed, while children who were younger at the time of persecution were inclined to remember (and cast later experiences into) states of helplessness, humiliation, and self-denigration. Consistent with recent infant microanalytic research, when caregivers are themselves depressed, highly stressed, and/or traumatized, transmission of negative emotional or unmentalized states, channeled nonverbally (as through rhythms of bodily tension) bears negative influence on the young child's self-regulation and the dyad's interactive regulation.

Prior researchers[35] found that children who were relatively older at the time of persecution coped better later in life since they were able to grasp the nature of their circumstances. It may be that these older children had a greater awareness of the dangers around them, linked to heightened experiences of mutilation anxiety rather than to a general or other subtype of anxiety. This greater level of perception and awareness of brutal realities in childhood understandably laid an experiential ground for persistence of related anxiety in adulthood. The link between younger age and greater shame anxiety and self-accusation depression highlights the vulnerability of the younger child exposed to trauma to self-diminution. Lacking anchors for trust, security, and basic safety, the child living through the Holocaust often lacked the benefits of responsive parenting and more typically emerging experiences of control. Caregivers (some of whom were parents, and some not), themselves highly stressed and/or traumatized, could not generate the emotional availability nor the affirming gaze and gestures that build a foundation of pride within a child. This very lack of prideful reflection likely contributed to the over-determined development of shame and anxiety.

Inadequate early development of security, pride and an anchored sense of self result in a lack of trust in oneself and others, as well as shame and insecurity about oneself, heightened difficulties managing anxiety states, and obstacles in the attainment of reflective functioning. Many interviewers and clinicians working with child survivors, including Kestenberg,[36] Fogelman,[37] Valent,[38] and Brenner[39] have commented on the sense of shame that persists in the psyches of young child survivor victims. For many, their own self-valuation was compromised as they held themselves responsible for experiences of abandonment, for identification with a scorned group, and for various forms of victimization suffered.

The correspondence between problematic attachment to caregivers and the development of shame has been explicated[40] psychodynamically as well as in empirical studies underscoring the relationship between the quality of early attachment relationships and the way shame-memories are structured.[41] Attachment disruptions between young children and caregivers likely contribute to the association between younger age at the time of trauma and experiencing shame anxiety in adulthood.

Though parents often went to great lengths to save their young children during the Holocaust, leaving them with other families or institutions, the children, nonetheless, often felt abandoned,[42] and some internalized a sense of being inherently rejectable, a self-state linked to shame.[43]

Younger children with worse prewar memories showed higher levels of anxiety and moderately higher levels of depression than their counterparts, suggesting that memories are internalized and impact functioning later in adulthood. No simple relationship was found between postwar physical and mental health and psychological well-being in adulthood. It seems likely that these large-scale factors do not have the specificity needed to predict long-term effects. They can be more fruitfully examined in conjunction with other postwar variables such as parenting and socialization. The postwar physical and mental health status of child survivors were in and of themselves outcome effects of the traumatic experience they endured. Similarly, no simple relationship was found between the familial/nonfamilial relationship with the individual who parented the child during the postwar period and mental health in adulthood. Perhaps the quality of caregiving (i.e., responsiveness, empathy, structure, support) was more important than the familial tie of those who actually took on the role of parenting the child. Additionally, many children had multiple types of postwar parenting, with many changes during a relatively short period of time.

A closer look at the nature of caregiving and nurturing during the postwar phase, as well as the impact of unpredictability and change, may prove meaningful. While no significant relationships were found between parental competence during the immediate postwar period and the broad facets of psychological well-being in adulthood, both maternal and paternal competences showed significant positive relationships with separation anxiety and separation depression later in life. Additionally, maternal adjustment to everyday life was found to be associated with depression of the child when he or she reaches adulthood.

These results underscore the importance of parental competence during the posttraumatic period in providing the child with a sense of security that potentiated developmental progress, especially along the pathway of separation-individuation. The reunification process between parents and children following the Holocaust was often complicated or even tumultuous. A child reunited with a parent could feel profound mixed emotions. Gratification could be entwined with anger at parents for abandonment. Children who had eagerly awaited reunifications with idealized figures often felt an amalgam of relief and disappointment. Children who had been in hiding with other families from a very young age were shocked to learn that they were in fact from a different family of origin, and they subsequently endured further loss on having to separate from their wartime caregivers. When reunification of parent and child was possible, parents recovering from their own trauma had difficulty functioning as parents. Intergenerational transmission of trauma[44] followed as children internalized their parents' difficulty in adjusting to personal, social, and work lives after the war, resulting in experiences of depression later in life and the periodic experience of unmentalized states.

In this study, age at the onset of persecution was not found to be a predictor for somatic complaints and health status. Along with conflicting findings in the literature, showing either older[45] or younger[46] children demonstrating more somatic complaints in response to trauma, it seems likely that if a relationship were to exist between these variables it is a more complex one, possibly curvilinear, and/or influenced by covariate factors.

Methodological Considerations

Employment of the Gottschalk-Gleser narrative analysis system along with the CDR *Code Book* offered some persuasive empirical findings. While qualitative factors were quantified in this mixed-methods study, the narrative content of the comprehensive interviews suggests that the nuances of trauma and individual experiences were not sufficiently captured by the quantifiable measures. Detailed accounts of personal life stories of child survivors of the Holocaust offered by qualitative researchers[47] highlight an array of complex influences that are not readily found to be consistent among subjects in quantified studies employing direct measurement. While quantification aims at the amplification of precision, it also involves inherent simplifications that do not easily capture the complexities of human coping resources and styles employed in response to persecutory trauma. To illustrate this point, two examples follow, reflecting subtleties of experience that could not be conveyed by the necessarily reductive methodology described above. They are both drawn from the interviews examined in the current study.

One subject discussed the wisdom of his parents in ensuring a gradual transition from his wartime parents to his parents of origin following liberation. He had been sent into hiding during his toddler years and had come to believe that the family with whom he was living was indeed his own. He spoke of the shock in learning of his true parents and the steps they took in fostering a strong relationship with his wartime family, arranging for him to have regular visitations with them, akin to a divorce situation. He explained that this enabled him to feel secure and not to feel torn between two sets of parents. He continued to maintain his relationship with his wartime family, sharing milestones of his life with them. He recognized the implications of this security in affording him a healthy and productive life.

Another child survivor described experiencing the war together with his parents, hidden with them and protected by them throughout the Holocaust. Early on he was hidden in a coffin and retrieved before burial, a scheme devised by his parents to smuggle him out of the ghetto. He recalled his parents responding to his every need both throughout the war and during the years that followed. While his parents showed high levels of competence, he endured significant difficulties separating and individuating in adulthood. Attachment, dependence, and a lack of exploration were quintessentially interwoven with survival; he never had the opportunity to practice separating.

These highly foreshortened examples both demonstrate psychological variables that are more complicated and intricate than those captured in the present study's quantifiable terms. They reflect the impact of patterns of attachment in childhood on the psyche and on object relations later in life. Well-framed case study approaches stay closer to each narrative, providing insight into child survivors' reflective thinking about the perceived intentions of their caregivers as they made various decisions regarding their welfare during and following the war.

One individual underwent complex processes of attachment to and separation from multiple caregivers who all had the insight to ensure for a modicum of resolution. This child survivor was thus able to integrate satisfactorily, leading to healthy development in adulthood. In the second account, there was almost an overattachment, albeit well intended and perceived as critical to survival that allowed him no opportunity to practice separating from caregivers. As a result, this child survivor endured great difficulty separating and individuating later in life.

Likert-type questions regarding postwar parental competence and parental adjustment did not capture the complex nature of attachment factors that were expressed by these individuals. Quantitative assessment that is even more comprehensive can supplement but not substitute for in-depth and individualized considerations of narratives. The language expressed by the survivors not only relates the events but also conveys the impact of personal experiences on their lives. The methodology applied in this study provides a working model for future explorations that could expand investigation of additional Gottschalk-Gleser Scales items and employ alternative narrative coding approaches.

An important factor in the postwar years, expressed in numerous interviews, was that children were often told not to talk about their experiences and to refrain from upsetting the adults in their lives. Some stories were not believed because they were told they were too young to possibly remember. Those who were at a preverbal age at the onset of the trauma recalled their prewar lives with broad brush strokes, often conveying sensory memories associated with their homes and loved ones in their lives. A powerful technique evident in interview transcripts (as suggested by Judith Kestenberg) was asking child survivors to imagine themselves as infants, often eliciting emotion-laden memories expressed nonverbally in their body language.

Limitations and Future Research

The Gottschalk-Gleser Scales provided an opportunity to analyze the language used in the survivors' narratives as a means of gleaning information regarding the mental health status of the interviewees as adults. Some limitations are evident, including an overlap between a number of the scales. For example, the PCAD's measures of depression and anxiety may not be sufficiently differentiated, sharing too many components. There is a significant amount of literature published about the Gottschalk-Gleser Content Analysis Scales. Gottschalk and his colleagues conducted the vast majority of the validation studies for these scales.[48] The original normative data was established using a sample from one urban community in the United States. Follow-up validation studies compared this normative sample to various clinical groups.[49] However, the latter also included fairly small sample sizes. Further scale development and a more diverse normative sample would benefit future applications of the scales.

In fact, the mean scores on the Gottschalk-Gleser PCAD obtained by the sample in this study were comparable to those obtained by the normative sample, though the standard deviations in this study were narrower than those in the norm group. Hence, while comparable to the general population, it may be that the Gottschalk-Gleser PCAD scales were compromised in their ability to differentiate historical Holocaust interviews, because of shared states of mind within the traumatized sample. Many interviewees employed themes calling up imagery consistent with "Depression," "Anxiety," and "Quality of Life" scale-items. In turn, the narrowed differentiation may have contributed to the lack of correspondence found between the PCAD variables and the wartime variables of age, prewar memories, and postwar situation.

As described, the dual quantification procedures of content analysis utilizing both the CDR *Code Book* Items and the Gottschalk-Gleser Scales proved valuable, yet were likely inadequate in capturing important nuances of a rich archival data set. Future studies regarding posttrauma sequelae may continue to strive to combine qualitative and quantitative methods in mixed-method designs by conducting interviews in addition to having participants complete quantitative measures, as well as by employing coding of the interview itself (e.g., for verbal and nonverbal features). Regarding more-recent (and future) atrocities, longitudinal study in which data are collected in the posttrauma period and at subsequent intervals thereafter would provide a rich foundation for further research that captures sequelae unfolding over time.

Other narrative coding methods, such as a modification of that applied to the Adult Attachment Interview[50] could be used to analyze this data set, because it may assess variables related to parenting, attachment, and reflective functioning with greater specificity. Plans to implement relevant aspects of Bucci and Maskit's DAAP method,[51] with the current data archive seems particularly promising, given that use of referential activity in the narrative reflects the speaker's relative degree of integrating nonverbally anchored feelings that have emerged in the telling. This may provide a quantitative approach to tapping unconscious elements conveyed in the interviews, such as those involved in the regulation of episodic memory activation, indexing, for example, defensive avoidance.

A review of these interviews indicates that many children were socioemotionally silenced after the war by adults who told them that they were too young to remember anything significant; those children who demonstrated recollections of the traumas they had endured were encouraged to forget their pasts and move ahead with their lives.

Central findings of this study proved the critical importance of postwar parental competence and maternal adjustment for the child's functioning later in life. This emphasizes the need for early intervention by mental health providers in the aftermath of massive trauma on behalf of both the child and the parents. The goals of such intervention are multifold. First, the child needs to process the traumatic experience and grieve rather than repress the experience and remain silent. The therapist needs to carefully modulate the rate at which the trauma is recalled and shared so the child is not overwhelmed by recollections of the trauma before being ready to integrate the memories into experience. Second, if and when children are reunited with their parents, the latter also need to process and grieve so that they heal rather than internalize their experiences and transmit their posttraumatic reactions to their children.

This examination of interview-derived narratives of child survivors of the Holocaust highlights how early childhood development lays the foundation for developing a healthy sense of self and for cultivating healthy relationships with others. When safety and security are shattered by traumatic separation, loss, and threat to survival, the developmental processes of attachment, separation-individuation, and identity formation are thwarted. Traumatized children need to be seen, heard, and validated in order to promote recovery and the resumption of growth into their adult lives.

Authors

Gila Sandler Saban received her doctor of psychology degree in school-clinical child psychology from Pace University, New York. She practices clinical psychology with children, adolescents, and young adults in Jerusalem and works in the Department of School Psychology in a nearby school district. Prior to moving to Israel, she served as the director of high school guidance at a large day school in New York. Her interest in trauma-related research and work is reflected in her doctoral dissertation on child survivors of the Holocaust, her clinical training, and her current practice.

K. Mark Sossin is professor of psychology and associate chair of the Department of Psychology at Pace University, New York. He is, in addition, a training analyst at the Contemporary Freudian Society, a member of the clinical faculty and supervisor at the Derner Institute of Advanced Psychological Studies of Adelphi University, and serves as the vice president of Child Development Research. He is the coauthor of *The Meaning of Movement: Clinical and Developmental Applications of the Kestenberg Movement Profile* (Routledge, 1999), and the coeditor of *Mothers, Infants and Young Children of September 11, 2001: A Primary Prevention Project* (Routledge, 2012), and most recently *Healing after Parent Loss in Childhood and Adolescence: Therapeutic Interventions and Theoretical Considerations* (Rowman and Littlefield, 2014). He is the codirector of the Pace Parent–Infant/Toddler Research Nursery and director of the Mind, Movement, Interaction and Development Research Group.

Anastasia Yasik is a licensed psychologist and professor in the Department of Psychology at Pace University, New York. She received her PhD in educational psychology from the Graduate Center of the City University of New York and completed her postdoctoral studies in psychiatric epidemiology at the Mailman School of Public Health at Columbia University. She teaches graduate courses in the School-Clinical Child Psychology PsyD program and has published and presented on topics relating to posttraumatic stress disorder, violence prevention/intervention, psychological assessment, school psychology, and early childhood issues.

Notes

We thank the following individuals for their editorial assistance: Yael Moskowitz, a doctoral student in the School Clinical Child Psychology Program at Pace University, New York City; Osnat Piro, an undergraduate LLB Law student at Hebrew University, Jerusalem.

1. Judith S. Kestenberg and Ira Brenner, *The Last Witness: The Child Survivor of the Holocaust* (Washington DC: American Psychiatric Press, 1996), 1.2; Judith S. Kestenberg and Eva Fogelman, Children During the Nazi Reign (Westport, CT: Praeger, 1994), xvii–xxi.
2. Lucy Berliner et al., "Children's Memory for Trauma and Positive Experiences," *Journal of Traumatic Stress* 16 (2003): 229–30.
3. Karen Appleyard and Joy D. Osofsky, "Parenting After Trauma: Supporting Parents and Caregivers in the Treatment of Children Impacted by Violence," *Infant Mental Health Journal* 24 (2003): 117; Jonathan Sandoval, ed., *Handbook of Crisis Counseling, Intervention and Prevention in the Schools*, 2nd ed. (Mahwah, NJ: Lawrence Erlbaum Associates, 2002), 247.
4. Gerard A. Jacobs et al., "Floods," in *Helping Children Cope with Disasters and Terrorism*, eds. Annette. M. La Greca et al. (Washington, DC: America Psychological Association, 2002), 157–161; Larry Kreuger and John Stretch, "Identifying and Helping Long Term Child and Adolescent Disaster Victims: Model and Method," *Journal of Social Service Research* 30 (2003): 94–97.
5. Susan W. Coates, Jane L. Rosenthal and Daniel S. Schechter, eds., *September 11 Trauma and Human Bonds* (Hillsdale, NJ: Analytic Press, 2003), 1–308; Wanda P. Fremont, "Childhood Reactions to Terrorism Induced Trauma: A Review of the Past 10 Years," *Journal of the American Academy of Child and Adolescent Psychiatry* 43 (2004): 383–84.
6. Panos Vostanis, "The Impact, Psychological Sequelae and Management of Trauma Affecting Children," *Current Opinion in Psychiatry* 17 (2004): 271; Isaiah D. Wexler, David Branski and Eitan Kerem, "War and Children," *Journal of the American Medical Association* 296 (2006): 579.
7. Alicia F. Lieberman, "Traumatic Stress and Quality of Attachment: Reality and Internalization in Disorders of Infant Mental Health," *Infant Mental Health Journal* 25 (2004): 341.
8. Theodore J. Gaensbauer, "Representations of Trauma in Infancy: Clinical and Theoretical Implications for the Understanding of Early Memory," *Infant Mental Health Journal* 23 (2002): 259–277; Abraham Sagi-Schwartz et al., "Attachment and Traumatic Stress in Female Holocaust Child Survivors and Their Daughters," *American Journal of Psychiatry* 160 (2003): 1089;

K. Mark Sossin, "Nonmentalizing States in Early Childhood Survivors of the Holocaust: Developmental Considerations Regarding Treatment of Child Survivors of Genocidal Atrocities," *The American Journal of Psychoanalysis* 67 (2007): 755.
9. Philip A. Saigh et al., "An Analysis of the Internalizing and Externalizing Behaviors of Traumatized Urban Youth With and Without PTSD," *Journal of Abnormal Psychology* 111 (2002): 462–70.
10. Karen Appleyard and Joy D. Osofsky, "Parenting after Trauma: Supporting Parents and Caregivers in the Treatment of Children Impacted by Violence," Infant Mental Health Journal, 24 (2003): 111–125.
11. Kestenberg and Brenner, *The Last Witness: The Child Survivor of the Holocaust* (Washington, DC: American Psychiatric Press, 1996): 1–238; Judith S. Kestenberg and Eva Fogelman, eds., *Children During the Nazi Reign: Psychological Perspective on the Interview Process* (Westport, CT: Praeger, 1994): ix–231.
12. Marianne Amir and Rachel Lev-Wiesel, "Time Does Not Heal All Wounds: Quality of Life and Psychological Distress of People Who Survived the Holocaust as Children 55 Years Later," *Journal of Traumatic Stress* 16 (2003): 296; Abraham Sagi-Schwartz, Nina Koren-Karie and Tirtsa Joels, "Failed Mourning in the Adult Attachment Interview: The Case of Holocaust Child Survivors," *Attachment and Human Development* 5 (2003): 400–401.
13. Louis A. Gottschalk and Goldine C. Gleser, *The Measurement of Psychological States through the Content Analysis of Verbal Behavior* (Berkeley and Los Angeles: University of California Press, 1979): 1–317; Paul F. Siegel, Mark Sammons and Hartvig Dahl, "Frames: The Method in Action and the Assessment of Its Reliability," *Psychotherapy Research* 12 (2002): 60–61.
14. Hartvig Dahl, Horst Kachele, and Helmut Thoma, eds., *Psychoanalytic Process Research Strategies* (Berlin: Springer, 1988): x–xvi; Gottschalk and Gleser, *The Measurement of Psychological States:* 91; Erik Hesse. The Adult Attachment Interview: Protocol, Method of Analysis, and Empirical Studies. In Jude Cassidy (Ed.), Phillip R. Shaver (Ed.), Handbook of Attachment Theory, Research, and Clinical Applications 2nd Ed. (New York, U.S.: Guilford Press), 552–598; Siegel, Sammons and Dahl, "Frames," 60–61.
15. Motti Cohen, Danny Brom, and Haim Dasberg, "Child Survivors of the Holocaust," *The Israel Journal of Psychiatry and Related Sciences* 38 (2001): 9–10; Rachel Lev-Wiesel and Marianne Amir, "Posttraumatic Stress Disorder Symptoms, Psychological Distress, Personal Resources, and Quality of Life in Four Groups of Holocaust Child Survivors," *Family Process* 39 (2000): 446.
16. Kestenberg and Brenner, *The Last Witness,* 1–201; Suzanne Kaplan, "Child Survivors and Childbearing: Memories from the Holocaust Invading the Present," *Scandinavian Psychoanalytic Review* 23 (2000), 249–282; Lev-Wiesel and Amir, "Posttraumatic Stress Disorder Symptoms," 446; Sarah Moskovitz, "Longitudinal Follow-up of Child Survivors of the Holocaust," *Journal of the American Academy of Child Psychiatry* 24 (1985): 403–407.
17. Esti Cohen, Rachel Dekel, and Zahava Solomon, "Long-term Adjustment and the Role of Attachment among Holocaust Child Survivors," *Personality and Individual Differences* 33 (2002): 300; Sagi-Schwartz, Koren-Karie and Joels, "Failed Mourning," 406; Rachel Lev-Wiesel and Marianne Amir,

"Secondary Traumatic Stress, Psychological Distress, Sharing of Traumatic Reminisces, and Marital Quality Among Spouses of Holocaust Child Survivors," *Journal of Marital and Family Therapy* 27 (2001): 444.
18. Kaplan "Child Survivors and Childbearing": 281.
19. Aviva Mazor and Yitzhak Mendelsohn, "Spouse Bereavement Processes of Holocaust Child 12Survivors: Can One Differentiate a Black Frame from a Black Background?" *Contemporary Family Therapy* 20 (1998): 80.
20. Kerry Bluglass, *Hidden from the Holocaust: Stories of Resilient Children Who Survived and Thrived* (Westport, CT: Praeger, 2003): ix–250; Judith S. Kestenberg, "Child Survivors of the Holocaust: 40 Years Later: Reflections and Commentary," *Journal of the American Academy of Child Psychiatry* 24 (1985): 410; Hans M. Reijzer, "On Having Been in Hiding," Antonie Ladan (Ed.). *The Dutch Annual of Psychoanalysis 1995–1996: Traumatization and War* 2 (1996), 66–67. (Amsterdam, Ne: Swets and Zellinger Publishing). Margrit W. Rustow, "From Jew to Catholic and Back: Psychodynamics of Child Survivors," in *Healing Their Wounds Psychotherapy with Holocaust Survivors and Their Families*, eds. Paul Marcus and Alan Rosenberg (New York: Praeger, 1989), 139.
21. Kestenberg, "Children Survivors of the Holocaust": 409; Yvonne Tauber, "The Traumatized Child and the Adult: Compound Personality in Child Survivors of the Holocaust," *Israel Journal of Psychiatry and Related Science* 33 (1996): 228–238: 226–227.n14
22. Nathan Durst, "Child Survivors of the Holocaust: Age Specific Traumatization and the Consequences for Therapy," *American Journal of Psychotherapy* 57 (2003): 512; Hans Keilson, *Sequential Traumatization in Children: A Clinical and Statistical Follow-up Study on the Fate of the Jewish War Orphans in the Netherlands* (Jerusalem: Magnes Press, 1992): 215–216. Lev-Wiesel and Amir, "Posttraumatic Stress Disorder Symptoms," 450–53; S. Robinson et al., "The Late Effects of Nazi Persecution Among Elderly Holocaust Survivors," *Acta Psychiatrica Scandanavia* 82 (1990): 313; Sagi-Schwartz et al., "Attachment and Traumatic Stress," 1090.
23. Keilson, *Sequential Traumatization in Children*: 79; Lev-Wiesel and Amir, "Posttraumatic Stress Disorder Symptoms," 450–53; Sagi-Schwartz et al., "Attachment and Traumatic Stress": 1091.
24. Kestenberg, Judith. What a Psychoanalyst Learned from the Holocaust and Genocide." International Journal of Psychoanalysis, 74 (1993): 1123; Durst, "Child Survivors of the Holocaust," 514; Krell, "Child Survivors of the Holocaust," 379; Kestenberg and Brenner, *The Last Witness*: 27–52.
25. CDR, *Code Book Child Survivor Study* 16. (Unpublished Code Book)
26. Gottschalk and Gleser, *The Measurement of Psychological States*,
27. CDR, *Code Book*
28. Gila Sandler, "Long Term Effects of Childhood Trauma: A Study of Child Survivors of the Holocaust Using Narrative Coding Analysis" (Order No. 3381439, Pace University, 2010, http://search.proquest.com/docview/305240028?accountid=14546, accessed December 20, 2016), 18106.
29. Keilson, *Sequential Traumatization in Children*: 37. Krell, "Child Survivors of the Holocaust," 380.

30. Louis A. Gottschalk, Carolyn N. Winget and Goldine C. Gleser, *Manual of Instructions for Using the Gottschalk-Gleser Content Analysis Scales: Anxiety, Hostility, and Social Alienation, Personal Disorganization* (Berkeley and Los Angeles, CA: University of California Press, 1969) : 23–170.
31. Nathan E. Lavid, Louis A. Gottschalk and Robert J. Bechtel, "Computerized Measurement of Neuropsychiatric Traits in Adolescents with Eating Disorders," in *Adolescent Eating Disorders*, ed. Pamela I. Swain (New York: Nova Science, 2005), 1–11; http://www.gb-software.com/pcad2000.html.
32. Louis A. Gottschalk, "Content-Category Analysis: The Measurement of the Magnitude of Psychological Dimensions in Psychotherapy," in *Language in Psychotherapy Strategies of Discovery*, ed. Robert L. Russel (New York and London: Plenum Press, 1987), 13–70; Louis A. Gottschalk, "The Application of Computerized Content Analysis of Natural Language in Psychotherapy Research Now and in the Future," *American Journal of Psychotherapy* 54 (2000): 306; Louis A. Gottschalk, Marsha K. Stein and Deane H. Shapiro, "The Application of Computerized Content Analysis of Speech to the Diagnostic Process in a Psychiatric Outpatient Clinic," *Journal of Clinical Psychology* 53 (1997): 428–31; Lavid, Gottschalk and Bechtel, "Computerized Measurement of Neuropsychiatric Traits:" 5–17.
33. Robert Bechtel, *Normative Data for PCAD 2000* (Unpublished, GB Software LLC, 2006). http://www.gb-software.com/pcad2000.htm; Louis A. Gottschalk, "Children's Speech as a Source of Data Towards the Measurement of Psychological States," *Journal of Youth and Adolescence* 5 (1976): 21–23; Louis A. Gottschalk and Julia Hoigaard-Martin, "A Depression Scale Applicable to Verbal Samples," *Psychiatry Research* 17 (1986): 217–18; Bechtel, *Normative Data for PCAD 2000*; http://www.gb-software.com/pcad2000.htm.
34. Louis A. Gottschalk, *Content Analysis of Verbal Behavior New Findings and Clinical Applications* (Hillsdale, NJ: Lawrence Erlbaum, 1995): 5–48.
35. Durst, "Child Survivors of the Holocaust," 502.
36. Kestenberg and Brenner, *The Last Witness*.
37. Kestenberg and Fogelman, *Children During the Nazi Reign*: 81; Eva Fogelman, "Transforming a Legacy of Loss," in *Daughters of Absence Transforming a Legacy of Loss*, ed. Mindy Wiesel (Downers Grove, IL: Dream of Things, 2012), 3–16.
38. Paul Valent, *Child Survivors of the Holocaust*, (New York: Brunner-Routledge, 1994): 1–7.
39. Ira Brenner, "Multisensory Bridges in Response to Object Loss During the Holocaust," *Psychoanalytic Review* 75 (1988): 573–587.
40. Clifford B. Yorke, "A Psychoanalytic Approach to the Understanding of Shame," *Sigmund Freud House Bulletin* 14 (1990): 14–28.
41. Marcela Matos, Jose Pinto-Gouveia and Vania Costa, "Understanding the Importance of Attachment in Shame Traumatic Memory Relation to Depression: The Impact of Emotion Regulation Processes," *Clinical Psychology and Psychotherapy* (2013): 149.

42. Anne Adelman, "Traumatic Memory and the Intergenerational Transmission of Narratives," *Psychoanalytic Study of the Child* 50 (1995): 343–367; Dori Laub and Nanette C. Auerhahn, "Failed Empathy: A Central Theme in the Survivor's Holocaust Experience," *Psychoanalytic Psychology* 6 (1989): 393–96.
43. Rosemary S.L. Mills, "Taking Stock of the Developmental Literature on Shame," *Developmental Review* 25 (2005): 38.
44. Peter Fonagy, "The Transgenerational Transmission of Holocaust Trauma," *Attachment and Human Development* 1 (1999): 101–10.
45. Durst, "Child Survivors of the Holocaust," 514–16.
46. Kestenberg and Brenner, *The Last Witness*; 1–29.
47. Eva Fogelman, "The Psychology Behind Being a Hidden Child," in *The Hidden Children: The Secret Survivors of the Holocaust,* Jane Marks (New York: Fawcett Columbine, 1993), 292–307; Eva Fogelman, "Effects of Interviews with Rescued Child Survivors," in *Children During the Nazi Reign: Psychological Perspective on the Interview Process,* eds. Judith S. Kestenberg and Eva Fogelman (Westport, CT: Praeger, 1994) 81–89; Eva Fogelman and Flora Hogman, "A Follow-up Study: Child Survivors of the Nazi Holocaust Reflect on Being Interviewed," in *Children During the Nazi Reign: Psychological Perspective on the Interview Process,* eds. Judith S. Kestenberg and Eva Fogelman (Westport, CT: Praeger, 1994) 73–80; Kestenberg, "Child Survivors of the Holocaust: 40 Years Later," 408–12; Judith S. Kestenberg, "Children of the Holocaust: Children Under the Nazi Yoke," *British Journal of Psychotherapy* 8 (1992): 374–390; Wilma Bucci, "The Referential Process, Consciousness, and the Sense of Self," *Psychoanalytic Inquiry* 22 (2002): 766–793.
48. Louis A. Gottschalk, "The Development, Validation, and Applications of a Computerized Measurement of Cognitive Impairment from the Content Analysis of Verbal Behavior," *Journal of Clinical Psychology* 50 (1994): 349–361; Gottschalk and Gleser, *Measurement of Psychological States*; Gottschalk and Hoigaard-Martin, "A Depression Scale," 213–227.
49. Gottschalk, *Content Analysis of Verbal Behavior*: 1; Gottschalk, Fox, and Bates, "A Study of Prediction and Outcome"; Gottschalk and Gleser, *Measurement of Psychological States*: 49–95. Gottschalk and Hoigaard-Martin, "A Depression Scale," 213–227; Louis A. Gottschalk, Ruth A. Fox, and Daniel E. Bates, "A Study of Prediction and Outcome in a Mental Health Crisis Clinic," *American Journal of Psychiatry* 130 (1973): 1107–1111; Kavita Gupta, Purnima Marthur and M. H. Chawla, "Evaluation of Schizophrenics vs. Non-Schizophrenics on Gottschalk-Gleser Social Alienation-Personal Disorganization Scale," *Journal of Personality and Clinical Studies* 6 (1990): 139–144.
50. Main and Goldwyn, *Adult Attachment Scoring*: 1.

References

Adelman, A. "Traumatic Memory and the Intergenerational Transmission of Narratives." *Psychoanalytic Study of the Child* 50 (1995): 343–367.

Amir, Marianne, and Rachel Lev-Wiesel. "Time Does Not Heal All Wounds: Quality of Life and Psychological Distress of People Who Survived the Holocaust as Children 55 Years Later." *Journal of Traumatic Stress* 16 (2003): 295–299.

Appleyard, Karen, and Joy D. Osofsky. "Parenting after Trauma: Supporting Parents and Caregivers in the Treatment of Children Impacted by Violence." *Infant Mental Health Journal* 24 (2003): 111–125.

Bechtel, Robert. *Normative Data for PCAD 2000.* Unpublished, GB Software LLC, 2006.

Berliner, Lucy, Ira Hyman, Ayanna Thomas, and Monica Fitzgerald. "Children's Memory for Trauma and Positive Experiences." *Journal of Traumatic Stress* 16 (2003): 229–236.

Bluglass, Kerry. *Hidden from the Holocaust Stories of Resilient Children Who Survived and Thrived.* Westport, CT: Praeger, 2003.

Brenner, Ira. "Multisensory Bridges in Response to Object Loss During the Holocaust." *Psychoanalytic Review* 75 (1988): 573–587.

Bucci, Wilma. "The Referential Process, Consciousness, and the Sense of Self." *Psychoanalytic Inquiry* 22 (2002): 766–793.

Child Development Research (CDR). *Code Book Child Survivor Study.* Unpublished Research and Data Collection Protocol, 1997.

Coates, S.W., J.L. Rosenthal, and D.S. Schechter, eds. *September 11 Trauma and Human Bonds.* Hillsdale, NJ: Analytic Press, 2003.

Cohen, Esti, Rachel Dekel, and Zahava Solomon. "Long-term Adjustment and the Role of Attachment among Holocaust Child Survivors." *Personality and Individual Differences* 33 (2002): 299–310.

Cohen, M., D. Brom, and H. Dasberg. "Child Survivors of the Holocaust: Symptoms and Coping After Fifty Years." *Israel Journal of Psychiatry Related Science* 38 (2001): 3–12.

Dahl, H., H. Kachele, and H. Thoma. *Psychoanalytic Process Research Strategies.* Berlin: Springer, (1988) 1–14

Dasberg, Haim. "Adult Child Survivor Syndrome: On Deprived Childhoods of Aging Holocaust Survivors." *Israel Journal of Psychiatry Related Science* 38 (2001): 13–26.

Durst, Nathan. "Child Survivors of the Holocaust: Age Specific Traumatization and the Consequences for Therapy." *American Journal of Psychotherapy* 57 (2003): 499–518.

Fogelman, Eva. "Effects of Interviews with Rescued Child Survivors." In *Children During the Nazi Reign: Psychological Perspective on the Interview Process,* edited by J. Kestenberg and E. Fogelman, 81–89. Westport, CT: Praeger, 1994.

———. "The Psychology Behind Being a Hidden Child." In *The Hidden Children: The Secret Survivors of the Holocaust,* edited by J. Marks, 292–307. New York: Fawcett Columbine, 1993.

———. "Transforming a Legacy of Loss." In *Daughters of Absence Transforming a Legacy of Loss*, edited by M. Wiesel, 3–16. Downers Grove, IL: Dream of Things, 2012.

Fogelman, Eva, and Flora Hogman. "A Follow-up Study: Child Survivors of the Nazi Holocaust Reflect on Being Interviewed." In *Children During the Nazi Reign: Psychological Perspective on the Interview Process*, edited by J. Kestenberg and E. Fogelman, 73–80. Westport, CT: Praeger, 1994.

Fonagy, Peter. "The Transgenerational Transmission of Holocaust Trauma." *Attachment and Human Development* 1 (1999): 92–114.

Fremont, W.P. "Childhood Reactions to Terrorism Induced Trauma: A Review of the Past 10 Years." *Journal of the American Academy of Child and Adolescent Psychiatry* 43 (2004): 381–392.

Gaensbauer, Theodore J. "Representations of Trauma in Infancy: Clinical and Theoretical Implications for the Understanding of Early Memory." *Infant Mental Health Journal* 23 (2002): 259–277.

Gottschalk, Louis A. "The Application of Computerized Content Analysis of Natural Language in Psychotherapy Research Now and in the Future." *American Journal of Psychotherapy* 54 (2000): 305–311.

———. "Children's Speech as a Source of Data Towards the Measurement of Psychological States." *Journal of Youth and Adolescence* 5 (1976): 11–36.

———. *Content Analysis of Verbal Behavior New Findings and Clinical Applications*. Hillsdale, NJ: Lawrence Erlbaum, 1995.

———. "Content-Category Analysis: The Measurement of the Magnitude of Psychological Dimensions in Psychotherapy." In *Language in Psychotherapy Strategies of Discovery*, edited by R.L. Russel, 13–70. New York and London: Plenum Press, 1987.

———. "The Development, Validation, and Applications of a Computerized Measurement of Cognitive Impairment from the Content Analysis of Verbal Behavior." *Journal of Clinical Psychology* 50 (1994): 349–361.

Gottschalk, Louis A., and Robert Bechtel. *PCAD 2000: Psychiatric Content Analysis and Diagnosis*. Corona del Mar, CA: GB Software LLC, 2002.

Gottschalk, Louis A., Ruth A. Fox, and Daniel E. Bates. "A Study of Prediction and Outcome in a Mental Health Crisis Clinic." *American Journal of Psychiatry* 130 (1973): 1107–1111.

Gottschalk, Louis A., and Goldine C. Gleser. *The Measurement of Psychological States through the Content Analysis of Verbal Behavior*. Berkeley and Los Angeles: University of California Press, 1969.

Gottschalk, Louis A., and Julia Hoigaard-Martin. "A Depression Scale Applicable to Verbal Samples." *Psychiatry Research* 17 (1986): 213–227.

Gottschalk, Louis A., and F. Lolas. "The Measurement of Quality of Life through the Content Analysis of Verbal Behavior." *Psychotherapy and Psychosomatics* 58 (1992): 69–78.

Gottschalk, Louis A., Marsha K. Stein, and Deane H. Shapiro. "The Application of Computerized Content Analysis of Speech to the Diagnostic Process in a Psychiatric Outpatient Clinic." *Journal of Clinical Psychology* 53 (1997): 427–441.

Gottschalk, Louis A., and C.N. Winget. *Manual of Instructions for Using the Gottschalk-Gleser Content Analysis Scales Anxiety, Hostility, and Social*

Alienation, Personal Disorganization. Berkeley and Los Angeles, CA: University of California Press, 1969.
Gupta, Raj K., P. Marthur, and M.H. Chawla. "Evaluation of Schizophrenics vs. Non-Schizophrenics on Gottschalk-Gleser Social Alienation-Personal Disorganization Scale." *Journal of Personality and Clinical Studies* 6 (1990): 139–144.
Jacobs, G.A., J.V. Boero, R.P. Quevillon, E. Todd-Bazemore, T.L. Elliott, and G. Reyes. "Floods." In *Helping Children Cope with Disasters and Terrorism*, edited by A.M. La Greca, W.K. Silverman, E.M. Vernberg, and M.C. Roberts, 157–174. Washington, DC: American Psychological Association, 2002.
Kaplan, Suzanne. "Child Survivors and Childbearing: Memories from the Holocaust Invading the Present." *Scandinavian Psychoanalytic Review* 23 (2000): 249–282.
Keilson, H. *Sequential Traumatization in Children: A Clinical and Statistical Follow-up Study on the Fate of the Jewish War Orphans in the Netherlands.* Jerusalem: Magnes Press, 1992.
Kestenberg, Judith S. "Child Survivors of the Holocaust: 40 Years Later: Reflections and Commentary." *Journal of the American Academy of Child Psychiatry* 24 (1985): 408–412.
———. "Children of the Holocaust: Children Under the Nazi Yoke." *British Journal of Psychotherapy* 8 (1992): 374–390.
———. "What a Psychoanalyst Learned from the Holocaust and Genocide." *International Journal of Psychoanalysis* 74 (1993): 1117–1129
Kestenberg, Judith S., and Ira Brenner. *The Last Witness: The Child Survivor of the Holocaust.* Washington, DC: American Psychiatric Press, 1996.
Kestenberg, Judith S., and Eva Fogelman, eds. *Children During the Nazi Reign: Psychological Perspective on the Interview Process.* Westport, CT: Praeger, 1994.
Koren-Karie, Nina, Avraham Sagi-Schwartz, and Tirtsa Joels. "Absence of Attachment Representations (AAR) in the Adult Years: The Emergence of a New AAI Classification in Catastrophically Traumatized Holocaust Child Survivors." *Attachment and Human Development* 5 (2003): 381–397.
Krell, Robert. "Child Survivors of the Holocaust: 40 Years Later Introduction." *Journal of the American Academy of Child Psychiatry* 24, no. 4 (1985): 378–380.
———. "Child Survivors of the Holocaust: Strategies of Adaptation." *Canadian Journal of Psychiatry* 38 (1993): 384–389.
———. "Holocaust Survivors: A Clinical Perspective." *Psychiatric Journal of the University of Ottawa* 15 (1990): 18–21.
Kreuger, Larry, and John Stretch. "Identifying and Helping Long Term Child and Adolescent Disaster Victims: Model and Method." *Journal of Social Service Research* 30 (2003): 93–108.
Laub, D., and N.C. Auerhahn. "Failed Empathy—A Central Theme in the Survivor's Holocaust Experience." *Psychoanalytic Psychology* 6 (1989): 377–400.
Lavid, Nathan E., Louis A. Gottschalk, and Robert J. Bechtel. "Computerized Measurement of Neuropsychiatric Traits in Adolescents with Eating Disorders." In *Adolescent Eating Disorders*, edited by P.I. Swain, 1–11. New York: Nova Science, 2005.
Lev-Wiesel, Rachel, and Amir, Marianne. "Post-traumatic Stress Disorder Symptoms, Psychological Distress, Personal Resources, and Quality of

Life in Four Groups of Holocaust Child Survivors." *Family Process* 39 (2000): 445–459.

Lieberman, Alicia F. "Secondary Traumatic Stress, Psychological Distress, Sharing of Traumatic Reminisces, and Marital Quality Among Spouses of Holocaust Child Survivors." *Journal of Marital and Family Therapy* 27 (2001): 433–444.

———. "Traumatic Stress and Quality of Attachment: Reality and Internalization in Disorders of Infant Mental Health." *Infant Mental Health Journal* 25 (2004): 336–351.

Main, M., and R. Goldwyn. *Adult Attachment Scoring and Classification Systems.* Unpublished classification manual. University of California, Berkeley, 1985/1991/1994/1998.

Matos, Marcela, Jose Pinto-Gouveia, and Vania Costa. "Understanding the Importance of Attachment in Shame Traumatic Memory Relation to Depression: The Impact of Emotion Regulation Processes." *Clinical Psychology and Psychotherapy* (2013): 149–165.

Mazor, Aviva, and Yitzhak Mendelsohn. "Spouse Bereavement Processes of Holocaust Child Survivors: Can One Differentiate a Black Frame from a Black Background?" *Contemporary Family Therapy* 20 (1998): 79–91.

Mills, R.S.L. "Taking Stock of the Developmental Literature on Shame." *Developmental Review* 25 (2005): 26–63.

Moskovitz, Sarah. "Longitudinal Follow-up of Child Survivors of the Holocaust." *Journal of the American Academy of Child Psychiatry* 24 (1985): 401–407.

Robinson, S. "Late Effects of Persecution in Persons Who as Children or Young Adolescents Survived Nazi Occupation in Europe." *Israel Journal of Psychiatry,* 17 (1979): 209–214.

Robinson, S., J. Rapaport, R. Durst, M. Rapaport, P. Rosca, S. Metzer, and L. Zilberman. "The Late Effects of Nazi Persecution Among Elderly Holocaust Survivors." *Acta Psychiatrica Scandanavia* 82 (1990) 311–315.

Rustow, Margrit W. "From Jew to Catholic and Back: Psychodynamics of Child Survivors." In *Healing Their Wounds Psychotherapy with Holocaust Survivors and Their Families,* edited by P. Marcus and A. Rosenberg, 271–286. New York: Praeger, 1989.

Sagi-Schwartz, Abraham, Nina Koren-Karie, and Tirtsa Joels. "Failed Mourning in the Adult Attachment Interview: The Case of Holocaust Child Survivors." *Attachment and Human Development* 5 (2003): 398–408.

Sagi-Schwartz, Abraham, Marinus H. van IJzendoorn, Klaus E. Grossmann, Tirtsa Joels, Karin Grossmann, and Miri Scharf. "Attachment and Traumatic Stress in Female Holocaust Child Survivors and Their Daughters." *American Journal of Psychiatry* 160 (2003): 1086–1092.

Saigh, Philip A., Anastasia E. Yasik, Richard A. Oberfield, Phill V. Halamandaris, and Margaret McHugh. "An Analysis of the Internalizing and Externalizing Behaviors of Traumatized Urban Youth with and without PTSD." *Journal of Abnormal Psychology* 111 (2002): 462–470.

Sandler, Gila. "Long Term Effects of Childhood Trauma: A Study of Child Survivors of the Holocaust Using Narrative Coding Analysis." 3381439. Pace University, ProQuest, UMI Dissertations, 2010.

Sandoval, Jonathan, ed. *Handbook of Crisis Counseling, Intervention, and Prevention in the Schools,* 2nd ed. Mahwah, NJ: Lawrence Erlbaum, 2002.

Siegel, Paul F., M. Sammons, and H. Dahl. "FRAMES: The Method in Action and the Assessment of Its Reliability." *Psychotherapy Research* 12 (2002): 59–77.

Sossin, K. Mark. "Nonmentalizing States in Early Childhood Survivors of the Holocaust: Developmental Considerations Regarding Treatment of Child Survivors of Genocidal Atrocities." *American Journal of Psychoanalysis* 67 (2007): 68–81.

Tauber, Yvonne. "The Traumatized Child and the Adult: Compound Personality in Child Survivors of the Holocaust." *Israel Journal of Psychiatry and Related Science* 33 (1996): 228–237.

Valent, Paul. *Child Survivors of the Holocaust.* New York: Brunner-Routledge, 1994.

Vostanis, Panos. "The Impact, Psychological Sequelae and Management of Trauma Affecting Children." *Current Opinion in Psychiatry* 17 (2004): 269–273.

Wexler, Isaiah D., David Branski, and Eitan Kerem. "War and Children." *Journal of the American Medical Association* 296 (2006): 579–581.

Yorke, Clifford B. "A Psychoanalytic Approach to the Understanding of Shame." *Sigmund Freud House Bulletin* 14 (1990): 14–28.

PART TWO

Immediate Postwar Period

 2

A Child's View
Children's Depositions of the Central Jewish Historical Commission (Poland)

Sharon Kangisser Cohen

> Night. A weak light of kerosene lamp lights up the dusk that reigns over the room. Suddenly I felt someone's touch. I opened my eyes. Over me stood mother, dear, unforgotten mother. I understood that the action, expected since a week, had come.[1]

Research on the experience of children during the Holocaust is both an emotionally and intellectually challenging task. The experiences of children during the war—the desperate circumstances in which they found themselves and their near-impossible struggle to survive—is for the most part incomprehensible to researchers who have been spared this awful fate. Testimonies taken from children are difficult to read because they represent the most vulnerable victims of the National Socialists (or Nazis) and the impotence of the adult world to fulfill their obligation to protect them. The question that this chapter addresses is, How did children who lived through the Shoah understand and interpret their bitter reality? While there are important theoretical models for understanding the cognitive development of children and how they make sense of their reality, there has been little work using these models to interpret children's responses and understanding of their victimization and persecution during the Shoah.

Early researchers from various disciplines who were engaged in the study of the trauma of children during the German occupation were very limited in documentation.[2] In order to fill the gap, Yaffa Eliach, a historian and herself a child during the Holocaust, initiated an oral history project at Brooklyn College in 1979. Judith Kestenberg, a psychoanalyst whose immediate family had been killed in German-occupied Poland, started an oral history project in 1981 that included group gatherings and eventually mushroomed into the Hidden Child Foundation and the World Federation of Jewish Holocaust Child Survivors and Descendants. The historian Debórah Dwork introduced the experience of children during the Holocaust into the academic discourse about children's experience. She, too, found it challenging to locate source material. In her study *Children with a Star: Jewish Youth in Nazi Europe*, she attempted to reconstruct children's experiences, reactions, and behavior during this difficult time. In the introduction, she acknowledged the challenges she had in finding source material: "For a number of reasons documentation on child life is fragmentary for this period. To put it one way: as the children were not old enough to wear stars, they were not old enough to be explicit objects of policy, and therefore they never became part of recorded history. That is to say, in the period prior to the implementation of the 'Final Solution' (i.e., until 1941–early 1942) . . . children were appendages to their parents, especially to their mothers."[3]

Therefore, for researchers attempting to study the experience of children during the war, an important question emerges: What source material is there to examine how children viewed their difficult and deadly reality? First, "Within occupied Europe, adult chroniclers who undertook to write historical journals in order to record the tragic madness of the times included commentaries on and depictions of child life."[4] Adults continued to write about children after the war. Second, there were some young adults who wrote diaries during this period in which they record their observations and express their feelings and thoughts.[5] While this gives us a picture of what children experienced and how they responded, it does not allow us to understand how children themselves viewed and experienced their reality. One contemporaneous source of children during the war is the Ringelblum Archive. According to Dalia Ofer, there are interviews conducted with children in the Warsaw Ghetto by teachers and members of Oneg Shabbat, the underground archive,[6] through which children's voices can be heard. Third, we have postwar interviews given by children who survived the war. These testimonies, conducted from liberation until the present day in different countries through different research and memorial institutions, provide scholars with insight into the experiences of children because they are based on the children's own memories. Most of the testimonies of child survivors were collected decades after the war, but there are also testimonies given by child survivors in the immediate postwar period. Boaz Cohen states,

> "Many collections of children's testimonies were initiated in the immediate postwar years. Benjamin Tenenbaum, a Polish-born Jewish prewar emigrant to Palestine, traveled to Poland in 1946. With the aid of a few friends, he collected 1,000 'autobiographies' written by surviving Jewish children. Dr. Helena Wrobel-Kagan, a survivor of Bergen-Belsen, started

a school at that camp in late 1945. She asked the children, themselves survivors, to write essays entitled 'My Way from Home to the Camp.' Similarly, the Jewish Historical Commissions in Poland and in the American Zone in Germany focused on children in their effort to collect survivor testimonies. Other Jewish organizations, such as the National Relief Committee for Deportees in Hungary and the American Jewish Joint Distribution Committee (JDC) in its children's homes in France, collected children's testimonies more sporadically."[7]

In their article on early postwar children's testimony, Horvath and Cohen write, "In fact, many of the Jewish testimony-collection projects of the postwar era specifically sought out children in order to record their experiences."[8] Based on a collection of depositions collected from child survivors and recorded by the Central Jewish Historical Committee in Poland in the immediate postwar period, this chapter explores how children understood and interpreted their wartime reality.[9]

These depositions give voice to the children's own perspectives of their experiences; they become the "central informants"[10] of their own lives. Researchers of children's experiences have long been advocating for research methodology that uses children's voices to understand their experience. Traditionally, children and childhood have been explored through the lens of the adult world that claims to speak for children. According to Pia Christensen and Allison James, "In part, this view was challenged by the perspective which sees children as possessing distinctive cognitive and social developmental characteristics."[11] Interviews with children reveal "children as social actors who are subjects rather than objects of enquiry."[12]

Depositions Taken by the Central Jewish Historical Commission

The Central Jewish Historical Commission (CJHC) in Poland began operating in 1944 with the aim "to collect evidence in order to combat fascism and to inform the world about the crimes committed by the Nazis."[13] In her article, Beate Müller wrote that of the approximately 7,300 testimonies collected first by the CJHC and then by the Jewish Historical Institute, its successor organization, more than four hundred were given by children.[14]

After her examination of the instruction booklet composed for the interviewers, Joanna Michlic outlined the main objectives of the interviewing project.[15] The objectives were broad and ranged from obtaining a historical account of what happened to the children during the war to examining the impact the war had on the children, on their ideological preferences, and on their attitudes toward other nations and those of Polish society toward Jews. In 1945 further instructions were added for interviewing child survivors.

Boaz Cohen explained how the interviewer would ask the survivor questions based on the questionnaire, and would then be required to "compose the testimony in the first person, and then have the witness approve and sign it."[16] The issues arising from the composition of such reports are obvious. Rachel Auerbach, one of the leading figures in the CJHC, regarded these accounts as highly problematic historical sources. According to Cohen,

> She [Rachel Auerbach] recounted that "the witness was retelling his experiences and the interviewer was, from time to time, reformulating the testimony in his own words and summarizing it. In this way, some unique personal characteristics of style and language would be lost." Moreover, the witness had to be stopped occasionally in order for the interviewer to write down what he heard. These pauses, she claimed, "exhausted the . . . tension, dramatic energy, and narrative" of the testimony. She wrote that more than once she felt that stopping the witness from talking was a "barbaric act."[17]

Researchers have thus begun to discuss how to relate to these depositions as historical sources. According to Beate Müller, "We should be careful when claiming that these testimonies offer a direct insight into the child's world, a direct access to a child's voice—they do no such thing."[18] For Müller, their value lies not in the historical account of the Shoah but in learning about what was deemed to be of interest at the time; in these texts the "contextual determinants emerge, telling us a much more complex story of the context in which the testimonies were created, how, why and by whom."[19]

While these interviews are undeniably constructed and influenced by the context in which they were recorded, transcribed, composed, and translated,[20] I would argue that we can still read the individual child's experience from these statements. Within these short and fragmented texts, nuggets of experiences are recalled and shared that provide scholars with valuable insight into the period, the issues that the children faced, and how they responded. Scenes, images, and behaviors are recalled then originated *then* and not *now*. They reveal memories that have remained significant in the minds and memories of those who recall them. They can be viewed as what Robert Kraft has termed "core memories," namely, "the representation of the original phenomenal experience in the form of perceptual, emotional, and physiological experience: visual images, sounds, smells, tastes, emotions, and bodily sensations—as vivid and as compelling as dreams." This is different from "narrative memory," which "is constructed from the images in core memory shaped in accordance with narrative conventions and conveyed primarily in language."[21] In the case of the postwar depositions of the CJHC, it is narrative memory that has been constructed by both the interviewer and the interviewee.

Structure of the Depositions

For the purpose of this chapter I examined sixty depositions from the CJHC in Warsaw that were translated into English from the original Polish and Yiddish. The translations were done under the auspices of the International Study of Organized Persecution of Children headed by Judith Kestenberg, a pioneer in the field of child survivors of the Holocaust.[22] Over 150 depositions from this collection are archived in the Oral History Division of the Hebrew University of Jerusalem. Maria Hochberg-Mariańska and Noe Grüss edited fifty-five of these testimonies, which were published in a volume entitled *The Children Accuse*.[23]

I observed various phenomena regarding the structure of these early depositions. They are relatively short, ranging from one to five typed single spaced pages; they focus on the individual's survival story, often including one or two near-death escapes. There is very little recollection of the prewar years, which is probably a reaction to the intentions of the project and the questionnaire that reveals the direct impact of the context of the interview on the ensuing narrative. In some of the interviews the first line or two hints at the socioeconomic situation of the family, but the religious or ideological position of the family is rarely disclosed. The depositions usually begin with a few sentences recounting the outbreak of the war, then proceed to the main focus of the war story and the children's account of survival, and end with a few thoughts or comments about the survivors' current reality.

While it is difficult to know how much of the narrative was edited, these depositions do seem to reflect the intent of the project. These child survivors are aware of the interviewer's interest in their wartime experiences, and therefore the emphasis was on relating that experience. However, it could be argued that the survival story is central for the children too. In her work on children's narratives, Susan Engel pointed out that the form of a story is closely tied to its function. In the stories children tell, there is a "dis-synchrony of time and space. One event takes up a huge amount place in the mind, and another long span of time takes up almost no time at all." Engel argued that some of this is a function of memory: "Children, we now know, do have a strangely jumbled sense of time and space. Meaning dominates over chronology."[24] Therefore, the actual stories they present are meaningful; they represent the scaffolding of their wartime experiences, illustrating what is important to them and how they grapple with the world.

It also became clear to me that running parallel to the survival story is an account of their relational world and how it was affected during this difficult time. This is obvious in that most young children would not have been able to survive on their own and needed the help of others; physical survival is inextricably linked to relationship. Children were able to gather information and an understanding of the developing reality through their interaction with others. Adult responses to the situation were observed by the children and sometimes informed their own decisions on how to behave and respond. Perhaps most significantly, the loss of relationships meant that the children's world was irrevocably altered, affecting not only their struggle to survive during the war but also their ensuing lives. The physical breakdown and loss of relationships as a result of the deportation and murder of their close family and friends is the emotional center of these narratives.

Interpreting Reality

One of my central questions while reading these depositions was, How did the children understand and interpret their reality? In accordance with the constructivist approach of developmental psychology, Lev Vygotsky proposed that knowledge is socially constructed and that children develop cognitive competencies through their interactions with adults who are available as teachers or models to guide them and help them make sense of their experience.[25] According to Willard Hartup and Zick Rubin, there are at least three areas in which relationships appear to be involved in children's development: the socialization process, the regulation of emotion, and the construction of the basic elements of the individuals' self-esteem. Relationships also are the foundations which inform children how to function independently in the world, and used in the development of subsequent relationships."[26]

It could therefore be assumed that children's normative process of cognitive development was operative during the war, since their knowledge of the wartime reality was constructed through their interaction with others, notably their parents, other adults, and friends who provided them with the language through which to understand their reality and the emotional cues informing them of how to respond.[27]

However, the questions remain: Were these processes challenged or affected during war or in situations of mass violence? If so, how were they challenged or affected? As children become victims, do they find alternative strategies and mechanisms to navigate their increasingly unrecognizable reality? Researchers writing on the effects of war on children have concluded that "Children of all ages attempt to understand the confusing events and experiences of war, but the strategies used differ by developmental level. A child's perception of war at an early age tends to be based largely on the perceptions of the attitudes of adults in the social environment, as well as on messages received through the radio, movies, and other mass media."[28] Children may therefore interpret their situation differently according to their cognitive abilities and development. Scheeringa and Zeanah explained: "Less mature cognitive appraisal abilities may lead young children to underestimate or fail to recognize some threatening situations as dangerous. . . . On the other hand, less dangerous events . . . may prove extremely frightening to young children who lack the ability to understand the meaning of perceptual stimuli they encounter."[29] A study of Soviet children in wartime similarly suggested that children take their cues from those around them, absorbing and reflecting the attitudes of those closest to them.[30] Even if parents try, it seems it is impossible for them to deceive children or keep information from them, because they are inevitably exposed to war-related news and programs. Parents are not able to protect their children from life, but they can help them face it. Uncertainty can often stimulate more fears and fantasies than the facts themselves.[31]

Based on previous research, I assumed that information about the war and what was happening would, for the most part, have been transmitted and filtered by their parents and that children would have directed their questions about their changing reality to the adults in their close surroundings. However, it is evident from these depositions that there were children who were not always told about the war and who did not recollect conversations about it. There were some instances where the child survivors did report attempts at communication but whose parents did not respond to their questions or were unable to talk about it.

In her deposition, Karolina Matecka, aged four at the outbreak of the war, relates, "The Germans entered and I asked daddy why he did not take me to preschool. He told me the war was on. I did not know what that meant and he did not explain it at all. I did not know I was Jewish. I did not know what that meant. I did not go outside often and I did not know why. I rarely played with children. I had one friend and I cried a lot after she died."[32] The child's age was likely to have been a factor in the parents' level of communication regarding what was happening. Interestingly, in Karolina's case, despite her young age, she still recalls her confusion and her father's inability to tell her what was going on. Even if children did not get explicit answers to their questions, many began to understand by observing their parents' reactions.

Halina Hoffman, aged five at the outbreak of war, recalls, "I do not remember when they took daddy to the camp. I know he was sick with his kidneys and I think he died, but mommy cried alone and did not want to tell me the truth so I would not be aggrieved. But anyway I felt it."[33] Her interview demonstrates how nonverbal communication signaled the fate of her father. It also signals how a parent's emotional reaction conveyed the bitter reality.

Likewise, Jerzy Hoffman, six at the time of the outbreak of war, explains: "Two days before the ghetto was liquidated, I saw them for the last time. Daddy seemed to have sensed it because he cried when he took leave of me."[34] Parents themselves might not have known or understood the unfolding reality and were therefore unable to explain their increasingly unrecognizable existence to their children, and yet they were compelled to navigate the situation both physically and emotionally.

From these depositions it seems that during the first phases of the war there was indeed a sense of confusion regarding the turn of events. However, because anti-Jewish legislation evolved in the months immediately following the outbreak of the war into ghettoization and deportation, and children began to witness the physical abuse and murder, many of them understood their vulnerability and the deadly reality to which they were inevitably exposed. Mania Steiner, aged three at the start of the war, relates that in the ghetto "the hunger was terrible and I saw myself how people fell on the street from hunger."[35] This awareness came from her position as a witness; many of the children who were in hiding were able to see what was happening to their family, friends, and communities. Likewise, Edward Keningsberg, two years old at the time of the outbreak of war, narrates: "I went to the window and saw the whole scene: I could see through the window that there was a cemetery there and there was a grave dug out there. On the grave lay a plank and on the plank stood 6 people. The Gestapo men shot at them with machine guns, terrified by this scene I began to scream: 'mama!' Mommy heard me and told me to be quiet or we will be shot and she went away."[36]

In some instances, children who had been sent into hiding or had escaped were surviving on their own, and therefore did not have adults to ask. They would gather information from people they met or from acquaintances who could provide some information regarding the fate of their families. From their depositions we learn how news of the death of their parents or other family members was often conveyed to them by people, often their non-Jewish neighbors or acquaintances, who had witnessed their deportation or murder.

Interestingly, the ways in which children acquired information highlights the intimate relationships and social networks that Jewish families had with their non-Jewish surroundings. In his deposition Jerzy Hoffman relates, "I escaped to Krakow and went to the janitor of the firm 'Spectrum' and found out from him that my uncle perished from hunger in some camp, but my auntie lived."[37] Likewise, Zygmunt Weinreb, aged four at the outbreak of war, recalls finding out about his mother's fate from the janitor of the brick factory: "In May 1944 mother left on a Wednesday and was supposed to return Thursday or Friday. . . . In the meantime as she left she did not return. When she was not here on Sunday I thought 'oho, bad.' . . . I thought to myself that it was very crowded and she could not get into the train. But after a few days Puchala came and told me that mother was at his house, and went out and never came back."[38]

Some of the children describe finding out about the fate of their family members from other Jews who were trying to hide and escape. Sondek Hochspiegel, aged seven when war broke out, recalls, "After 3–4 days it happened that I went to a householder for bread. My brothers remained on the road. They waited for me. After that I could not find them. Only after meeting Jews I knew I found out that the Germans caught my brothers. From that time on I never heard from them."[39] Rozalia Barnet, aged nine at the outbreak of war, recalls how she was in hiding with a Pole in a village and learned of the fate of her parents from her brother who had come to find her:

> One day I chased a cow to a pasture and there I saw my brother. He found out that from Ciechanowska where I was and found me. He told me then that he was with the partisans. I asked him for mother and he cried then and told me how our parents perished. The Germans took them to the Jewish cemetery and told them to dig a hole. Who could jump over the ditch, could save his life. The hole was very deep and wide. Mother jumped and fell in. After her jumped father and the Germans shot them both. My brother stood behind the fence and saw it all. We both cried and I told my brother that I will go and register as a Jew and they should kill me too, because I don't want to be alone in this world. My brother consoled me that maybe we will survive and he will take care of me. I ran to the house to bring him sour milk and biscuits. Suddenly I hear shots. I returned and already my brother was dying. A

Ukrainian noticed him and shot at him. I washed his wounds and he lived for five minutes more.[40]

While deportation could sometimes be confirmed, the actual fate of these adults was only learned after the war. Jerzy Hoffman recounts, "In Plaszow, O.D. Wahrenhaupt told me that daddy and mommy were deported no one knew where. [A] few days ago, a lady I know, Sala Krunholz, told me that she saw my parents in Auschwitz."[41]

In order to survive the children's *aktion* (round up prior to deportation) Mirka Bram's mother gave three-year-old Mirka to a peasant woman in Adampol. The camp was close to the woman's house, and hence Mirka's mother could visit her. Mirka recalls how she learned of her mother's fate from her rescuer: "Once, returning from a visit to mommy I met a carriage full of Germans. I thought nothing bad, but people were saying that the Germans surrounded Gajow and will shoot Jewish women. Then I cried a lot and was afraid for mommy. Our landlord consoled me that this might not be true and the next day he went to look. He came back and told me that if I wanted to see mommy the last time, I should go with him, because mommy lays in the river where she has been shot down. But I did not want to see mommy shot down."[42]

These depositions also reveal how children learned about their difficult reality though their parents' emotional and psychological reactions. Many of these young children witnessed their parents' emotional collapse as well as their great efforts to remain alive. Dwojra Frymet explains:

> We were poor before the war, but now after father's death we had nothing at all to eat. . . . When we moved to the ghetto, we had our furniture, but in this room where we had to live, there was no room and the furniture was in the court yard. I and my siblings were glad that we were moving. There was great enjoyment for us to take the furniture and different things out of the apartment. My mommy cried a great deal then and said that we were going to our death. She buried the best we had, the Passover dishes, because she thought that maybe one us children will survive and will take these things perhaps. Mommy was sick constantly from worry. My older brothers has to carry her to the ghetto (because she could not walk) to our new apartment. Other Jews could gather staples but we had no money, Mommy and the children were swollen from hunger.[43]

Dwojra's testimony is a painful rendition of the emotional and physical collapse of her mother, a harrowing portrait of the loss of the parents' ability to protect their children. This extract illuminates a noted phenomenon in the ghetto whereby children often took over their parents' role by becoming providers and protectors not only of their siblings but also of their own parents who could not withstand the harsh reality.[44] Some depositions reveal how children often made their own decisions that contrasted with those of their parents. Edward Keningsberg gives one such example:

> In our house lived a Jewish mason. Mommy and daddy asked him to repair our *szuber* [stove] because it was out of order. But in reality they wanted to poison themselves. I began to ask what will be done with this *szuber*. Mommy answered that the *szuber* is fixed we will go to sleep. And I asked what will happen after we go to sleep. Mommy told me that when we fall asleep we will never wake up. I asked mommy why we will not wake up. Mom did not answer me and I guessed that we will be dead. Then I began to scream that I want to live. When I was crying, Trembowelski said that he would not repair the *szuber*, that it may be still good. Mommy, daddy and other Jews resigned themselves.[45]

In many of the interviews, at the same time as recalling their parents' ingenuity and bravery in the struggle to survive, the children also show insight into the physical and emotional toll of their ordeal. Wladyslaw Siekierka, five years old when war broke out, recalls: "Mother dressed as an Aryan and went to the town to beg from people she knew. We died of fear before mother would return, because we could never be sure that she will come back. . . . When mother was supposed to come at night we didn't sleep. . . . Mothers' legs were swollen from all this walking and she moaned for a long time and told us about her wanderings and how she deceived the Germans."[46]

The depositions thus not only relate the children's stories of survival but also document the experiences and fates of others: grandparents, parents, and siblings. They are testaments to the reactions of the adult world to their terrifying reality and to the relations that developed between family members as witnessed by children. The adults' reactions were a source of information for these children, helping them to understand their wartime reality and possibly providing a model for their own behavior and responses.

Children's Relational and Emotional World

Relational memory is not only connected to children's awareness and understanding of their reality, but is also the emotional core of their experience. Relationships united children with their prewar normal life, and the destruction of these relationships signaled prewar life's radical demise and their changed reality. This can be seen in the structure of the depositions; many begin with a relational memory that signals a changed reality. For example, Hieronim Majzlisz recalls, "I well remember the start of the ghetto on the 12.14.1941, because that was the last time I saw my friend Rysia Schatz."[47] Likewise, in his deposition Jurek Adin recalled, "I still remember the bombardment of Warsaw in 1939. A friend came to visit me. We sat in the shelter and a bomb fell and killed the friend who was walking home."[48] The depositions often end with a comment on the relationships they have lost and the new ones they have formed. C, for example, was hidden for most of the war by Poles and evaded capture by wandering together with a young girl, Marysia, "from one corner to another." He concludes his deposition: "In the end Marysia went to Krakow without leaving her address. Our paths parted. The old generation partially perished, but we the young ones we are building a new society which knows how to love and obtain freedom."[49]

Another example of relational memory from is from Syda Furnschein's deposition: "My worst experience was the time when I lost my mother and I became a total orphan even though I had a father. Continuously I dream of pictures of my house. I dream about my parents, about holidays and that we are going with the family to grandma etc. My yearning right now is not to separate from my caretakers and to go my family and be together with grandma."[50] Pearl Freitag, the sole survivor of her family, ends her testimony in the following way: "I entered the children's residence, at 25 Narutowich Street. I like this place very much; I am with many children. We work together, and study together. Here I do not feel so lonely, and I am no more depressed."[51]

In her discussion of the deposition collection, Beate Müller noted a "relative rarity of emotional comments in the children's stories."[52] She argued that "the narratives do contain signs of emotion, but they are not foregrounded and therefore have to be deduced from the surface text."[53] Müller used traumatic memory to relate to the noticeable absence of expressed emotions, attributing this to the editing of the testimonials that may have been done by the interviewers after the interviews were conducted. This "related both to legal practices of the time . . . and to then prevalent epistemological traditions in historiography and (Polish) social science, as well as to modes of writing about the self in East European Jewry."[54] While it is clear that there is no obvious outpouring of emotion in these depositions, the events described are, in my opinion, very emotional. More specifically, the expression of emotion is located in the relational moments, particularly those times of separation from or the loss of their parents.

In his deposition Henryk Weinman, born in 1941, recalls the highly emotional separation from his parents. Such separations were excruciating and even the parents could not contain their emotions:

> We lived in a small apartment, a room with a kitchen. I slept in such a big bed with mommy and daddy, I had a nice suit, a sailor suit. Mommy gave me the best food they had at home. She told me that a man wants to take me away from her and he is a Jew. . . . I told mommy that I would not leave for anything in the world. She told me several times "do not return to the Jews." Once Witek came and told me he will be my brother. I cried a lot and screamed that I will not go away from mommy. Mommy cried a lot and daddy too. All three of us were crying, only Witek did not, he took me without my coat and put me into the car by force. I screamed, I cried, I asked: "To whom? What for? Why? Where do you take me, Sir? I want to go back to mommy, but Witek did not listen.[55]

Zofia Kessler witnessed the death of her family members and the desperation of her mother. In her account, she recalls her emotional reaction to the loss of her mother:

> In the summer of 1940 the Germans came to us and they began to shoot. I ran away with Mommy and my brother. Mommy got wounded when the Germans chased us. Me and mommy hid in the bathroom. Both ran away in the opposite direction. Through the slit in the bathroom I saw how they shot brother and took out people from the barracks. Among them was also daddy. When it calmed down we went to my sister in the village. Mommy was wounded on the leg but walked still. We told sister everything but she was afraid to keep us. We went to my brother. My brother's landlady gave us food and I went to my landlady where we sold various things. . . . When I returned to my brother the next day, he told me that mother went to the Germans herself because she said she could no longer suffer since she had an infection. I remained with my brother. We both sat down and cried. My brother said: "You go to the landlady and don't admit to them you are Jewish" and told me to go. It was winter, I had no shoes and was cold.[56]

In some of the depositions, emotion is expressed in relation to the children's rescuer who hid them and kept them safe until the end of the war. Some of the child survivors speak of their emotions when having to leave their Christian caretakers and of the emotional support they received from them during these difficult times. One of the intentions of the CJHC was to document the behavior of the local population toward the murder of the Jews. These depositions reveal a gamut of responses, as pointed out by Joanna Michlic in her work on Jewish children in Nazi-occupied Poland based on their early postwar recollections: "Overall, the eyewitness testimonies bring a new dimension to the well-recognized issues of betrayal, hostility and indifference on the one hand, and of sacrifice, dedication and compassionate care on the other. They reveal that sometimes these seemingly opposing reactions intersected."[57]

Conclusion

There are multiple layers to these short and powerful depositions. They give voice to child survivors' memories of their experiences during the war years while also testifying to the responses and reactions of the adult world to the difficult reality that invariably impacted on their own. They detail the children's personal struggles to survive alongside a testimony of the death and destruction of their loved ones. The children do not relate conversations with their parents through which they learned about the changing reality, but rather they articulate the gradual acquisition of knowledge through the scenes and reactions that they witnessed and the information they gathered, showing how they often had to make sense of the chaos on their own.

Central to these interviews is the child's relational world in which their emotional experience is located. In light of Vygotsky's work, this is not surprising as relationships form the foundation of the child's emotional and cognitive world. It is therefore understandable that the disruption, loss, and destruction of relationships during the Shoah, which altered the world of these children irrevocably, is the emotional core of their experience. The loss of adult protection signified death for many young children, and the absence of emotional protection forced children to survive on their own or find other people with whom to connect. However, their feelings of loneliness are a source of distress throughout all of these texts. It is evident from the depositions that the children's narration of their experience is usually in relation to someone. Relationships that are threatened and destroyed are also reconstructed and reformed as their story of survival progresses.

The centrality of their relational world can also be explained through their postwar experiences. After the war, many of them found themselves alone, having to rebuild their lives with no family and without a basic feeling of belonging or connectedness. In the early postwar years, child survivors were charged with finding a way to reconnect and build a network of relationships as they embarked on the arduous journey of rebuilding their lives. Thus, the centrality of relationship in their depositions also sheds light on the primacy of the context of telling and speaks to the wider field of oral history and narrative. These child survivors are telling their stories from the vantage of their present concerns: coming to terms with their losses and finding ways to rebuild social and familial networks, either in the reconstruction of relationships after extended periods of separation from family members or in their integration into the institutional world of orphanages or children's homes. The postwar reality may therefore inform how they frame and present their past experiences.[58] Their relational world is in the foreground and is a central concern, playing an important part in the way they understand and make meaning of their past. Geoffrey Hartman explained that narrative memories are not only a means to communicate memories of experience, but also "can be a source for historical information or confirmation, yet their real struggle lies in recording the psychological and emotional struggle for survival, not only then but also now."[59]

Finally, the relational world could have been expected to still occupy the minds of survivors in the years that followed liberation. Scheeringa and Zeanah pointed out, "Young children experience a variety of positive and negative stressors under the watchful eyes of their caregivers. They will navigate these stressors in large part based upon the nature of their primary caregiving relationships. Further, parents are likely to be the most important and useful agents of change to aid their children's recovery."[60] This important issue is beyond the scope of this chapter, but it suggests the use of the Kestenberg Archive of Testimonies of Child Holocaust Survivors to examine if and how the relational world of child survivors influenced their postwar recovery and adaptation.

Author

Sharon Kangisser Cohen is the Director of the Diane and Eli Zborowski Centre for the Study of the Holocaust and Its Aftermath and the Deportation Project at The International Institute for Holocaust Research, Yad Vashem. She is, in addition, a lecturer at Haifa University and the Rothberg School for international students at the Hebrew University of Jerusalem. She holds a PhD from the Hebrew University in the field of Holocaust studies, and has published numerous articles relating to the postwar lives of survivors of the Holocaust. Her most recent book, *Testimony and Time: Survivors of the Holocaust Remember*, was published in 2015 by Yad Vashem.

Notes

All interviews quoted in this chapter were held at the Oral History Division, Hebrew University of Jerusalem. The original material is to be found in the Jewish Historical Institute, Poland.

1. Testimony of C, (257) 29-4735
2. Dwork, *Children with a Star*, xvii–xxii.
3. Ibid., xvii.
4. Ibid., xxv.
5. For more on this, see Zapruder, *Salvaged Pages*.
6. For more on this archive, see Kassow, *Who Will Write Our History?*; Sakowska, *Archiwum Ringelbluma*; Kermish, *To Live with Honor*.
7. Cohen, "The Children's Voice," 74.
8. Cohen and Horváth. "Young Witnesses in the DP Camps," 103.
9. Over 150 depositions from the Central Jewish Historical Committee were received as part of the Kestenberg Child Survivor Archive. These depositions were translated into English from the original Polish and Yiddish.
10. Christensen and James, *Research with Children*, 2.
11. Ibid., 2.
12. Ibid., 1.
13. Michlic, "The Children Accuse," 15.
14. Müller, "Trauma, Historiography and Polyphony," 160.
15. Michlic, "The Children Accuse," 15.
16. Cohen, "The Children's Voice," 76–77.
17. Ibid., 77.
18. Müller, "Trauma, Historiography and Polyphony," 159.
19. Ibid., 184–185.
20. This can be said to hold true for Holocaust survivors' testimonies and indeed for all oral history interviews. For more on this issue refer to Greenspan, *On Listening to Holocaust Survivors*.
21. Kraft, *Memory Perceived*, 26.
22. It is important to point out that there are numerous issues involved in testimonies that have been translated. It is beyond the scope of this chapter to describe these issues, but I would argue that this is a marginal issue for my work; I do not use a linguistic close reading of the language but rather an exploration of the stories that are told.
23. Hochberg-Mariańska and Grüss, *The Children Accuse*.
24. Engel, "Narrative Analysis of Children's Experience," 203.
25. Woodhead and Faulkner, "Subjects, Objects or Participants?," 27.
26. Hartup and Rubin, *Relationships and Development*, 1–2.
27. This type of interaction would then also inform the child's emotional development and interaction after the war, however this is outside the scope of this chapter.
28. Bender and Frosch, "Children's Reactions to the War," 12; Jensen and Shaw, "Children as Victims of War," 32; Barenbaum, Ruchkin, and Schwab-Stone, "Psychosocial Aspects of Children Exposed to War," 46.

29. Scheeringa and Zeanah, "Relational Perspective on PTSD in Early Childhood," 808.
30. Bender and Frosch, "Children's Reactions to the War."
31. Beverly, "The Reaction of Children and Youth to Wartime"; Barenbaum, Ruchkin, and Schwab-Stone, "Psychosocial Aspects of Children Exposed to War," 46.
32. Testimony of Karolina Matecka (257) 32-5313. 1947
33. Testimony of Halina Hoffman, (257) 32-3638.
34. Testimony of Jerzy Andrzej Hoffman, (257) 32-1520.
35. Testimony of Mania Steiner, (257) 32-3698. 1948
36. Testimony of Edward Keningsberg, (257) 32-3342. 1948
37. Testimony of Jerzy Hoffman, (257) 32-3342.
38. Testimony of Zygmunt Weinreb, (257) 32-406. 1945
39. Testimony of Sondek Hochspiegel, (257) 32-2762. 1947
40. Testimony of Rozalia Barnet, (257) 32-2740. 1943
41. Testimony of Jerzy Andrzej Hoffman, (257) 32-1520.
42. Testimony of Mirka Bram, (257) 32-3638. 1945
43. Testimony of Dwojra Frymet, (257) 32-2794. 1947
44. For more on this issue, see Ofer, "Cohesion and Rupture"; and Kangisser Cohen, "Family Relationships in the Nazi Ghetto."
45. Testimony of Edward Keningsberg, (257) 32-3342. 1948
46. Testimony of Wladyslaw Siekierka, (257) 32-3681. 1947
47. Testimony of Hieronim Majzlisz, (257) 32-1519.
48. Testimony of Jurek Adin, (257) 32-3685. 1948
49. Testimony of C, (257) 32-4735.
50. Testimony of Syda Furnschein, (257) 32-3618.
51. Testimony of Pearl Freitag, (275) 32-3616. 1946
52. Müller, "Trauma, Historiography and Polyphony," 170.
53. Ibid.
54. Ibid.
55. Testimony of Henryk Weineman, (257) 32-3362.
56. Testimony of Zofia Kessler, (257) 32-1267. 1947
57. Michlic, Joanna B. *Jewish children in Nazi-occupied Poland: survival and Polish-Jewish relations during the Holocaust as reflected in early postwar recollections.* Yad Vashem, 2008.
58. The story as told by the survivors is their memory and their interpretation of the event, and it is in constant negotiation and dialogue. The meaning that individuals attribute to their past is likely influenced by various factors, including the contemporaneous context in which their self is being negotiated and constructed.
59. Hartman, *The Longest Shadow*, 142.
60. Scheeringa and Zeanah, "A Relational Perspective on PTSD in Early Childhood," 813.

References

Barenbaum, J., V. Ruchkin, and M. Schwab-Stone. "The Psychosocial Aspects of Children Exposed to War: Practice and Policy Initiatives." *Journal of Child Psychology and Psychiatry* 45 (2004).

Bender, L., and J. Frosch. "Children's Reactions to the War." *American Journal of Orthopsychiatry* 12, no. 4 (1942): 571–586.

Beverly, B.I. "The Reaction of Children and Youth to Wartime." *Journal of Pediatrics* 20 (1942).

Christensen, P., and A. James, eds. *Research with Children: Perspectives and Practices.* London: Routledge, 2008.

Cohen, B. "The Children's Voice: Postwar Collection of Testimonies from Child Survivors of the Holocaust." *Holocaust and Genocide Studies* 21, no. 1 (Spring 2007): 73–95.

Cohen, B., and R. Horváth. "Young Witnesses in the DP Camps: Children's Holocaust testimony in context." *Journal of Modern Jewish Studies* 11 (2012): 103–125.

Dwork, Debórah. *Children with a Star: Jewish Youth in Nazi Europe.* New Haven, CT: Yale University Press, 1991.

Engel, S. "Narrative Analysis of Children's Experience." In *Researching Children's Experience. Approaches and Methods,* edited by S. Greene and D. Hogan, 199–216. Thousand Oaks, CA: Sage, 2005.

Greenspan, H. *On Listening to Holocaust Survivors: Beyond Testimony.* Saint Paul, MN: Paragon House, 2010.

Hartman, Geoffrey. *The Longest Shadow: In the Aftermath of the Holocaust.* New York: Palgrave, 2002.

Hartup, W.W., and Z. Rubin, eds. *Relationships and Development.* Oxford: Psychology Press, 1985.

Hochberg-Mariańska, M., and N. Grüss, eds. *The Children Accuse,* translated by Bill Johnston. London: Vallentine Mitchell, 1996.

Jensen, P.S., and J. Shaw. "Children as Victims of War: Current Knowledge and Future Research Needs." *Journal of the American Academy of Child and Adolescent Psychiatry* 32 (1993).

Kangisser Cohen, Sharon. "Family Relationships in the Nazi Ghetto: Kovno—A Case Study." *Journal of Family History* 31, no. 3 (2006): 267–288.

Kassow, Samuel D. *Who Will Write Our History?: Emanuel Ringelblum, the Warsaw Ghetto, and the Oyneg Shabes Archive.* Bloomington: Indiana University Press, 2007.

Kermish, Joseph. *To Live with Honor and to Die with Honor.* Jerusalem: Yad Vashem, 1986.

Kraft, Robert N. *Memory Perceived: Recalling the Holocaust.* Westport, CT: Praeger, 2002.

Michlic, Joanna. "The Children Accuse (Poland, 1946): Between Exclusion from and Inclusion into the Holocaust Cannon." *Society for the History of Children and Youth Newsletter* 9 (2007).

———. *Jewish Children in Nazi-Occupied Poland: Survival and Polish-Jewish Relations during the Holocaust as Reflected in Early Postwar Recollections*. Jerusalem: Yad Vashem, 2008.

Müller, Beate. "Trauma, Historiography and Polyphony: Adult Voices in the CJHC's Early Post-War Child Holocaust Testimonies." *History and Memory* 24, no. 2 (2012): 157–195.

Ofer, D. "Cohesion and Rupture: The Jewish Family in the East European Ghettos in the Holocaust." *Studies in Contemporary Jewry* 14 (1998): 143–165.

Sakowska, Ruta, ed. *Archiwum Ringelbluma*. Vol. 2 *Dzieci—tajne nauczanie w getcie warszawskim*. Warsaw: ŻIH, 2000.

Scheeringa, M.S., and C.H. Zeanah. "A Relational Perspective on PTSD in Early Childhood." *Journal of Traumatic Stress* 14 (2001).

Woodhead, M., and D. Faulkner. "Subjects, Objects or Participants?" In *Research with Children: Perspectives and Practices*, edited by P. Christensen and A. James,. London: Routledge, 2008.

Zapruder, A. *Salvaged Pages: Young Writers' Dairies of the Holocaust*. New Haven, CT: Yale University Press, 2002.

 3

Starting Over
Reconstituted Families after the Holocaust

Beth B. Cohen

Introduction

In the year 2000 the United States Holocaust Memorial Museum and its Second Generation Advisory Group hosted a conference entitled "Life Reborn: Jewish Displaced Persons, 1946–1951."[1] It was the first such gathering to address the Jewish displaced persons (DP) experience as a legitimate topic for academic inquiry.[2] As its title "Life Reborn" suggests, an important theme framing the conference was how Holocaust survivors in the DP camps began the process of starting anew immediately after the war. Many noted how quickly the DPs married and began families. Indeed, scholars have documented the historically high birthrate in the DP camps that has come to symbolize survivors' resilience as well as postwar renewal of Jewish life.[3]

A 1949 article from the *New York Times*, however, offered an alternative view of DP families. In her description, the journalist noted the arrival of Vilna ghetto survivors Mr. and Mrs. Schwartzenburg and their fourteen-year-old daughter who sailed into New York harbor after three years in a DP camp. The report recorded that among the refugee families lining the decks were thirty-nine children between the ages of six and sixteen.[4] The examples of the Schwartzenburgs and others in this story suggest a different model of postwar Jewish families: one composed not of newlywed survivors bringing a post-Holocaust generation of babies into the world but one made up of the rejoining of parents and children of preexisting families that had been ruptured by the war. For the latter, starting over meant the complex cobbling together of the remains of what had been rather than starting anew.

This chapter explores the reconstruction of these Jewish families in the wake of the Shoah. I scrutinized reconstituted families that include children born before or during the war from the perspective of the children themselves. What were some of the consequences for children who became part of (in today's parlance) blended families composed uniquely of survivors? How did the dynamics of a two-generation survivor family affect the youngsters, their role in the family, and their self-perception as survivors? To explore these questions, I drew from a variety of sources. This includes the newly accessible Kestenberg Holocaust Child Survivor Archive at the Hebrew University of Jerusalem, video testimonies from the University of Southern California (USC) Shoah Foundation, my own oral history collection, and contemporary archival material from Jewish communal organizations.[5] Synthesizing these varied sources allows patterns to emerge that repeat themselves across different oral history collections. That these patterns repeat across families' experiences in a variety of sources illuminate and reinforce the complexity of post-Holocaust Jewish family groups. They also challenge preconceived models of survivor families in the aftermath of World War II, models that emphasized Jewish renewal and neglected the aftereffects of the Holocaust on Jewish children and their parents.

Background

The murder of between one million and one and a half million children, perhaps 90 percent of the prewar population, reflects the particular vulnerability of Jewish children and the irrevocable rupture of prewar Jewish families.[6] Those children who endured comprised, therefore, a tiny shred of the Shoah's surviving remnant: an estimated 150,000 were alive in 1945.[7]

Although the contemporary media showcased the plight of Jewish war orphans, especially for the sake of American fundraising campaigns, most of the surviving children fell outside this category. In fact, in 1948 Leo Wulman, a physician and member of both the World Jewish Congress and American Oeuvres de Secours aux Enfant (OSE), noted that roughly 20 percent of those in the range of five to ten years old were orphans.[8] Approximately 80 percent in this group, then, were not orphans but had one surviving parent (rarely two[9]), which sharply contrasts with both the image of the orphan child survivor in the postwar contemporary media as well as the later popular and scholarly depictions of families as articulated at the "Life Reborn" conference noted earlier.[10]

Reunion with Birth Parents and Separation from Foster Parents

Many, though not all, children survived because they spent the war in hiding. Because it was harder, for many reasons, for a group to hide, few families remained together during the war. While some intact nuclear families still existed after the war, this was the extremely rare exception. In some instances, one parent was able to hide with a child. The perception that it would be easier to survive if separated or for practical purposes (i.e., the availability of a hiding spot only for one) meant that children were frequently separated from their parents.[11]

Usually, the surviving parent's first step after the war—if separated from offspring during the war—was to find his or her child. This process was often far from straightforward and could take months, if not longer. Sometimes, but not always, a parent knew exactly where a child had spent the war years. A parent might search for months or even years before finding children who had been hidden in multiple or unknown locations, for example. Natalie Gold's experience illustrates this. Her parents smuggled her out of the Radzimin Ghetto in 1943 at the age of eighteen months. Moving from one hiding place to another, they grew desperate and decided to try to at least save their baby. They placed a necklace with a cross around her neck and abandoned her on the doorstep of an acquaintance. Soon after her mother was deported to Treblinka. By then, unbeknownst to her parents, Natalie had been placed with nuns. After the war her widowed father had nearly given up after a year of searching when he found her at a convent among hundreds of unclaimed children.[12]

Eva Brettler, a survivor of Ravensbruck and Bergen-Belsen who was ten years old when the war ended experienced a similarly prolonged postwar separation from her father. In 1945 she was sent from Germany to a Jewish orphanage in Sweden. She was certain her mother was dead and believed her father was too. After a year spent adjusting to her new Scandinavian environment, she learned that her father was alive and returned to him in Budapest.[13] Other examples confirm that there was often a temporal gap beyond the war years before a parent claimed a child. This lapse in time often had significant consequences for the child.

If finding children was complicated logistically, reunions between the generations were psychologically thorny. For one, foster parents were familiar whereas biological parents, depending on the child's age and wartime experiences, could be strangers. In a 1948 report from the Jewish Family and Children's Services, Denver, Colorado, a social worker captured Mr. M's comments about his son Bob who was six when he retrieved him after a three-year separation. The social worker wrote, "When they [Mr. and Mrs. M] were able to take Bob back, he, of course, was frightened at the very beginning and did not want to leave the house where he was living." But, she added, Mr. M reported (as parents often reflected later) that "shortly afterwards, he adjusted himself."[14]

As this social worker recorded, it was not only the renewed contact with a biological parent that was fraught but also, simultaneously, the sometimes hurried separation from the family that had sheltered them. The experience of Lea Eliash and her daughter Asya, is one of many that speaks to this point. While in the Lithuanian ghetto of Kovno, Lea managed to arrange for a childless gentile couple to hide two-year-old Asya on their condition that they would raise her as a Christian but return her after the war should her parents survive. Lea smuggled her daughter out of the ghetto to the place where Asya would live for the duration of the war. When Lea was finally able to reclaim her daughter after a two-year separation, Asya was reluctant to leave the only mother she knew to go with Lea, who was, by then, a stranger. Asya's rescuer, however, honored her promise and, over the course of a few months, gradually relinquished the girl. Again, as in the case of Mr. M, Lea remembered that after an initial distance Asya readjusted quickly and well to her mother.[15]

The quality of wartime care was not necessarily a predictor of a child's reaction to the shift back to a birth parent. RF offers an example of a child whose wartime experiences were not positive, but whose reunion with her mother was hardly a smooth transition. Rather, it highlights that these postwar meetings were sometimes less about new beginnings and more often about complicated familial reconnections.[16]

RF was born in Vienna in 1937. When she was an infant her father left for America in the hope of sending for his wife and daughter once he was established in the new country. With the worsening political situation, this plan came to naught, as did an attempt to send RF on a *Kindertransport* (children's transport). Eventually, RF and her mother went to Belgium to be with her mother's family. When the family went into hiding, three-year-old RF was placed in a convent. Over the next few years she was moved to a series of hiding places. She was sporadically taken for brief visits to her mother who was usually in transit to a different refuge. She spent the last part of the war in an orphanage in Belgium where she recalls feeling isolated and withdrawn. After the war an American soldier took an interest in her and began visiting. He wanted to adopt her and, although she told him she had a father in America, he did not believe her. As he continued to explore the possibility of adopting her, the Red Cross confirmed her father's existence. During that period, RF's mother also returned from Auschwitz and told her now eight-year-old daughter that she would be resuming life with her mother. Was she pleased by this turn of events? "I really don't know," she recalls in an interview. "No," she clarifies, "it [her mother] was another person coming into my life. . . . I was very excited that this soldier was going to adopt me. . . . He was the closest person that I had ever been to. . . . I spent the longest amount of time with him than I had ever spent with anyone in my whole life." Over the course of the soldier's visits to the orphanage he took the girl for Jeep rides and brought her chocolates. RF reflects, "I developed a sort of relationship with this man. . . . He became a real caretaker for me and then my mother arrives and she interrupts this and now I have to go with her and all of this is behind me."[17]

RF had no choice but to go, however unwillingly, with her mother. Soon after she returned to her mother, her father managed to locate them. This, too, was not, it transpired, a welcome development. After finding his wife and child, RF's father served his wife with divorce papers. Despite her mother's bitterness, she and her daughter emigrated to the United States. Her parents did, in fact, reunite and remained together because of her, she believes, even though, according to RF, they never truly reconciled.[18] Moreover, she expressed that her father's long absence left her feeling that "a father figure didn't mean that much to me anymore." In fact, she clarifies, "it didn't mean anything to me."[19]

It would seem, therefore, that RF had a tenuous and ambiguous connection with both father and mother. She had to contend with tremendous challenges. In addition to a mother who had been in Auschwitz, her parents' fractured marriage, and emigration to another country, RF had spent the war years in a series of institutions; by the time she and her parents were finally reunited, she had had little experience of being part of a nuclear family.

In A-FH's oral history, she offers a different picture of a child parting from the sheltering family to reunite with her father, a stranger, which was initially complicated but, according to her, proceeded relatively smoothly. Her Polish foster family did not want to surrender her after the war but not, she learned, because they were deeply attached to her.[20] Rather, they had hoped to save her soul and prevent her from returning to Judaism. When it became clear that her father was intent on reclaiming her, they moved her to a secret location. Her father tracked her and had a friend "literally kidnap me." Yet, A-FH does not recall this separation from her foster family as traumatic. This seems surprising because, until the age of six, she had never seen her father. Perhaps it was because, as she later learned, she was bruised, ill, and emaciated when her father found her, the result of apparent neglect and abuse by her "rescuers."[21] For both A-FH and RF, the wartime years were harrowing ones that would fundamentally affect them later when they rejoined their families.

New Parents, New Siblings: Postwar Family Constellations Reconfigured

In the instances where parents, such as Mr. M and Lea Eliash, comment on their reunions with their offspring, they tend to minimize the child's transition back to the parent as they recall the joy they felt at having their children back. While A-FH's memories support a seemingly smooth change, many child survivors, like RF and others, recollect the return to their birth parents as difficult, even traumatic. In addition to the possible wrench of leaving the foster family or the challenge of resuming life in yet another strange setting, much had happened—not just during but also after the war—that had profound effects on the child. For example, Eva Brettler, the previously mentioned child in Sweden, was surprised to learn that not only was her father alive in Budapest, but also that she now had a new mother and baby brother.[22]

Eva's experience was not uncommon. Just as unattached, single survivors in DP camps married quickly after liberation, so did young widows and widowers in the interim between the war's end and the recovery of a surviving child. These unions soon produced children. As a result, the surviving children found themselves not only adjusting to resumed contact with a biological parent and, for some, the pain of separation from the rescuing family, but also the difficulty of coping with a new stepparent and half-sibling born after the war, the stepparent's "real" child. In her testimony, Ellen Zitkin articulates the feeling of being a fifth wheel in her postwar family constellation. The expression on her face belied the superficiality of this cliché, suggesting the pain still fresh fifty years later.[23] Others echoed this sense of marginalization experienced in the new dynamic created as adult survivors rebuilt their postwar family with new partners. While many child survivors grew to love and become deeply attached to stepparents and half-siblings, they also acknowledged that this relationship, particularly early on, was laden with complex emotions.

A-FH voiced another perspective that speaks to family divisions created by reconstituted families. Although her stepmother insisted she treated her as if her own child, A-FH's memories challenge this. She recalls that her parents "always fought disgustingly," which provoked her stepmother to accuse her husband and A-FH— "you and her"—of siding against her.[24] Child survivors repeatedly emphasize that having one surviving parent was not necessarily a positive reconnection or beginning for them. For those whose parents remarried, the replacement of a deceased parent with a stepparent could evoke confusing emotions in the child.

RL's interview captures some of the bewilderment she felt toward her stepmother.[25] In 1942, at the age of five, she went into hiding in an attic with a large group of immediate and extended family members. She witnessed her mother's death there shortly before the end of the war. After the war, her father remarried another survivor. Regarding her stepmother, RL remarks, "I never considered her my mother; she was just not mother material. . . . She had her own stuff to deal with and I never felt love for her." RL also reveals that she could not understand why her father remarried because her childhood self imagined her mother might return to them. When asked to name her worst experiences, she does not describe the two years she spent in an attic with fourteen people but rather her father's marriage to her stepmother, her perception of her father's postwar deterioration, and her own profound struggle with depression as she was growing up in the United States.[26]

Family Secrets and Taboos

A-FH's interview reveals another dynamic of the new family configuration. She was approximately three years old when her mother died in Auschwitz. As noted, she met her father for the first time when she was six. She mourns that she has few, if any, memories of her mother. Her father, however, "refused to talk about her. He lost her, he remarried." Her added comment, "It's a whole mess," hints at the layers of difficulties that shadowed them. According to A-FH, her father, like RL's, never recovered from his first wife's death and could not bring himself to speak of her to his daughter. As a child, A-FH desperately wanted to know more about her mother but had no one to whom she could turn. The father of Natalie Gold, the little girl discovered in the convent, also remarried another survivor. Natalie, too, found that her dead mother was a forbidden topic of conversation but for different reasons. Natalie believes her stepmother was jealous of her husband's dead spouse, perceiving her memory as a rival in her marriage. Eva Brettler also recalls the tension aroused in her postwar family by the mention of her dead mother. It was traumatic enough that she had lost her mother when she was six years old, but when her deceased parent became a taboo subject, "it was," Eva laments, "like she never existed."[27]

Many, many other survivors echo these recollections. The children quickly learned that neither their surviving parent nor their stepparent would allow them to raise questions about the dead parent. This silence often led to the fiction that the stepparents were not stepparents at all, but the child's only mother or father, which further erased the memory and the reality of the murdered parent's connection to the child. While in A-FH's eyes her stepmother was wonderful, she remembers that her stepmother did not want A-FH's children to know that their mother was not her biological daughter or that A-FH and her sister, born to her father and stepmother after the war, were half-siblings. Natalie and Eva's stepmothers behaved similarly. In the example of the former, Natalie's children learned the true nature of their grandfather's wife when they stumbled across an interview about their mother in a magazine. Eva's children also discovered the truth by accident, when her teenaged son noticed that his grandparents' wedding anniversary did not align with his mother's age. And with this revelation, the younger generation experienced feelings of betrayal by the older generation.

Hiding the true nature of relationships is a phenomenon, however, that ripples repeatedly through child survivor testimonies and one with which many struggled profoundly and continuously throughout their lives. Eva N's story illustrates this secrecy at the family's core and the long shadow it cast. Eva was born in 1941; she and her mother were sheltered in several hiding places near Budapest. Her father died in a labor camp and after the war, CF-N, a close friend of her father's, moved in with them. CF-N and her mother decided that it would be best for four-year-old Eva if they maintained the fiction that he was her biological father. When her sister was born in 1953, Eva overheard a visiting relative comment that "maybe now he [CF-N] will be happy having a child of his own."[28] Those words prompted twelve-year-old Eva to check the family safe where she found her birth certificate listing her biological father's name. She also found adoption papers. She then learned the truth from her mother; her father had been murdered in a Hungarian labor camp and the man she believed to be her father was, in fact, her stepfather. "My step-father loved me very much," states Eva, but when she learned his true identity she was thrown into turmoil.[29] She now understood why there was so little physical resemblance between herself and CF-N. She felt betrayed by her parents and wondered what other secrets they had kept from her. Eventually she learned at least one: the relative that occasionally visited was her paternal grandmother and not, as she had been told, a distant cousin. By the time she knew this, this relative had passed away. Even today, many decades later, Eva still feels the lingering effects of this denied connection to her paternal grandmother and of what she considers her mother's loyalty to her stepfather over both Eva and her deceased father.[30]

The reasons for fostering these untruths varied. A-FH believes it was her stepmother's need for self-protection. Acknowledging the truth "will kill my [step] mother, it will destroy her," she states.[31] In A-FH's opinion, her stepmother believed that her stepdaughter would love her less without a biological connection, even though A-FH largely expresses her utmost admiration for the woman who she says "epitomizes great courage and heroism" in becoming her stepparent.[32] Some of the secrecy, though, may have reflected societal norms of the times when families were less open about matters they believed were best left unspoken. Certainly, too, the late 1940s–1950s was an era in which the traditional family was idealized.[33] While blended families existed, they were much more of a departure from the norm than they are today. Perhaps survivor stepparents, negotiating the process of acculturating to life in the United States, were especially sensitive to the external image they projected and believed they would be more accepted if perceived as biological parents, as a "real" family. Possibly they thought that revealing their true relationship would invite unwanted questions. Child survivors still struggle, however, to accept the shroud of secrecy; many survivors perceive that their parents maintained secrecy at the expense of honesty, and that this secrecy undermined and effaced their memory of deceased parents.

Unanswered Questions

At times, additional complications arose in reconstructed families provoked by unanswered questions concerning wartime experiences. An example from the archives of the Jewish Family and Children's Services in Denver sheds light on the effects of doubts that lingered in the minds of some parents long after the war ended. While details are scanty, we learn from the social worker's report that Polish survivors Mr. B and daughters Joann and Ann arrived in America in 1951. Once settled in Denver, Mr. B believed he was unable, for both financial and emotional reasons, to properly care for his two daughters. Joann, aged fourteen, was placed in the National Jewish Home for Children. Buried in her file is an alarming statement: Joann's father, who had "lost sight" of his daughter during the war when she was placed in a convent, was not positive that she was, in fact, his biological daughter. The social worker noted, "There had been definite signs of rejection on part of Mr. B which had intensified Joanne's personality difficulties."[34] It is unclear whether Joann knew of or shared her father's suspicions, but it certainly affected Mr. B's attitude toward her. Likewise, Natalie Gold never discussed with her father her fears that she might not be his. Yet given that he had not seen her for three years when she was a toddler, she did indeed wonder. And this lingering doubt, accompanied by the unfulfilled need to know about the mother she could not remember, shadowed her childhood and adolescence.[35]

Other Models of Reconstructed Families

Sometimes adults created families with children who they knew were not their biological offspring. These examples offer different models of familial units in the wake of the Shoah. Archival sources detail adults who pieced together a two-generation family comprising themselves as parents with orphans, usually blood relatives, as their children. Orphaned brothers Anshel and Jankel G speak to this situation. During the war Anshel assumed the role of protector over Jankel, who was eight years younger.[36] Jankel in fact attributes his survival in hiding to his brother's contacts and arrangements with a Russian peasant. Toward the end of the war, Anshel was hospitalized for typhus and on recuperation, was in danger of being drafted into the Russian army. Jankel, fearful of the separation and threat to Anshel's safety, went to the authorities where he recalls crying, "'Look, this is my father. Without him I wouldn't have survived,' which is the truth."[37] Anshel managed to evade the army and, soon after, met and proposed to his future wife. But the proposal came with conditions. According to Jankel he said, "I want you to know that you are marrying me but I have an eleven-year-old son. . . . I just want you to know in advance." Jankel notes that the young woman understood the relationship and accepted his brother's proposal. Eventually relatives of their mother sent them affidavits so they could immigrate to America. The newly married couple in their twenties, along with their now fourteen-year-old "son," arrived in New York in 1948 and continued on to Philadelphia where their American sponsors lived. Once in Philadelphia, their aunt encouraged Anshel to leave Jankel with her until he had established himself. For the next four years, Jankel lived with his aunt and uncle, visiting his brother and sister-in-law during summers. He finally returned to his brother in 1952 when he was eighteen years old. Jankel appears to have accepted the arrangement that separated him from his brother, perhaps because his childhood, like others, was not cohesive but rather a series of interruptions to which he had become accustomed. He notes that he grew up at an early age.[38] Indeed, the sense of an interrupted or missing childhood is a common yet significant theme among child survivors.[39]

Like Jankel, Lya Frank and her younger sister were orphaned by the war, and became part of a new family composed of survivor relatives that reflects yet another type of postwar dynamic. Lya was born in Utrecht, Holland, in 1936.[40] Just before her parents' deportation to Westerbork and Auschwitz in 1943, they arranged for Lya and her younger sister to go into hiding with separate families. By the end of the war she and her sister were orphans. An uncle and his wife and daughter had also survived in hiding in Holland. According to Lya, her uncle searched Red Cross lists and within a few months he had located his two nieces. Because living quarters were difficult to obtain, Lya joined her sister's foster family for six months while her uncle petitioned successfully to become the girls' guardian. Soon after, the girls moved into their aunt and uncle's home. The consequences of having had multiple families in her short life, as well as the impact of joining a family where her survivor aunt and uncle became her parents, were not lost on Lya. By the time she was nine years old, she notes, she had had four sets of parents. Reflecting on the range of experience, she recalls, "My own parents were affectionate—hugging, kissing, expressive. My hiding parents were kind but did not readily show emotion. My sister's hiding parents were strict in their religion, but affectionate."[41] And as for the relatives with whom she remained after the war, she notes, "My uncle and aunt were distressed by the war, and my aunt was constantly unstable. . . . They had lost most of their family and were traumatized."[42] Her aunt and uncle became her new parents and she, as in the case of other children, became part of a family composed of two generations of survivors. While her maternal aunt and uncle believed they were fulfilling their obligation to their murdered sister's children, it was an arrangement that unfortunately brought little comfort to Lya. In addition to the emotional instability of her new parents, she, like so many, had to adjust to new familial configurations. In this case, it was both her surviving biological cousin (now her "sister") as well as a new baby cousin also called "sister." Lya remembers that she went from a situation where she was "the center of attention" to one where she had to get used to being on the fringe of a volatile family.[43]

PS is another example of an orphan who had a surviving relative of her parents' generation, but unlike Lya's relatives, they did not feel the same sense of obligation toward her.[44] Born in 1932, PS was ten when her parents paid an acquaintance to hide her. She ended up in a Belgian convent where, on liberation, she was reunited with a cousin who had been hidden in an orphanage.[45] One day the girls were told that a mother had come to get them. PS soon saw, much to her grief, that it was her cousin's mother and not hers. Though thirteen-year-old PS hoped that her aunt would claim her too, the woman, an Auschwitz survivor, felt otherwise. PS recalls, "Eventually she was able to take her daughter back with her. . . . She had one little room. . . . This is what always hurt me that she didn't take me as well, she only took her daughter."[46] PS's pain was compounded by learning that her uncle had come back and she recalls saying, "This is the injustice of the world. How could both of them come back and not one of my parents or other aunts or uncles come back?"[47] PS's aunt did feel some responsibility toward her niece and reported her to the Joint Distribution Committee, which helped PS connect with a maternal uncle who had immigrated to America years before the war. As a result, PS moved to the United States in 1949 and settled in New York.

The example of PS encapsulates the experiences of a child survivor who desperately wanted to be part of her surviving relatives' family but who, due to their own limited material and emotional resources, did not include her as they rebuilt their own nuclear family. PS, Lya, and Jankel were all orphans, yet each of their experiences reveals a different picture of reconstructed postwar families. Echoing these examples are the 1950 records of the New York Association for New Americans (NYANA) that report that while the majority of their family caseloads were nuclear families, 11 percent of two-generation families were not made up of parents and their biological children.[48]

Violence toward Child Survivors by Survivor Parents

The Holocaust left its victims with scars that often deeply affected their behavior as parents. Much as it is comforting to believe that the act of surviving and the subsequent family reunions would draw parents (or adult relatives) and children closer, cement relationships, and foster appreciation for renewed family life, this notion does not reflect the profound consequences of the war for those who endured it. In some tragic and extreme instances children became victims after the war. Peter Daniels, born in Germany in 1936, exemplifies this situation.[49] His father abandoned his wife and child before the war, and mother and son survived together in Terezin. After the war his mother became physically abusive toward him. The beatings began in the DP camps after she remarried, and continued in the United States until Peter finally left his mother and stepfather's home at the age of fourteen. His mother, he notes, told him years later that his departure eased the tension between her and her new husband.[50]

Marie Kaufman recalls beatings from her father after they settled in Los Angeles, a result, she believes, of the frustration he felt at his displacement and his struggle to support his family in America.[51] This domestic violence prompted her to leave home and marry at an early age. Others, who wish to remain anonymous, indicate that they were victims of sexual abuse perpetrated by survivor stepparents. One survivor sadly relates that her mother protected her during the war but could not do so afterward.[52] Whether this abuse can be attributed to wartime experiences is impossible to determine. What seems clear, however, are the child survivors' strong feelings of parental betrayal. The same parents who had seemingly done everything to save their children during the war failed to do so afterwards when the children still desperately needed protection. Again, it is impossible to determine the root of the abuse—or its prevalence—but the younger generation of survivors in these instances certainly believe that their parents' behaviors were the result of postwar trauma and tensions brought on by new or renewed family dynamics.

Identity as Survivors

Survivor parents generally dismissed the idea that their children were survivors or even that they were much affected by their past, which added to an already burdened dynamic between the generations. Child survivors articulate a near universal agreement that their experiences went unacknowledged by the older generation. What caused parents to minimize or ignore their children's wartime experiences and memories? Initially, parents may have accepted the general consensus of the day that only concentration camp survivors were true survivors and there were, of course, few child camp survivors. Even those like Ravensbruck survivor Eva Brettler, however, note that their age undermined external recognition of their experiences. Many parents believed that their children were too young to remember events, and that they had, therefore, come out of the war relatively unscathed emotionally.[53] The fact that many children survived because gentiles sheltered them led some to conclude that the younger generation had experienced the best of human behavior rather than the worst. It comes as no surprise, however, that, as we have seen, personal accounts repeatedly challenge this notion regarding both children's wartime experiences and their memory of the events.

The postwar traumas suffered by adult survivors underscore one woman's comment that her father "never really recovered,"[54] and the possibility that the parents' own personal postwar struggles overshadowed their children's. Many child survivors express as adults that they were well aware of their parents' pain and subsequently learned to hide their own. Eva N recalls one Yom Kippur when her mother lit ninety-one *yahrzeit* (memorial) candles, one for each of her murdered relatives. How could her own concerns, she wondered, compare to her mother's wounds?[55]

Perhaps because their parents' memories dominated, or so they were told, many children believed that their memories were relatively inconsequential, despite the fact that the confluence of war and postwar factors indelibly influenced their lives and the contours of their reconstructed families. Numerous child survivors now express the feeling that they were alone, that there were no others who had experienced what they had. When they eventually met other child survivors with whom they had a common language, they felt as if they had discovered long-lost family.[56] At the same time, they began to identify as survivors and finally received recognition from older survivors and the wider public.[57]

Conclusion

After the Holocaust, surviving adults quickly married and had children. This postwar renewal of Jewish families, as shown by the unprecedented number of births in DP camps, has been described as a triumph by scholars, and a testament to human resilience. Less attention has been paid to a different and more complicated model: reconstituted families that included survivors and their children born before or during the war. Rather than symbolizing renewal, these families were rebuilt by those whose prewar connections had been fundamentally ruptured by the Holocaust.

Jewish children were particularly at risk during the Shoah. Estimates indicate that as many as 90 percent were murdered. Of the surviving children, approximately 80 percent had one surviving parent, which underscores the utter breakdown of prewar Jewish family life. Just as Jewish children were especially vulnerable during the war, so were they vulnerable afterward. My work shows that the road back to some semblance of family life was fraught with complications. In the first instance, reuniting with a parent often meant leaving a familiar—and sometimes happy—rescuing family to live with a parent who was a stranger. Children found themselves in families where, in the vast majority of instances, the adult generation was not only different from the sheltering family but also different from their birth family. The new family group might comprise a parent and stepparent, aunts and uncles as parents, older siblings as parents, or even strangers, all of them survivors of the Holocaust.

Critical to these reconstituted families is the fact that both adult and child survivors existed in the same family constellation. Two generations of survivors under one roof had a deep and lasting impact on family dynamics and on child survivors on many levels. Parenting roles had been disrupted and traumatic wartime experiences sometimes left mothers and fathers ill-equipped to resume their parental role. Parents' divided affections between old and new family members eclipsed and diminished children's memories of their birth parents. Children felt the long-lasting effects of their own as well as their parents' traumatic experiences. While, according to child survivors, the aftereffects of the Holocaust shadowed and shaped them, the older survivor generation was generally blind to the war's influence on their children.

Rather than seeing the postwar rebuilding of Jewish family life as a study in triumphant renewal, my study depicts a nuanced and complicated portrait that highlights the multifaceted challenges experienced by children in these reconfigured postwar families, challenges that resulted from the creation of a familial mosaic composed not of new brides, grooms, and babies, but of widowed men and women, and children, irrevocably altered by the war and imperfectly pieced back together in its aftermath. To see it otherwise effaces what children experienced once the war ended.

Author

Beth B. Cohen received her doctorate in Holocaust history from Clark University's Strassler Family Center for Holocaust and Genocide Studies. After completing her graduate studies, she was a "Life Reborn" postdoctoral fellow at the United States Holocaust Memorial Museum. She lives in Los Angeles where she has taught at UCLA, Loyola Marymount, Chapman University; she currently teaches at California State University, Northridge. Her publications include *Case Closed: Holocaust Survivors in Postwar America* (Rutgers University Press and United States

Holocaust Memorial Museum) as well as contributions to the volumes *We Are Here: New Research on Displaced Persons*; *The Myth of Silence*; *Childhood and Material Culture*; and USC Casden Institute's annual review on the Holocaust in American life.

Notes

The interviews quoted in this chapter include those held at the Oral History Division, Hebrew University of Jerusalem, the USC Shoah Foundation: The Institute for Visual History and Education, and the author's collection.

1. Most of the interviews quoted in this chapter were held at the Oral History Division, Hebrew University of Jerusalem.
2. Rosensaft, *Life Reborn*.
3. Ibid. This number topped one thousand births per month from 1946–1948.
4. Samuels, "DP Chief arrives in Land of Choice."
5. Besides interviews conducted by the author, these sources include the USC Shoah Foundation Visual History Archive Online (http://vhaonline.usc.edu), the Jewish Family and Children's collection found in the archives of the American Jewish Historical Society (http://www.ajhs.org/), and the New York Association for New Americans (NYANA) found at the YIVO Institute for Jewish Research.
6. "Children During the Holocaust," *Holocaust Encyclopedia*.
7. Lavsky, "Role of Children in the Rehabilitation Process of Survivors."
8. Wulman, "European Jewish Children in the Postwar Period," 4.
9. As far as I know, there are no statistics available on these numbers.
10. This raises the question of what age designates a child survivor. Stefanie Seltzer, president of the World Federation of Jewish Child Survivors of the Holocaust and Dr. Robert Krell, psychiatrist and child survivor, defined a child survivor as one who was born in or after 1928. This has now been expanded to include those born in 1927.
11. See Dwork's *Children with A Star* for an analysis of children's experiences during the war, and the decisions and circumstances surrounding placing children in hiding.
12. Natalie Gold, interview by Beth B. Cohen, Los Angeles, CA, May 27, 2009.
13. Eva Brettler, presentation to Beth B. Cohen's class, Holocaust and Genocide for Educators. California State University, Northridge, California, April 27, 2013. According to Eva, Mrs. Grosz, a former neighbor from Budapest, had seen her alive in Bergen-Belsen and notified Eva's father when she returned to Hungary.
14. Case file AM-48, Jewish Family and Children's Services, 3.
15. Lea Eliash, VHA Interview Code 9900, USC Shoah Foundation Visual History Foundation, December 11, 1995.
16. Testimony of RF-JK/MK, (257) 16–19. December 4, 1993 6–8.
17. Ibid, 8.

18. Ibid.
19. Ibid, 10.
20. Testimony of A-FH, (257) 14-2.
21. Ibid.
22. Eva Brettler, presentation to Beth B. Cohen's class, April 27, 2013.
23. Ellen Zitkin, VHA Interview Code 13577, USC Shoah Foundation Visual History Foundation, May 16, 1996.
24. Testimony of A-FH, (257) 14-2, 3.
25. Testimony of RL, (257) 19-19 July 31, 1992.
26. It is interesting to note that while research has been conducted on the mental health of the second generation and the transmission of trauma from their parents, research seems to be absent regarding child survivors who grew up with survivor parents.
27. Eva Brettler, presentation to Beth B. Cohen's class, April 27, 2013.
28. Ibid.
29. Ibid.
30. Eva N, interview by Beth B. Cohen, Los Angeles, CA, May 3, 2013.
31. Testimony of A-FH, (257) 14-2, 1.
32. Ibid. Interestingly, A-FH noted in her interview that when she finally told her stepmother this (when her own children were already adults) her stepmother did not remember demanding this of her, although she did not deny it. Eva B, as noted, also stated that her stepmother insisted on keeping the true nature of their relationship hidden from her grandchildren. Confirmed Eva B.
33. Maynes and Waltner, *The Family*.
34. JB, Case File 102, Jewish Family and Children's Services.
35. Natalie Gold, interview by Beth B. Cohen, May 27, 2009.
36. Testimony of JG, (257) 17-7.
37. Ibid, 12.
38. Ibid.
39. Kellermann, *Holocaust Trauma*, 54.
40. Lya Frank, interview by Beth B. Cohen, Los Angeles, CA, February 19, 2013.
41. Ibid.
42. Ibid.
43. Ibid.
44. Testimony of PS (257) 2-22 A,B, 26.
45. Ibid., 27.
46. Ibid.
47. Ibid.
48. NYANA, "Demographic Characteristics of the Recent Jewish Immigrant." NYANA was a postwar Jewish communal agency created in 1949 to help resettle Holocaust survivors in New York City. See Cohen, *Case Closed*, for a fuller history of the organization.
49. Kaufman, *How We Survived*, 43–52.
50. Ibid.
51. Kaufman, *How We Survived*, 203–212.

52. Interview by Beth B. Cohen, March, 2014. Interviewees wish to remain anonymous.
53. Kellermann, *Holocaust Trauma*, 54.
54. Testimony of A-FH, (257) 14-2, 3.
55. Eva N, interview by Beth B. Cohen.
56. Stefanie Seltzer, president of World Federation of Jewish Child Survivors of the Holocaust and Descendants, interview by Beth B. Cohen. March 26, 2014.
57. According to Stefanie Seltzer (ibid.), child survivor groups began in the United States in the early 1980s around the time of the publication of Sarah Moskowitz's *Love Despite Hate*. Adult survivors had begun to organize into New American and *landsmanschaften* (mutual aid) groups in the late 1940s and early 1950s soon after arriving in the United States.

References

Center for Advanced Holocaust Studies. *Children and the Holocaust Symposium Presentations*. Washington, DC: United States Holocaust Memorial Museum, 2004.
"Children During the Holocaust." Holocaust Encyclopedia, United States Holocaust Memorial Museum. http://www.ushmm.org/wlc/en/article.php?ModuleId=10005142
Cohen, Beth B. *Case Closed: Holocaust Survivors in Postwar America*. New Brunswick, NJ: Rutgers University Press, in association with the United States Holocaust Memorial Museum, 2007.
Cunningham, Hugh. *Children and Childhood in Western Society Since 1500* (Studies in Modern History). London and New York: Longman, 1995.
Durst, Natan. "A Child Survives . . . and Then What?" In *A Global Perspective on Working with Holocaust Survivors and the Second Generation*, edited by John Lemberger, 289–304. Jerusalem: JDC-Brookdale Institute of Gerontology and Human Development in cooperation with the World Council of Jewish Communal Service, 1995.
Dwork, Debórah. *Children with A Star: Jewish Youth in Nazi Europe*. New Haven, CT: Yale University Press, 1997.
Jewish Family and Children's Services, Denver. American Jewish Historical Society Archives, Newton, MA.
Kaufman, Marie, ed. *How We Survived: 52 Personal Stories by Child Survivors of the Holocaust*. Los Angeles: Child Survivors of the Holocaust, Los Angeles Organization, 2011.
Kellermann, Natan P.F. *Holocaust Trauma: Psychological Effects and Treatment*. New York: iUniverse, 2009.
Krell, Robert. *And Life Is Changed Forever: Holocaust Childhoods Remembered*. Detroit, MI: Wayne State University Press, 2006.
Lavsky, Hagit. "The Role of Children in the Rehabilitation Process of Survivors: The Case of Bergen Belsen." In *Children and the Holocaust Symposium Presentations of the Center for Advanced Holocaust Studies*, 103–116. Washington, DC: United States Holocaust Memorial Museum, 2004.

Maynes, Mary Jo, and Anne Waltner. *The Family: A World History*. New York: Oxford University Press, 2012.
Moskovitz, Sarah. "Children in the Holocaust and After." Paper presented at Holocaust conference, Yale University, New Haven, CT, October 28, 1984.
———. *Love Despite Hate: Child Survivors of the Holocaust and their Adult Lives*. New York: Schocken, 1983.
New York Association for New Americans (NYANA). "Demographic Characteristics of the Recent Jewish Immigrant." NYANA Executive Report, 1950, NYANA Executive Meeting, NYANA Archives, New York.
Rosensaft, Menachem. *Life Reborn: Jewish Displaced Persons 1945–1951*. Conference proceedings. United States Holocaust Memorial Museum, Washington, DC, January 14–17, 2000.
Samuels, Gertrude. "DP Chief Arrives in Land of Choice." *New York Times*, February 17, 1949.
Wolf, Diane. *Beyond Anne Frank: Hidden Children and Postwar Families in Holland*. Berkeley: University of California Press, 2007.
Wulman, Leo. "European Jewish Children in the Postwar Period." Paper presented to the 19th Yearly Conference of the Yiddish Scientific Institute, January, 1948. *American OSE Review* 5, no. 1–2 (1948).
Zara, Tara. *The Lost Children: Reconstructing Europe's Families After World War II*. Cambridge, MA: Harvard University Press, 2011.
Hidden Child Newsletter

Archives

European Jewish Children's Aid: http://www.ajhs.org/
Jewish Family and Children's Services, Denver, CO. American Jewish Historical Society Archives, Brandeis University, Waltham, MA. http://www.ajhs.org/
Kestenberg Archive of Testimonies of Child Holocaust Survivors, The Oral History Division, Hebrew University of Jerusalem, Jerusalem, Israel.
New York Association for New Americans Archives (NYANA), New York, NY. http://www.ajhs.org/new-york-association-new-americans-nyana
USC Survivors of the Shoah Visual History Foundation, Los Angeles, CA: http://vhaonline.usc.edu

"Both Valuable and Difficult"
A Meeting Point between Historical and Psychological Interviews
Rita Horváth and Katalin Zana

The Kestenberg Project in Hungary

In Hungary at the end of the 1980s and the first half of the 1990s, well-known Hungarian psychotherapists conducted interviews primarily with child survivors of the Holocaust as part of the Kestenberg Holocaust Child Survivor Archive.[1] The psychological focus of the Kestenberg interviews in general made the entire Kestenberg project special among the numerous projects in the United States, Israel, and Western Europe.[2] In Hungary, however, psychologists and sociologists initiated the first oral history research projects on the Holocaust in the early 1980s.[3] The Kestenberg project—an international undertaking, engaging Hungarian psychotherapists who already had experience with Holocaust-related work and oral history projects—fit therefore the contemporary Hungarian scene very well.

Teréz Virág's famous presentation at the meeting of the Hungarian Psychological Society in the Hungarian Academy of Sciences[4] in 1982 marked the beginning of the visible phase of the heightened psychological interest in Holocaust research in Hungary. Therapy always dominated Virág's highly influential work, but from then on, projects were also designed in order to collect psychologically relevant oral history data concerning the Holocaust. The data collection by various oral history projects conducted mainly by psychoanalytical workgroups in Hungary, similarly to the data collection by the Kestenberg project, remained intimately connected to the therapeutic work of the interviewers and their processes of identity construction throughout the entire period of taking down and working with the interviews. The main goal of the projects was to reveal the psychological impact of the Holocaust on survivors and their descendants.[5] It is therefore illuminating to analyze the interviews in one another's context viz. together as a corpus.

Historical Contexts

The historical period in which the Kestenberg interviews took place was very turbulent: before, during, and directly after the collapse of the communist/socialist regime in Hungary. In the midst of the drastic political and social changes, large segments of Hungarian society had started to rethink and reconstruct their identities as well as their relationships to earlier events and periods of the twentieth century. The vast majority of the approximately 100,000 Jews living then in Hungary also faced a severe identity crisis, but unlike for the rest of the society, it was the organized persecution of the Holocaust that was at the center of their crisis.

The special characteristics of the destruction of the majority of the Jewish community in Hungary—its lateness, speed, and efficiency—raised questions that have tortured survivors and their offspring ever since.[6] The testimonies collected in the Kestenberg Archive of Testimonies of Child Holocaust Survivors, for example, show very clearly that the trauma of the Holocaust continues to be central to the lives of survivors and their descendants. The fact that Hungarian society completely excluded the Jews from the community of Hungarians during World War II constituted a crucial part of the Holocaust trauma of the thoroughly assimilated Hungarian Jews—Orthodox, Status Quo Ante, and Neolog alike. This trauma of rejection had formed the basis of the post-Holocaust identity crisis of the Jews of Hungary that became even more complex by the end of the 1980s as a consequence of the various phases of the communist/socialist dictatorship between the years of 1948 and 1989. The post-Holocaust identity crisis was experienced by the overwhelming majority of Hungarian Jews and encompassed personal, communal, cultural, and existential definitions of their Jewishness.

Psychoanalyst György Vikár, for example, used the simile of the "double sandbag" to describe the psychological weight many Jews felt they were carrying. This was a weight that consisted of the trauma of the Holocaust as well as the burden left by the subsequent communist era. Scholars have called attention to the phenomenon that belief in the communist ideals was instrumental for many formerly persecuted Jews in order to be able to survive in the aftermath of the Holocaust. Vikár also noted that many Jews had joined the Communist Party enthusiastically because it promised them freedom and equality, and some even rose to high ranks in the new regime. After the exposure of the crimes of the regime, "at the time when the structural insufficiency and the economic bankruptcy [of the communist/socialist system] manifested themselves," in addition to being stigmatized as Jews, Jews were also stigmatized as having supported a guilty system.[7] Vikár here talked only about the generation growing up after the war, whose parents believed in the communist ideals, but his statement holds true for the larger Jewish community as well. The Kestenberg interviews that were collected in Hungary, for example, demonstrate clearly that the majority of the interviewed child survivors are also burdened with the loss of the communist ideals, which became impossible to mourn due to feelings of guilt and shame associated with the actual realization of the ideals. Ferenc Erős, taking up Vikár's terminology, also stressed that the communist system did not pay attention to the trauma of the Holocaust and marginalized all ethnic and/or religious group identities.[8]

Various aspects surrounding the fall of the communist/socialist regime in 1989 aggravated and highlighted the severe and pervasive identity crisis of Hungarian Jewry, but one specific element stood out in the minds of the contemporaries: the rise of political anti-Semitism with its endorsement by the right-wing social elite. This made the crisis especially acute because people, particularly survivors and their descendants, felt that it repeated one of the most crucial aspects of the events leading to the destruction of the Jews of Hungary during the Holocaust. Psychoanalyst Judit Mészáros, one of the interviewers for the Kestenberg project who was also immersed in her own research and therapeutic work concerning the Holocaust, wrote in an article summarizing developments from 1989 to 1994 about the hostile environment and the prevalent feeling of dangerous historical repetitions:

> Citizens who are members of minority groups, who are seen as "other"—the Jew, the Gypsy, the Arab—no longer feel safe. Many speak of their anxieties. For example, a woman who was severely abused in a Gestapo prison said, "in recent weeks, I have been suffering from insomnia. When I go to sleep, I have nightmares and wake up all in a sweat." To the questions why her anxieties have been renewed, she replied with just a name: "Csurka." What does this name represent, and how has it gained a symbolic meaning? The answer is very simple. At that time, the bearer of this name belonged to the social elite and to the government. History shows that anti-Semitic forces can achieve significant influence only if they gain the approval of the social elite, or at a minimum, if they do not meet resistance from that quarter. During the rule of a government that, after having been elected democratically, shifted to the right, this fear was likely to be realized. It is not difficult, therefore, to understand why the patient invoked the name of a writer-politician with a leading role in the governing party as an explanation for her anxious state.[9]

Even the fact that Mészáros in this quote drew on an example (the example of the woman who was severely abused in a Gestapo prison) given by psychoanalyst Teréz Virág, whose name by the time of writing the summarizing article had become synonymous with Holocaust-related trauma, is a statement in and of itself.

Awareness of a wave of anti-Semitism was so obvious that, for example, psychoanalyst EJ, whose Kestenberg interviews the authors of this chapter have analyzed in depth, talked about it as a given with Á, her thirteen-year-old interviewee:

> EJ Then, you have said that it [being Jewish] does not signify anything bad. You know that you are Jewish, but you think that it is nobody's business.
> Á Well, not that it is nobody's business, but . . . well, . . . how . . . how to say this. . . . For example now, *since nowadays anti-Semitism is already strong, isn't it,* and if I said it [that I am Jewish] amongst my circle of friends then it is possible that they would be anti-Semites and that would be the end of our relationship. Well, *this can happen nowadays already.* . . .
> EJ Then you think that it is better not to talk about it, because now the atmosphere, the political situation, is such that saying it [that you are Jewish] would result in rather bad things.
> Á Yes, well, it is likely.[10]

EJ interviewed the young teenager because she was interviewing three generations of a child survivor's family. The grandmother was the child survivor, and EJ interviewed not only the survivor, but her daughter and two granddaughters as well.[11]

Historical and/or Psychological Interviews

The at-once historical and psychological interviews conducted in the framework of the Kestenberg project in Hungary give us a special opportunity to explore the complex theoretical issue regarding the differences and the similarities between psychological and historical interviews, especially in cases of large-scale social traumas such as the Holocaust. This is a very important—not only theoretical but also practical—issue, since historians need to employ both psychological and historical interviews as oral-historical sources for researching large-scale social traumas. And in order to employ source criticism, we need to know the relationship between the two.

Historians traditionally consider testimonies to be sources of highly questionable value, saying they are merely anecdotal evidence, mainly because they are hopelessly subjective and riddled with problems pertaining to the workings of memory and individual psychology. Trauma narratives, such as Holocaust testimonies, that test the boundaries of representation as well as those of memory are viewed with even more profound skepticism than other kinds of testimonies. From the point of view of traditional historical research, the value of children's testimonies, especially when given much later in life, is even more questionable.[12]

Nonetheless, testimonies have become crucial to Holocaust research and documentation since they are an almost exclusive record of the reactions and special individual as well as group characteristics of Holocaust victims that are otherwise unavailable in the numerous official sources prepared by the perpetrators concerning the destruction of the Jews. In addition, there are major events of the Holocaust, especially toward its end, that are barely documented by any sources other than oral-history interviews, testimonies, and other types of life writings.[13]

Judith Kestenberg emphasized that while the Kestenberg project aimed at historical documentation, it had a psychological focus—not only because psychotherapists served as the interviewers but also because the project concentrated on psychological research questions.[14] This holds true also for the contemporary, locally initiated Hungarian oral history projects with their focus on issues of transgenerational transmission of large-scale social traumas.

The psychologists engaged in the Kestenberg project, Judith Kestenberg herself, Eva Fogelman, Ilka Quindeau, Charlotte Kahn, and others, laid the groundwork for a definition of the various genres of psychological and historical interviews primarily from the psychological point of view. They delineated the differences between various psychological types of interviews: the first interview for a therapy, the therapy itself, and interviews such as those in the Kestenberg project that focus on both psychological research questions and historical documentation. To this work, we aim at adding our theories based on the information encoded mainly in the Hungarian Kestenberg interviews.

One of the major differences between historical and psychological interviews becomes inscribed in the different roles of the interviewers and interviewees and the different dynamics that follow from those roles. In an interview that is conducted in the framework of a historical project aiming at documentation, the interviewee is the locus of authority with the power to impart knowledge to those who do not or cannot know. The interviewer, by contrast, takes on the role of a reverent and appreciative student. The interviewer is also a representative of the public who needs the knowledge that only the survivor possesses. This makes the interview, in a sense, more formal (somewhat impersonal). The overall picture is slightly altered when the interviewer is also a survivor, but the structure should remain largely intact for the interview to be informative for historical research.[15]

In the case of psychological interviews, however, the interviewer, a psychotherapist, is in control and is the locus of authority. The psychological interview-situation in itself causes regression. The survivor regresses to the role of a child who is in search of an understanding and committed parent figure as well as a community to belong to. This makes the interview much more personal than a historically focused interview.[16]

The fact that the overwhelming majority of the interviewees in the Kestenberg project are child survivors makes this dynamic even more marked and complicated. Judith Kestenberg even stated that one of the crucial goals of the interviewer was to address the child in the survivor.[17]

Thus, the basic power relationship between interviewer and interviewee differs between typical historical and psychological interviews. In a classic historical interview situation, it is the interviewer who comes to the witness to ask for help, in other words, to ask for information—knowledge. In a psychological interview, however, it is the patient who seeks the psychotherapist's help. In the Kestenberg interviews, both are true, but as a result of standard psychotherapist attitudes and the fact that the interviewees knew that they were being interviewed by psychotherapists, the relationship between the interview partners is more similar to a regular psychological than to a historical interview.

The underlying narratives of historical and psychological interviews are, therefore, different. In a historical interview, the aim of the survivor is to impart knowledge, to initiate the interviewer and, through him or her, to initiate others into something unimaginable, to share knowledge and to allow people partake in it. In a psychological interview, the aim is to find a warm and loving community, to alleviate loneliness, and to share a community of fate. According to the underlying narrative informing interviews of most historical testimony-collecting projects, survivors aim at sharing knowledge, while according to the narrative basis of psychological interviews, survivors want to share their selves.

For psychotherapists it is obvious that in all types of interviews (primarily psychotherapeutic or historical) the psychotherapist interviewer collects objective, subjective, and scenic information, thus automatically activating a number of psychological processes.[18] In the case of interviews that are both psychological and historical, the therapist-interviewer must check these processes very carefully. This is because in a usual psychological setting, the psychological interview is a closed system with only two participants: the patient and the therapist. In a historical interview, however, the later presence of an audience is an integral part of the interview-setting. And the existence of an audience in a setting that is usually emphatically private, and, therefore, feels private, renders the interviewee very vulnerable. In addition, it is imperative to try not to initiate psychological processes that the therapist cannot deal with and conclude during the time of the interview.

During therapy, the psychotherapist collects information in order to understand the psychological processes of the patient, and by drawing on that information, the therapist aims to bring about a personal cure for the patient. This, however, is a long process requiring a number of sessions. By contrast, during a historical interview, the primary goal is the collecting and recording of information in order to create a nonpersonal knowledge base. Moreover, the very psychological processes of the interviewees are themselves crucial pieces of information about both the traumatic historical eras and their aftermath. Psychotherapist-interviewers therefore have to use the tools of their trade to extract as many pieces of information as possible without causing harm to the witness that could lead to retraumatization.

One of the ways in which psychotherapists conducting historical interviews tackle this problem is by maintaining a group historical focus. Even though psychologists routinely stress the individual focus of the so-called psychohistorical approach, it turns out not to be the case. By reading the Kestenberg interviews taken in Hungary together as a corpus, which is the usual way for historians to approach testimonies, it is evident that the focus on the individual is far from unequivocal. For example, the interviewers who aim at appraising the effects of long-term traumatization do that by not concentrating on the regular focal point of psychological interviews—namely, the individual. We can see this at work mainly when we identify the trains of thought that the interviewer does not follow through. The interviewer lets certain pieces of information holding the promise of being decisive for the witness's personal present go unnoticed/unmarked, deeming them too personal (and potentially harmful for the individual) for being compatible with the group focus.

The analyzed interviews show that the interviewer EJ, for example, was acutely aware of both the latent presence of the future audience and the potential harm of taking up far-reaching issues. We discern her constant awareness of the future audience and the nontherapeutic nature of the oral history interviews from the fact that she did not take up several topics that she would undoubtedly have followed through in a purely psychological interview, as the operating rules of analytically oriented psychotherapy calls for it. In her interview with M for instance,[19] EJ did not take up such topics as M's especially troubled relationship with her father and, in turn, her son, even though it is evident that the tortured complexities of these relationships have much to do with the trauma of the Holocaust and, therefore, contain information about the long-term effects of the historical calamity.

The special historical circumstances during the era of the drastic social and political changes in Hungary in the 1980s and 1990s exacerbated the dangers of psychological harm and retraumatization during or as a consequence of participating in a Holocaust-testimony-collecting project. The Kestenberg interviews conducted in Hungary had a double focus: the Holocaust and the contemporary social-political turmoil. They are prominent oral history sources for both. However, the double focus was also paradoxical, since perceiving the situation at the end of the 1980s and the beginning of the 1990s as one that repeats crucial aspects of the era leading up to the Holocaust turned the Holocaust into the unequivocal focus. And this paradoxical nature of the double focus, the overwhelming sense of repetition, made the interviews potentially explosive and harmful for the participants. The pervasive sense of being trapped in a recurrence left the participants with less and at times even no distance from the trauma of the Holocaust. Past and present were mixed together in a way that threatened the boundaries of the self and, indeed, all boundaries. Psychotherapists had to record this phenomenon, and, most importantly, use their expertise to protect the interviewees from retraumatization.

On the other hand, while harm was a very real concern, the special situation caused by the omnipresent sense of repetition also made this a very useful time to take Holocaust testimonies. As literary trauma theorist Cathy Caruth posited, the process of repetition affords the opportunity to get more information about the trauma by allowing a witnessing voice to emerge. In her analysis of Tasso's story (used by Freud in *Beyond the Pleasure Principle*), Caruth focused on "the moving and sorrowful voice that cries out, a voice that is paradoxically released through the wound."[20]

The historical situation in Hungary at the end of the 1980s and the beginning of the 1990s also strengthened the psychological dynamics compelling the participants of Holocaust testimony interviews to search for a community. The feelings of danger and historical repetition forged a special alliance between interviewers and interviewees. In this context it is possible to understand a salient feature of the Hungarian Kestenberg interviews: interviewees frequently and inventively asked their interviewing psychotherapists to confirm any similarities in their mutual backgrounds or identities. M, for example, even asked the therapist whether they had attended the same high school and whether she knew her former headmistress and other teachers.[21] As seen above, EJ's thirteen-year-old interviewee also asked for conformation of a shared opinion concerning Jewishness by employing a question tag: "Isn't it?"[22]

One of the most characteristic pieces of scenic information in the text of the interviews is the overwhelming feeling of frustration at being stuck in a crisis of identity. EJ's interview with M is a typical example of this phenomenon. While throughout the interview M demonstrates no change regarding her feelings of being trapped in a Jewish identity crisis, the sense that the interviewer goes through a process of transformation as a consequence of observing M's crisis is noticeable.

When we read the Hungarian Kestenberg interviews together as a corpus, we can see that the person who actively and consistently perceives these interviews as historical and intended for posterity as well as narrative tools for bringing about a positive change concerning the all-encompassing identity crisis of the Jews of Hungary is the interviewer. Incidentally, the interviewer is the one who, like the later audience, also experiences the interviews that he or she had conducted, in one another's context. Therefore, we would like to show an example in which we can identify that the interviewer—who is viewed by the interviewee as a fellow Jew of a similar age and background and who is acutely aware that she is conducting a historical interview that will be read by historians and other researchers—apparently slips into the interview a personal opinion that differs from that of the interviewee who is paralyzed by her identity crisis concerning Jewishness.

In EJ's interview with M, M struggles for a long time to put into words why she thinks that Jews are different from everybody else. She keeps stammering and finally asks the interviewer, "What do you think about this?"[23] The interviewer answers with a clarifying or structuring question, which is typical in a psychoanalytical situation when the therapist is directly addressed: "As if the question [meaning, M's question] would center around the issue whether *you* might be different now."[24] The interviewee continues to stammer as if the interviewer has not said anything: "Well . . . that . . . why do they feel us to be different?"[25] M does not react to EJ's clarifying question even though it was she who directly addressed the interviewer. At this point, the interviewer cuts in with further clarification that offers alternatives for the trapped interviewee: "And that there is this difference [concerning Jewishness] that is *both valuable and difficult.*"[26]

This is a very significant moment in the interview, completely unnoticed by the interviewee who, even after the statement, continues to struggle as if there has been no intervention at all. But for the interviewer, stating that being different as a Jew is "both valuable and difficult" is momentous. It was a psychological intervention, aiming to offer alternatives. However, it was also possibly an interjection of the interviewer's own opinion on the issue of being Jewish. This is particularly significant when taking into account that in interview after interview the interviewer had recorded the various representations of being paralyzed by an identity crisis regarding Jewishness. In our opinion, then, the interviewer's statement concerning being Jewish—"And that there is this difference that is both valuable and difficult"—has a psychological function within the interview situation, but is also a recording of the interviewer's opinion for the future researcher. Moreover, we think that the interviewer's recorded opinion is, at least partly, the result of being involved in the work of interviewing.

A statement by Ferenc Erős, a famous researcher of the Holocaust trauma in Hungary who started to conduct interviews very early in the beginning of the 1980, helps to interpret the previous example. Erős claimed that the process of interviewing Holocaust survivors during times of profound identity crisis of the Jewish community of Hungary had a liberating effect on the interviewers. He said in an interview, "Now I do not have any severe identity problems. I must say it [my identity] has developed parallel with my interview work, with thinking about it, with the related dialogues. I would constantly compare the interviewees' answers to my own possible ones, and this, in turn, helped me to clarify many of my viewpoints as to previously unanswered questions. The starting point was only blindness, not any kind of certainty."[27]

Conclusion

The Kestenberg project in Hungary together with the majority of the local oral history projects of the 1980s and 1990s concerning the Holocaust were conducted amidst great political, social, and economic changes. Throughout the period, the psychotherapists who had been involved in these projects conducted psychotherapy with both survivors and their descendants and created individual psychological and social theories on the basis of their work as therapists and interviewers, while simultaneously working on understanding and reconstructing their own identities in connection to their work. Katalin Pető's scientific article, "Identitás és Történelem" [Identity and history],[28] containing her personal example, demonstrates this phenomenon very well. The multilayered, both personal and scientific working processes of the therapist-researchers of the Holocaust oral history projects of the 1980s and 1990s are so effectively encoded in the interviews, that they invite us, researchers of the interview collections, to approach the interviews in a similarly complex, scientific, involved, and committed manner.

The intensity of the historical period and the multilayered involvement of the participants of these oral history projects concerning the Holocaust deeply informed the interviews and created meaningful and complex connections between individual psychological, social, and sociohistorical processes, revealing the theoretical and practical characteristics of psychological and historical interviews in relation to one another.

Authors

Rita Horváth is a literary scholar and historian. She received her doctorate from Bar-Ilan University (Israel) in 2003. She has served as a scholar-in-residence at the Hadassah-Brandeis Institute, Brandeis University where she continues to be a research associate. She is currently a research fellow at the International Institute for Holocaust Research at Yad Vashem and is also involved in the Children's Holocaust Testimony Project. She is cowriter of *Previously Unexplored Sources on the Holocaust in Hungary*, published by Yad Vashem in 2007. Since 2004 she has taught in the Holocaust Studies Program at Eötvös Loránd University, Budapest and, since 2005, has run English literature courses at Bar-Ilan University.

Katalin Zana is a specialist in psychotherapy and radiology. She received her doctorate in 2002 from Semmelweis University, Budapest. She works as a radiologist and a psychotherapist, and has conducted research in the field of neuroscience at the Centre Universitaire de Recherche et d'Exploration (CURE), Lille, France. Her research has focused on psychoanalytical themes, such as trauma, narrative, and creativity, as well as on developing a modernized version of Ferenczi's concept of mutual psychoanalysis. She is also involved in creating models by fMRI to observe psychological phenomena.

Notes

1. All interviews with child survivors that were collected in the framework of the Kestenberg project and are quoted in this chapter are held at the Judith Kestenberg Child Survivor Archive, The Oral History Division, Hebrew University of Jerusalem.

2. For example, the Spielberg Project (Visual History Archive of the USC Shoah Foundation), Yaffa Eliach's testimony collecting project in The Center for Holocaust Studies, Documentation and Research at Brooklyn College, the Fortunoff Video Archive for Holocaust Testimonies, Yad Vashem's testimony collecting project, the project of the Documentation Centre of Austrian Resistance (DÖW) in Vienna.
3. Éva Kovács, András Lénárt and Anna Lujza Szász called attention to this remarkable phenomenon in their article (Éva Kovács, András Lénárt and Anna Lujza Szász, "A magyar holokauszt személyes történetének digitális gyűjteményei," [Digital Collections of the Personal History of the Hungarian Holcaust], 336). In this article the authors surveyed and analyzed the major Hungarian Holocaust oral history projects from the 1980s on. The revised version of this article was published in English as Éva Kovács, András Lénárt, Anna Lujza Szász: "Oral History Collections on the Holocaust in Hungary.
4. "I held my first lecture on the experiences I had gained conducting psychotherapy with Hungarian Holocaust survivors on 9 November 1982" (Virág, *Children of Social Trauma*, 11). Virág also stressed that this was a crucial date for her from the point of view of her personal history because her mother was deported on that day in 1944.
5. György Vikár wrote, "The inquiries commenced with the deep-interview-survey of Ferenc Erős and his colleagues (1985). At about the same time, Teréz Virág began to collect the cases of second and third generation survivors from her psychoanalytical work (1983, 1984, 1988). The case study published by Judit Mészáros also belongs here (1990)" (Vikár, "Zsidó Sors," 142). Vikár also called attention to the work of Júlia Szilágyi, István Cserne, Katalin Pető and György Szőke, about which he heard for the first time on October 4, 1989, at the Hungarian Jewish Cultural Association. Szilágyi and colleagues collected forty analytically oriented deep interviews with Holocaust survivors, their children, and their grandchildren, aiming at tracing the transgenerational influences of trauma (ibid.). The first version of the article was presented on October 4, 1989, at the Hungarian Jewish Cultural Association. Éva Kovács, András Lénárt, and Anna Lujza Szász add that the project of Szilágyi, Cserne, Pető, and Szőke started as early as 1986–1987. Éva Kovács, András Lénárt, and Anna Lujza Szász also describe the first project Vikár mentioned as follows: "Ferenc Erős and András Stark were interested in how the first-generation descendants of Holocaust survivors coped with the anxiety stemming from their Jewishness or from its concealment. With the help of András Kovács and Katalin Lévai they started conducting interviews." They also wrote, "Soon after the Jewish foundation schools were established in 1991, Éva Kovács and Júlia Vajda embarked on exploring the Jewish identity among second and third generation Holocaust survivors by applying the technique of narrative life history interviews which they conducted with two dozen families. In each case, they spoke with both the parents and the children" (Kovács, Lénárt, and Szász, "Oral History Collections on the Holocaust in Hungary," 5)
6. The Holocaust in Hungary victimized less than 6 percent of Hungary's total population, because the Jewish inhabitants of Hungary, including

the recently annexed territories, consisted of 725,007 Jews of the Jewish faith and 61,548 Jews who had converted to Christianity according to the last census that was taken before the German occupation of Hungary. The census was conducted in January 1941. The first phase of the Holocaust in Hungary, the phase of the Hungarian anti-Jewish policy, began in the spring of 1938, when the first anti-Jewish law was passed in the Hungarian Parliament. During this phase, the Hungarian regime, by using anti-Jewish legislation, gradually and systematically eliminated the Jews of the country from the economic and social spheres. Moreover, the Hungarian regime unequivocally demonstrated its murderous hatred toward the Jews by the 1941–1942 deportations to Galicia and the massacre at Délvidék (Novi Sad and in its vicinity in the Bačka region), as well as by the institution of forced labor in the Hungarian army.

The second phase of the Holocaust, the phase of the German anti-Jewish policy, began abruptly on March 19, 1944, when the German army occupied Hungary in order to ensure Hungary's by-then wavering alliance. The Hungarian administration remained intact and in force after the German occupation, and the new Hungarian prime minister, Döme Sztójay, his government, and the entire administrative apparatus, implemented quickly and efficiently the anti-Jewish measures of Nazi Germany. The ghettoization and deportation of the majority of the Jews of Hungary happened within the span of a few months, between April and July 1944. The overwhelming majority of the Jewish population of the Hungarian provinces were deported to Auschwitz.

From the end of June 1944, the more than 200,000 Jews of Budapest were forced to live in houses marked by yellow stars. The situation of the Jews of Budapest changed for the worse when Governor Horthy tried to pull out of the war in October 1944. The German answer was to assist the coup of the extremist right-wing Hungarist Arrow Cross Party headed by Ferenc Szálasi. From then on, the terror of the Arrow Cross men was let loose and two ghettos were set up in Budapest. Many Jews were murdered in the streets or shot into the Danube. Forced labor and the notorious death marches characterized the last period of the Holocaust of the Jews of Hungary taken from Budapest during the Szálasi-era or taken from Hungary earlier. About 600,000 Hungarian Jews were murdered in the Holocaust.

7. Vikár, "Zsidó Sors," 143.
8. "Az asszimiláció a holokauszt után is folytatódott" (Assimilation has continued after the Holocaust as well), Pál Várnai's interview with Ferenc Erős in *Szombat*, November 1, 2005. In another study about the post–World War II Jewish identity crisis, Erős and Ehmann wrote, "In some families—for some reason or other—the parents were loyal to the Communist regime. An alternative to deny Jewish background completely was to find brand new, 'progressive,' and viable narratives instead of the lost and banned one. The 'we are not Jews, we are Communists' type of strategy seemed to be a good solution" (Erős and Ehmann, "Jewish Identity in Hungary"). In addition, at the time of the drastic social and political changes at the end of the 1980s, numerous aspects of the post-Holocaust coping mechanisms

gave rise to frightening feelings of historical repetitions or, in other words, historical continuity as demonstrated even by the title "Assimilation Has Continued after the Holocaust As Well."

9. Mészáros, "Antisemitism and Jewish Identity in Hungary," 97.
10. Testimony of ÁG, ÁG-EJ 4/5/90, 1–2. It is also significant that the interviewee says "*it*" several times instead of saying the word "Jewish." The italics are ours. The main text contains our own translation from the Hungarian original, but we also found an English translation in the Kestenberg Archives: AG-EJ 4/5/90.
11. Testimony of VG (the grandmother), 4/05/1990; testimony of AG (the mother), 4/05/1990; testimony of ZG (the older daughter), 4/05/1990; and testimony of ÁG (the younger daughter), 4/05/1990. EJ's interviews with three generations are especially illuminating if we research them together with the interviews of the project of Éva Kovács and Júlia Vajda in which interviews were conducted with more than twenty families, including parents and children.
12. Most influentially, Raul Hilberg argued for basing historical research solely on documents.
13. A characteristic example of this phenomenon are the infamous death marches of Jews from Budapest toward the inner parts of the Third Reich. Kinga Frojimovics, for instance, has reconstructed the main routes of the death marches on the basis of early postwar testimonies given to the Deportáltakat Gondozó Országos Bizottság (National Relief Committee for Deportees, DEGOB) in Hungary in 1945–1946. See on the following website: "Forced Labor Service in Hungary during WWII." http://www.tm-it.co.il/avodat-kfiya/show_item.asp?levelId=65137. (in Hungarian and Hebrew), accessed in May 8, 2010.
14. The psychological focus of the interviews with trauma survivors are also obvious, because supportive listening is one of their main features. Supportive listening can have a therapeutic effect, but, at the very least, it can help to avoid retraumatization during the interview.
15. Kinga Frojimovics, for example, analyzed in her paper "Holocaust Survivor Self-interviews, 1940s and 1950s" the self-interview and the other interviews of one of the interviewers of the DEGOB, Teréz Alexander, herself a former deportee. Frojimovics demonstrated how deeply Alexander's status as a concentration camp survivor together with her views on what sort of knowledge constitutes a valuable testimony affected her work as an interviewer and the power relationship between interviewer and interviewee.
16. The reasons for these parent-child roles and the regression of the interviewee are not to be found mainly in the contents of the interviewer's questions but rather in the therapeutic attitude, and thus we learn about this relationship primarily from the scenic information encoded in the interview and not from what was literally said.
17. Kestenberg, "Overview of the Effect of Psychological Research Interviews on Child Survivors," 27–28. The situation in the Kestenberg Hungarian interviews is further complicated by the fact that in many of the cases the

interviewers themselves were either child survivors or second-generation survivors.
18. Ilka Quindeau described these processes in her theoretical article, "Narration as a Construction of Identity," 39–40. Quindeau also posited that as a consequence of these processes, the ideal readers of psychological and psychohistorical testimonies taken by psychotherapists are also psychotherapists, because they can fully decode the information that had not been interpreted during the interview. As a literary scholar, I would question this point, since literary works in general rely on scenic information that is interpreted and analyzed by the reader rather than by the characters or participants.
19. Testimony of MÁ, MÁ-EJ (257) 7-7-92, 1992.
20. Caruth, *Unclaimed Experience*, 2–4.
21. Testimony of MÁ, MÁ-EJ (257) 7-7-92, 1992., 10, 12.
22. Testimony of ÁG, ÁG-EJ 4/5/90, 2.
23. Testimony of MÁ, MÁ-EJ 7-7-92, 1992. 22.
24. Ibid. Italics are the authors.
25. Ibid., 23.
26. Ibid. Italics are the authors'. This quotation constitutes a part of the title of this article.
27. Szántó, "A zsidó szellem" 9. Erős's formulation is so accurate and important that Meszáros also quotes it in her summarizing article (Mészáros, "Antisemitism and Jewish Identity," 95.
28. Pető, "Identitás és Történelem."

References

Caruth, Cathy. *Unclaimed Experience: Trauma, Narrative, and History*. Baltimore: Johns Hopkins University Press, 1996.
Cserne, István, Pető Katalin, Szilágyi Júlia, and Szőke György. "Az elmaradt gyász," [Mourning that did not Take Place] *Múlt és Jövő* (1989): 1, 31–32.
Erős, Ferenc, and Bea Ehmann. "Jewish Identity in Hungary: A Narrative Model Suggested." In *Ambiguous Identities in the New Europe. Replika Hungarian Social Science Quarterly. Special Issue,* edited by Hadas Miklós and Vörös Miklós, 121–132. Budapest: Replika Circle, 1997.
Frojimovics, Kinga. "Holocaust Survivor Self-interviews, 1940s and 1950s." Paper presented at Imperial War Museum conference "Beyond Camps and Forced Labour: Current International Research on Survivors of Nazi Persecution." London, January 2012.
Kestenberg, Judith S. "Overview of the Effect of Psychological Research Interviews on Child Survivors." In *Children during the Nazi Reign: Psychological Perspective in the Interview Process*, edited by Judith S. Kestenberg and Eva Fogelman , 27–28. Westport, CT; London: Praeger, 1994.
Kovács, Éva, András Lénárt, and Anna Lujza Szász. "A magyar holokauszt személyes történetének digitális gyűjteményei", [Digital Collections of the Personal History of the Hungarian Holcaust] *BUKSZ* 2011, 336–351.

Kovács, Éva, András Lénárt, and Anna Lujza Szász. "Oral History Collections on the Holocaust in Hungary." *S:I.M.O.N.—Shoah: Intervention. Methods, Documentation*, October 15, 2014: 1–18. http://simon.vwi.ac.at/index.php/working-papers/43-kovacs-eva-lenart-andras-szasz-anna-lujza

Mészáros, Judit. "Antisemitism and Jewish Identity in Hungary Between 1989 and 1994." In *Children Surviving Persecution: An International Study of Trauma and Healing*, edited by Judith S. Kestenberg and Charlotte Kahn, 90–101. Westport, CT; London: Praeger, 1998.

Pető, Katalin. "Identitás és történelem".[Identity and History]In *A társadalmi traumatizáció hatásai és pszichoterápiájának tapasztalatai*, [The Ramifications of Social Traumatization and the Experience of its Psychotherapy] edited by Teréz Virág, 80–84. Budapest: Animula, 1999.

Quindeau, Ilka. "Narration as a Construction of Identity." In *Children during the Nazi Reign: Psychological Perspective in the Interview Process*, edited by Judith S. Kestenberg and Eva Fogelman, 35–53. Westport, CT; London: Praeger, 1994.

Szántó, Gábor T. "A zsidó szellem az európai gondolkodás kiirthatatatlan része: Interjú Erős Ferencnccel" [The Jewish spirit is an ineradicable part of European thought: Interview with Ferenc Erős], *Szombat* 6, no. 9 (1994).

Szilágyi, Júlia, Cserne István, Pető Katalin, and Szőke György. "A második és a harmadik generáció holocaust túlélők és gyermekeik" [The Second and Third Generation Holocaust Survivors and their Children]. *Psychiatria Hungarica* 2 (1992): 117–129.

Várnai Pál. "Az asszimiláció a holokauszt után is folytatódott." [Assimilation has continued after the Holocaust as well]. Interview with Ferenc Erős in *Szombat*, November 1, 2005. http://www.szombat.org/archivum/%E2%80%9Eaz-asszimilacio-a-holokauszt-utan-is-folytatodott-1352771429

Vikár, György. "Zsidó sors(ok) az analitikus rendelés tükrében" [Jewish Fate(s) as reflected in Analythical Therapy Sessions]. *Thalassa* 1–2 (1994): 139–146.

Virág, Teréz. *Children of Social Trauma: Hungarian Psychoanalytic Case Studies.* London and Philadelphia: Jessica Kingsley, 2000. translated by Emma Roper-Evans. The Hungarian original: *Emlékezés egy szederfára* [Remembering a Mulberry Tree], edited by Klári László. Budapest: Animula, 1996.

———. "Kollektív trauma—egyéni öngyógyítás" [Collective Trauma—Individual Self Therapy]. *A Magyar Pszichoanalitikus Egyesület tudományos előadásai, 1991–1992* [Scientific Lectures of the Hungarian Psychoanalytical Association], 23–35. Budapest: Animula Kiadó, 1993.

———. "Soá és ősbizalom" [Shoa and Basic Built-in Trust]. In *Magyar megfontolások a Soáról* [Hungarian Thoughts about the Shoa]. edited by Hamp Gábor, Horányi Özséb, and Rábai László, 281–284. Budapest—Pannonhalma: Balassi Kiadó–Magyar Pax Romana Fórum, 1999.

Archive

Kestenberg Archive of Testimonies of Child Holocaust Survivors, The Oral History Division, Hebrew University of Jerusalem, Jerusalem, Israel.

PART THREE

Postwar Memory, Coping Mechanisms, and Adjustment

 5

Performative Memory-Making and the Future of the Kestenberg Archive
Stephenie Young

> Interviewer: "Tell me whatever you remember, from your first memory."
> Survivor: "I can't remember exactly, but I can tell you what happened."
> Testimony of GE, Kestenberg Archive[1]

> The Archive: if we want to know what that will have meant, we will only know in times to come.
> Jacques Derrida, *Archive Fever*[2]

Archives

"What good is the memory archive? How can it deliver what history alone no longer seems to be able to offer?"[3] Andreas Huyssen's questions, more than a decade old, are inevitable to those concerned with memory studies. Now, more than ever before, we understand that the concept of memory is slippery, and that to archive the memory of a survivor is to add yet another layer to the chaotic "truth" of an event. And the Holocaust is no exception to the questionable "truth" of memory.

Survivors' memories of the Holocaust, inexact as they may have been in the first place, fade quickly with the passing of generations. Their memories have been intercepted, interrupted, and fused with family stories and photographs, rumors and hearsay, popular anecdotes, and all of the news about other traumatic events that has hit the headlines since the 1940s—the tragedy of the gulags in Stalinist Russia, famine in Mao's China, atrocities in Bosnia, Darfur, Syria—too many to list here. To consider a Holocaust narrative as a memory document and as an asset to the archive in the twenty-first century is to also take into account how those memories have come to us in a post–Cold War or a post-Rwanda world. It is to take note of the substantial influence that the post-Holocaust world has on its survivors' memories and testimonies, and the way that these other events add to the complexities and instabilities that are part of creating a Holocaust memory archive that is also subject to the crucial influence of provenance: the question of when the testimonies were taken, for what purpose(s), and by whom is crucial in any discussion about the oral history of the Holocaust.

But the possibility for a reliable memory archive is also tested by ever-shifting fashions in the kinds of stories that the public wants to read and watch, the must-reads about the Holocaust that have varied over the past sixty years. Stories that held the attention of the U.S. public, such as Elie Wiesel's *Night* (1958) and Primo Levi's *Survival in Auschwitz* (1947), now compete with other kinds of narratives. Especially influential have been contemporary Hollywood films (many loosely adapted from survivors' stories) such as Steven Spielberg's now classic *Schindler's List* (1993), Quentin Tarantino's bawdy and edgy *Inglourious Basterds* (2009), and the film adaptation of Tatiana de Rosnay's novel, *Sarah's Key* (2006). Although there is more than one type of audience for Holocaust testimony, the mainstream success of certain stories over others is important to mention because a survivor's memory, a testimony, often does not have a sustaining power unless it is translated into a different genre that is more readable or watchable by a wider audience. In other words, it must fulfill certain expectations about what is an emblematic Holocaust story, such as a readable plot and setting, a clearly defined protagonist and antagonist, and the ability to provoke an emotional response in the reader/viewer. Thus, the successful stories correspond to a popular perception—in other words, the aesthetic of a Holocaust meta-narrative—one that is reinforced by the constant reproduction of itself as the truth of the event, leaving little room for alternative narrative interventions.[4]

Does this mean that the few popular stories that survive in the publishing and film market (and very few stories actually make it into the public realm) are the only memory archives of the Holocaust that we can hope for? Should we console ourselves with the fact that it is better the general public is familiar with some version of some of the stories than few or no stories of the Holocaust? Or is that not enough? Perhaps we should give due attention to the texts (unpublished, forgotten, ignored) that fall outside the borders of the popular Holocaust aesthetic. Maybe we should seek out the stories that lack the well-edited finesse of a Wiesel or Levi, or the popular appeal of a Spielberg film. Yet, when we locate them, what are we to do with these testimonies that do not find a home inside the protected borders of discursive fashion?

A group of testimonies that highlight the need for more reflection on the relationship between the influences of popular demand, mediated survivor memory, and the future for a more inclusive Holocaust memory archive is the Kestenberg Archive of Testimonies of Child Holocaust Survivors. By taking a close look at testimonies in this archive, I wish to consider both the potential value of this collection to add to what we think we already know about memory discourse as well as to the future for testimonies like these that fall outside the popular culture aesthetic. Not surprisingly, the Kestenberg interviews are far removed from the eloquence of a Wiesel book, and they certainly have no captivating soundtrack playing the likes of David Bowie's song "Cat People" in the background as in a Tarantino film. Films, novels, poetry, visual art and the rest of the cache of the multitude of genres in which the memory of Holocaust is expressed may have many different audiences searching for numerous ways to engage with the subject matter. Yet, although testimony is an altogether different genre, the Kestenberg testimonies are also idiosyncratic, provocative, and captivating in their own way. On the one hand they are traditional oral testimonies transferred word by word, sound by sound, from cassette tapes onto the blank page by the transcriber using a manual typewriter, like many other oral transcriptions of this type. But on the other hand, they seem to go against the grain of the current popular culture Holocaust aesthetic: that aesthetic presents a smooth dialogue in a chronological narrative, often omits negative personifications of its protagonist, and offers some type of closure for its audience. In the Kestenberg testimonies the reader is faced with manuscripts that relentlessly interrupt the flow of any kind of story, with typos, question marks, ellipses, and interjected comments where the typist cannot understand the discussion—all in stark contrast to the effortless, edited Holocaust narratives that are widely circulated. The disparity is made stronger by the fact that the Kestenberg archival documents are full of tense and uncomfortable exchanges between the interviewer and the interviewee as each struggles to distill experience and conceptualize the meaning of memory for an imagined future archive. These raw, unrefined and unfiltered testimonies potentially execute for us, as the reader, the chaotic process of witnessing and place us in the position "of being a witness to the process of witnessing itself."[5] Rather than presenting us with a polished, chronological text that has very few incongruities or gaps in the way the story is told, these Kestenberg testimonies actually perform—or act out, if you will—just how difficult memory recall is. They enact the struggle for both the interviewer and the interviewee to seek a kind of truth to the event. Both come to the table with all their cultural baggage and their conflated memories to search for and perhaps find a common tongue in which to talk about a trauma decades after the event.

Yet the "truth" is always already inaccessible, and I am therefore more interested in looking at how the Kestenberg archive performs memory-making through an unconventional aesthetic lens. I assert that because of its performative aspect, where we witness the interviewer's and the child survivor's struggles in the late 1980s, more than forty years after the war, to negotiate memory resulting in several outcomes, the archive adds a significant voice to the cacophony of opinions about how the Holocaust memory archive is negotiated for a twenty-first-century audience; at the same time, the archive perhaps acts as an intermediary calling for the dissemination of more texts like it. After all, what good is a memory archive if it only appeals to the fashions of the time and is essentially closed off, hermetically sealed, from the texts that grapple with the very issues more-popularized representations of the Holocaust gloss over?

Performative Memory

> You can't ask a [child] survivor, 40 years later, to distill his experiences through the mind's eye of the child. Everything he does and thinks is colored by his later life as an adult.[6]

It is a widely held belief that the age or era of the witness can be traced back to Eichmann's trial in the 1960s that "revolved essentially around the testimony of survivors [and] inaugurated nothing less than a cultural turn towards testimony—the speech of the witness, the first-person narrative of suffering or trauma."[7] Yet the so-called era of memory studies as connected to survivor testimony and trauma as a research focus was not on the radar of writers and researchers until well into the late 1980s and early 1990s when writers and theorists who focus on testimony, witnessing, and trauma such as Dominick LaCapra, Cathy Caruth, Dori Laub, and Shoshana Felman published ground-breaking works in the field.[8] By the 1990s this traumatic turn, this focus on the witness and on memory, not only brought attention to stories about the post-traumatic stress disorder (PTSD) of soldiers of war that have become so common (as with the Vietnam War and the 1990s Gulf War from a U.S. perspective), but also shone a light on other kinds of survivors of mass atrocities, war, and traumatic events, including the Holocaust.[9]

However, before these shifts in public perception about who was designated a survivor and why his or her memories might be important, things were very different for those who had withstood National Socialist (or Nazi) extermination attempts, and as late as the 1980s "many child survivors of the Holocaust did not see themselves as survivors."[10] The Kestenbergs set out to change this view. They were pioneers in the burgeoning field of child psychology, working during a time when the long-term effects of trauma from childhood were just beginning to be studied as part of a legitimate discipline. As they began their work taking the testimonies of Holocaust survivors who had been babies or young children during the war, now known as the 1.5 generation,[11] they faced the challenges discussed above, exacerbated by the fact that their subjects oftentimes did not consider themselves survivors of the Holocaust and may have been only vaguely aware of terms such as "childhood trauma," "Holocaust," or "Shoah."

Another issue the Kestenbergs faced was the need to account for the fact that these were adults who were being asked to make connections between traumatic childhood experiences and the effect it had had on their lives, all filtered or mediated through others' memories: parents, extended family, and cultural identifications, and conflated with the mediated representations of post–World War II atrocities. The latter point was addressed by Miriam Hansen in her perceptive essay, "*Schindler's List* Is Not *Shoah*: The Second Commandment, Popular Modernism, and Public Memory," where she wrote, "Whether we like it or not, the predominant vehicles of public memory *are* the media of technical re/production and mass consumption."[12] According to Hansen, the Shoah has always been somewhat "dependent on mass-mediated forms of memory."[13] I agree with Hansen that this mass-mediated memory has been working more or less with a blank slate since the time of the Shoah due to the fact that the Nazis achieved one of their goals even if they lost the war: they eliminated any potential for "communities of survivors."[14] The Nazis destroyed the "very basis and structures of collective remembering and . . . unlike most of the 'ordinary massacres' committed in the course of the German genocidal war all over Europe, the Shoah left no *communities* of survivors, widows and children, not even burial sites that would have provided a link with a more 'organic' tradition of oral and collective memory."[15] This void of community in the postwar era, as Eva Hoffman writes, often leads to memories that are "blunted by overfamiliarization"—a deluge of films, books, plays, operas.[16]

The 1.5 generation, the child survivors, are victim to this in particular. Although they were physically present during the Holocaust, some of them were very young, and their memories are partially supplied, often significantly or wholly, by stories and photographs passed down by family who survived and (like the general population who were not part of the Holocaust) who have memories from the media. Thus, these child survivors have a tendency to sometimes filter their own trauma through other events that they were not necessarily part of. This could, of course, be the type of pitfall Michael Bernard-Donals referred to as "conflations of memory." These kinds of memories, "a curious conflation . . . that involves impossible connections between the events of the Holocaust and other events sometimes only tangentially related to it,"[17] have the potential to adversely affect both the survivor, who must filter his or her story of the past through a mediated experience, and the audience (reader/listener/viewer) of the story who faces some of the same dangers.[18] Yet, one could also argue that comparing certain events from Guatemala or Rwanda, for example, might enhance the testimony of survivors who are then able to draw on other kinds of traumatic experiences to better connect with their own.

I have selected two representative testimonies from the Kestenberg archive that were conducted in English to further examine the complexities of constructing a memory archive with all of the accompanying cultural baggage, including mass-mediated memories and the struggle of the survivor and interviewer to find common ground. Although there are many testimonies that could be said to address the complexities that I outline, I believe that these two Kestenberg testimonies parallel each other in many instances and create an interesting conversation that presents a type of witnessing that opens up the possibility for an alternative post-Holocaust aesthetic that stresses the performative process of memory making, moves against a widely accepted popular version of the Holocaust, and stresses the need to pay greater attention to testimonies that are more experimental.

Both of the interviews were conducted in English in the United States in the late 1980s and are with adult survivors who were infants in Eastern Europe during the war. Although their experiences were different, it is the interview process itself that I am concerned with: the performativity of the conversation that shows how much they share. I highlight, in particular, three commonalities: First, the child psychologist who runs each interview approaches memory through association, imagination, and fantasy. Second, the interviewees appear to have little or no recollection of the events from their childhood, and this lack leads them to regard memory differently from how their interviewers regard memory. The interviewees prefer to draw on the memories of parents or grandparents, on old photographs, and/or on what they have learned about the Holocaust (and other events that they associate with the Holocaust) through the media. And third, in both interviews a tension is created through this struggle with the framing of memory that leads to the development of a kind of raw, tension-filled, anti-aesthetic that necessarily falls outside the twenty-first-century cache of Holocaust texts.

Interview with GE

The first interview was conducted in 1987 with GE[19] who was born in August 1943 in Budapest, Hungary, to a Reform Jewish family; he was only eight months old when the Germans invaded the country. His father, a coachman before the war began, was eventually forced under the Arrow Cross government to work for the Germans as part of a Jewish battalion.[20] He was then most likely taken to the Flossenbürg camp in Germany, then to Mauthausen in Austria, and released after liberation in late spring 1945. GE's mother was able to evade capture during the war, but it is assumed that his maternal grandmother and other family members died in Auschwitz. The first part of the interview is an attempt to recall memories of his childhood during and immediately after the war, and the second part turns to his later years as a teenager who was ashamed to be Jewish due to cultural bias and teenage angst. Judith Kestenberg, the interviewer, talks with GE about his adult life as an immigrant in the United States with an American wife and two children, and how the Holocaust may have affected the way that he lives. Also of note is that GE is a history professor who lives and works in California and who did not really begin, in his opinion, to consider his relationship to the Holocaust as a child survivor until he started research for a book about the war.

The interview with GE tellingly begins with a prompt about remembering, as many testimonies do with survivors—adult or child. The interviewer asks GE, "Tell me whatever you remember, from your first memory."[21] GE at first lists some facts and dates, but soon says, "I have absolutely no recollections."[22] Kestenberg, who often focuses on imagination and fantasy in her work with survivors of traumatic events, interrupts GE's denial of recollection to ask if he was breastfed, to which he briefly answers, "I was breastfed. At that time you didn't have a choice."[23] He then moves on to describe life in Budapest as he understands it during the war. This is an important moment in the dialogue; what commences here and continues throughout the interview is a parallel conversation that draws attention more to the back-and-forth discussion between the interviewer and interviewee about what memory is and how it can be evoked rather than to the factual or historical information gleaned from the witness.

GE's initial responses are deeply connected to what I mentioned earlier—namely, that in the late 1980s, when these interviews were conducted, the concept of a Holocaust survivor as understood today did not exist as such a well-defined identity group. Hence, GE never really thought of himself as a survivor until later in his life when, as a history professor in the United States, he started to write about the Holocaust. And although through his writing he began to reconceptualize his identity as that of a survivor and as part of an identity group, he maintains that almost all of his memories are actually the memories of others—that is, they are received memories. Several times throughout the forty-six-page manuscript of his interview GE attempts to acknowledge his disconnect from the past by talking about received memories through the media and his own work in the field of Holocaust studies. For example, he tells Kestenberg, "I never realized until I started to write this book, that I'm part of the Holocaust, basically. . . . I grew up with stories of the Holocaust; nights, evenings, winter evenings. . . . I was glued to my parents' stories."[24] When Kestenberg reacts with, "OK, you still can have a memory," he maintains, "I don't remember anything whatsoever."[25] He insists that he has no memories of his own and that his only role is to pass down the stories he heard from his surviving family.

GE's insistence that he has no memories of his own does not, however, lead Kestenberg to accept his claims as the final truth of the interview. Instead, when GE makes a comment about his inability to remember, Kestenberg interrupts him and attempts to extract unconscious childhood memories from him. This shift in the discussion is a direct allusion to her work on transposition that Kestenberg describes as "an organization of the self in relation to time and space. It is a mechanism used by a person living in the present and in the past."[26] More simply put, transposition is the term used for the complex mourning process that children of survivors undergo when they show symptoms of having suffered through a traumatic event in which only their parents were present. Children of Holocaust survivors take on the trauma of their parents as if it were their own and even show symptoms of having lived through it. Thus, Kestenberg uses the theory of transposition to get GE to reconsider the way that he organizes time and to ask him to recognize that his past and his present may not be as separate as he believes them to be.

Kestenberg refers mainly to the second generation in her discussion of transposition and points out in her interviews that the children of survivors want to "rescue" their parents "from the psychic death of continuous, unresolved mourning" that they suffer as survivors.[27]

Although in theory this applies only to the children of survivors, she also acknowledges that this could apply to the youngest members of the 1.5 generation: "In contrast [to the second generation], adult and child survivors continue to live in the past, not on the basis of fantasies alone, but on the basis of memories, verbal and nonverbal. The difference becomes hazy for those who are both survivors and children of survivors. Those who were very young during persecution have to depend on their parents to tell them what happened. They too have to supplement what meager body memories they have."[28] Kestenberg recognizes that on some issues it is difficult to discern between second and 1.5 generation survivors because the latter may have been too young to have conscious memories of the Holocaust. Consequently, as with the second generation, members of the 1.5 depend on their parents to tell them what happened. For this reason, child survivors exist in a liminal space in relation to their memories—a hazy past of both verbal and nonverbal memories but also dependent (though it is impossible to measure the extent) on the memories of the parents. But Kestenberg still believes that they can supplement their "body memories"[29] through imagination, and this is what she is trying to do in the interview with GE: to evoke these body memories by asking him to try to imagine different scenarios from when he was a small child.

On the one hand, we see GE's insistence on his mediated memories, and on the other, we see Kestenberg's attention to transposition and the verbal and nonverbal signs that she associates with child survivors. The latter accounts for the many passages in this interview where she asks GE to imagine an event from infancy rather than asking him to tell her what he believes that he actually remembers. For example, in this following dialogue GE finds recall of his time as a baby difficult, so Kestenberg asks him to imagine something else instead:

JK   It's not a question of remembering, but it's a question of imagining. Can you imagine yourself in a crib?
GE   No.
JK   Can you imagine yourself being carried?
GE   Yes.
JK   OK, who is carrying you?
GE   My mother.
JK   How is she carrying you?
GE   Very close to her, because she told me, and now we're talking about . . . she mentioned when she had to run down to the shelter . . . the bomb shelter, or coming up; that's how I visualize it.[30]

Kestenberg believes that if GE can imagine his mother holding him, it will bring other memories to consciousness because, for her, imagination is a way of stimulating memory. But it can also be problematic because suggestions might implant false memories rather than prompting those of the interviewee.

Kestenberg's theories and methodologies provoke a lot of questions about the process of taking testimony and memory recall. We see that the interviewer must maintain equilibrium in this manner of questioning and not push the survivor too far. However, in these interviews it appears that using theories of transposition seems to add tension to the conversation rather than help survivors come closer to understanding their past. We see this in the ways that memory is supplemented. A supplement to memory (a photograph, a story from a relative, or even imagining a memory) helps the survivor to recall his own experience and what the supplement is can differ greatly between the interviewer and survivor in these testimonies. For example, while GE seems to go along with Kestenberg to some extent when he tries to imagine his mother carrying him, he ultimately comes back to his claim that his mother had told him about a bomb shelter and that must be the reason that he is able to imagine a moment like this at all. In order to solidify his personal story, GE clearly wants to connect with real events that his mother has told him and/or through what he has learned in the public sphere about the Holocaust since the war years. However, Kestenberg continues her questioning along the same lines and the conversation moves back and forth between Kestenberg's attempt to capture body memory through the supplement of fantasy and GE's attempt to construct his individual Holocaust experience by supplementing it with his own wartime memories, family stories, and public sources of information.

Photographs are another way that survivors call on the past, and the stories GE was told by his family become even more solidified on discovering some family photographs while researching his book in 1985. These images give GE another real supplement and a certainty about his past that he did not seem to have before finding them:

GE ... Maybe '85, or a little bit earlier, I found the first baby picture I ever had. I never had a baby picture, you see. And this baby picture was with my ... I don't remember. It's a family ... very immediate family and my grandmother on there, which I never saw.
JK This is your mother's mother?
GE Yes, who died in Auschwitz. So it was done apparently some time ... I seem to be maybe six to eight months.[31]
GE ... I can't remember exactly, but I can tell you what happened.[32]

In the very same sentence GE recognizes his inability to recall the past but also his belief that he knows what happened. While it is obvious that he cannot remember exactly what happened because he was just an infant, he is sure about his grandmother's transport to Auschwitz because he has that photo (which is not of the transport, of course) and because of a story told to GE later by his brother who escaped the transport by jumping from the train. The photo and his brother's story are enough evidence for GE, even if none of this is his own actual memory and the only family member that he recognizes in the photograph is his maternal grandmother. This photograph, as an object of memory and a document of the past, becomes a real memory for him.

This act in which photographs become a real memory was dubbed by Hirsch "postmemory." She describes it as "the relationship of the second generation to powerful, often traumatic experiences that preceded their births but that were nevertheless transmitted to them so deeply as to seem to constitute memories in their own right."[33] Hirsch explains how the photograph tends to be more powerful than other narratives: "More than oral or written narratives, photographic images that survive massive devastation and outlive their subjects and owners function as ghostly revenants from an irretrievably lost past world. They enable us, in the present, not only to see and to touch that past but also to try to reanimate it by undoing the finality of the photographic 'take.'"[34]

GE is a slightly different case: Hirsch was describing the second generation, and as a child survivor (and a child of survivors), he is technically the 1.5 generation. However, in common with the second generation who had not experienced the war, he can only imagine his and his parents' experiences. The photograph is essential to his identity. Without it he would lack the certainty that the supplement provides to such survivors. GE is able to add one more layer to his story because he believes in the truth or power of the photographs, yet he still understands that the stories that his parents told him are separate from his own memories. It does not seem that GE wishes to reanimate the past, the moment of the photograph, but rather that he wants to use the photographs to justify the memories of his family and to prove that he lived during this time. It seems that if GE exists in a photograph with his family, even if most members are unidentifiable to him, then his story of his past and what he tells the interviewer about it must hold some truth.

In addition to this use of oral stories and family photographs to support his testimony, there is one more key element to how GE constructs memories of his childhood during the Holocaust—his post-Holocaust mass-mediated memory. This becomes apparent when although Kestenberg returns again and again to questions about his time as a very small baby, hoping to evoke other kinds of memories through further imagination exercises, she does not get the results that she seems to be looking for. Her questioning, instead, leads GE, who is still attempting to feel something from his infancy, to consider another influence on this memory:

> GE Somehow I feel that at the time . . . again, maybe I'm biased, you see.
> JK Why are you biased? In which way?
> GE Because I read so much material on children in the Holocaust, but at the time . . .
> JK This kind of material you read, that I'm asking you about?
> GE Maybe not.
> JK Maybe? I'm sure not!
> GE No, no, don't be sure.
> JK Where? Where would you read it?
> GE Don't be sure.
> JK About mothers holding children and how they rocked them?
> GE No, not how they rocked them, but they picture themselves and the reason I think . . . perhaps I wasn't wrong . . . because especially in wartime Budapest, bombs falling, a mother instinctly [sic], perhaps, holding close, the child.[35]

Thus, GE claims to know how mothers held their babies, but this is not from his memory. Rather, it seems that he strongly identifies with what he has read in books or seen in other media since the war. GE's rational mind tells him that what he knows about the Holocaust, what he remembers, is predominantly, if not completely, due to the filtering of these events through the post-Holocaust era. So it might have been from his readings, or from images he has subsequently seen. It might be simply from being out in the world and observing the very act of mothers holding their babies. Hence, what arises from this part of the interview is that it is not GE's imagination that informs his testimony, but knowledge acquired from post-Holocaust experiences.

GE's interview with Kestenberg is captivating not because it tells a smooth, chronological Holocaust story, but because it allows us to observe a conversation between two people with very different conceptions of how memories are reconstructed. The dialogue is at its most interesting when it reveals a somewhat contentious and uncomfortable exchange. As readers, we watch them perform the messy struggle of recalling memories for an archive. It should therefore be noted that the interview could be read as less about what GE recalls or remembers, such as his mother holding him or his grandmother's transport, and more about the way that their discussion exposes the process of witnessing. GE does not have all of the facts straight. He draws from any source that he can think of—family memories, long-lost photographs, and post-Holocaust observations of the world, as well as his own reading and experiences—to solidify what he knows and to supplement the absence that was left in the wake of the Holocaust. At the same time, Kestenberg uses her technique of transposition to help GE to recall unconscious memories using imagination and fantasy. Together they perform the chaos of memory discourse and the complexities of the archival process.

Interview with DE

In the second interview we can observe much of the same attention to these different approaches to memory. In this testimony the survivor DE is described as living in the Los Angeles area but as originally coming from Lublin, Poland, the second-largest Jewish settlement in Poland at the start of World War II.[36]

As with GE, issues about memory arise at the very beginning of the interview as DE shares some facts about where and when he was born. The interviewer, JC, also provides some guidance about how the interview should proceed and the angle from which the interviewer wants DE to think about the concept of memory: "I'd sort of would like first for you to give me an overall sketch of what you know about your family during the Holocaust, what you know about yourself, and about your parents, and siblings if there were any. And afterwards, I'd like to ask you questions specifically about your memories, not what you were told. Sometimes children at the age you were, they have stories or pictures, and they have their own memories."[37] The interviewer notes that there are different ways that memories are created and sees a distinction between "stories or pictures" and the children's "own memories." This is an extremely problematic distinction, opening up many questions: How can adult survivors clearly separate their own memories from what they were told? What is the difference between what they were told and what they remember? Where do we draw the line between the two? Should we even try? While these may be valid questions, of interest to me is that this testimony discloses a curious tension between the interviewer and survivor that draws attention to the different conceptualizations of memory that result from these interviews.

To return to the current interview, DE responds to JC: "Well, of course, whatever happened to me during the years of the Holocaust, I only know from what I'm told."[38] His comment echoes elements from GE's interview: the interviewer's pattern of suggestions about the ways in which to evoke memory, and the survivor's almost absolute insistence that his only memories are not actually his own.

The interviewer in this case, resembling Kestenberg but with a little less insistency, still utilizes imagination and fantasy as discovery tools throughout the interview with DE. For example, JC attempts to get DE to make a connection between an attempt to protect his parents (transposition) and a recurring dream:

> DE   But I do remember, I guess as a result of all the discussions and information from my parents I do remember some recurring dream that I had in those years. Well, I shouldn't say those years, but in the last year or two, maybe, if I remember a dream of uh, German soldiers and tanks uh, coming down the street and then uh, stopping around the street of our section, and uh, telling all the Jews that they were arrested and that the whole thing was going to happen again sort to speak. I do remember that.
>
> JC   . . . Can you remember the dream now? I mean, ca—, you picture the dream, can see the— the, see the pictures. Was the dream in color or black and white?
>
> DE   I don't. It's been so long. Forty years.
>
> JC   . . . Did you have a sense of wanting to protect them [his parents] from it?
>
> DE   I don't, I can't say yes or no.[39]

DE admits that the dream is old and indistinct and that he really does not have his own memories. He does not seem to believe that the dream comes from an actual experience but maintains that it must have come from a discussion with his parents instead. As with GE, DE determines that his memories are nothing more than received memories from his family.

One of the most interesting parts of the interview is DE's description of his separation from his parents during the war. Here, he clearly relies on stories told to him by his parents to relate one of the most traumatic experiences he suffered as a child. He tells of his birth to Orthodox parents in 1940–1941 in the Lublin Ghetto and of his parents handing him over to a gentile Polish neighbor in 1942 in the hope that he would remain safe. There was a neighbor, he says, who "threw me out with the garbage, sort [sic] to speak."[40] By chance, he was discovered by "some policeman" who "turned [him] over to some Catholic orphanage."[41] DE has no direct memory of this event, so once again he relies on his parents' memories. He does admit to having some fleeting memories of the orphanage: "I remember just a piece of dark bread, and some bitter dark liquid," referring also to a "dining hall," "a glimpse memory of the courtyard," and "the Cloister, or the church itself."[42] He restates that he has "a tremendous amount of knowledge that [his] parents gave [him]."⁴³ The interviewer asks him whether he has seen any photographs or even has any images of people in his memory from this time, but DE notes only these vague memories of rooms and food, in addition to the information that he learned from his parents.

In contrast to GE, DE also makes reference in his interview to public memories that mention both the Holocaust and post-Holocaust traumatic events, including a comparison to Biafra. The latter comes up when he describes how he looked when his parents picked him up from the orphanage at the end of the war:

DE   The only thing I remember is when they got me from the orphanage I was uh, I was a horrible sight to look at because I had this gigantic belly from—
JC   Starvation.
DE   Malnutrition.
JC   Uh, huh.
DE   And I had uh, I had uh, some terrible hair problems with lice all over and just blotchy hairs of some kind . . . .
JC   . . . This is stress.
DE   Yeah, apparently I just eh, I looked horrible the way they described me. I looked like these, these posters.
JC   Biafra.
DE   Yeah, Biafra. Yep.⁴⁴

Here it is the interviewer that suggests Biafra, but DE, as the survivor, quickly agrees with this image of how he must have looked—a lice-ridden, starving child from Africa. There are many general parallels that can be made between various modern tragedies and the Holocaust, but it seems that DE agrees with the reference to Biafra because it is closer to his contemporary experience. It also seems that because DE does not have the ability to describe what he experienced in Poland due to the absence of any photographs to prove what he saw, the visualization needs to come from something that both he and the interviewer have actually seen in the media and thus knowledge about the Holocaust is mediated through the reference to Nigeria. He does not appear to suffer from a conflation of memories here; rather, this reference to Biafra, a small moment in the interview, implies signification. It demonstrates the ease with which a survivor might reference other more-recent events to find some common ground, some language, by which to convey his story to others.

Mass-mediated memory is referenced again in another section where DE refers to Claude Lanzmann's 1985 film *Shoah* in a discussion about his feelings toward the Nazis and Ukrainians, with a particular adversity toward the Poles:

JC That angry feeling towards what the Polish people—do you have that same with the *German [sic]* or not?—Not really.

DE It's strange. I, you know, as far as the Nazis or as far as older Germans that you see in government that you know were Nazis, I have the same feeling, if not more so but, I don't have the same sense of the language like when I se— when I think of Poland, and Polish people, and the Ukraine and Ukrainians, what those people did. It was . . .

JC That's the stronger thing that comes up for you. That's sort of more—

DE That's—

JC Put away.

DE Well, there's stronger than my hatred for the Nazis and what they did, obviously, but uh, I can differentiate uh, that quite easily from the uh, from the way that the Pollacks uh, and the Ukrainians uh, did to the Jews, to the Jewish survivors. That's something that I cannot accept. So, there's different levels of anger. . . .

JC Talk about what the Ukrainians and the Pollacks did. . . .

DE . . . the insanity of the Nazis and the, the cruelty of the Nazis after the humane [sic] thing that they did, but as far as Pollacks are concerned, that movie, Shoah, . . . you go back . . .

DE And you talk and you talk to these people. Anti-Semitics.[45]

This exchange is notable because DE employs *Shoah* to perhaps validate his feelings that the Poles are anti-Semitic and to explain why he has such an adverse reaction to them. He does not have a direct memory of the Poles to draw on, but he has been told numerous stories by his parents, he has read newspaper articles, and has lived in a culture that is full of references to the extreme situation in Poland during the war. Here he does not conflate a different event with his own experience but instead conflates a version of that event with his own trauma.

Both of these survivors, GE and DE, and the many others who were interviewed for the archive were asked to do the impossible: to recount forty years later their experiences "through the mind's eye of the child."[46] But equally problematic, they were also asked to discuss experiences that they were far too young to remember. As a result, they have absolutely no recourse but to articulate this absence of memory through the stories of others. The interviewers think otherwise or at least use a very different approach. This results in a performative narrative that emphasizes the tensions that exist between the varying approaches to understanding how the memories of the witness may act as a source of truth—call it historical if you wish—about the Holocaust and the struggles of remembering. GE and DE both insist that as child survivors they are dependent on the stories of others to fill in the blanks of their memories. They turn not only to their parents or photos of their families but also rely on mediated versions of the Holocaust and post-Holocaust disasters, such as Biafra, to describe impressions and scenarios that they themselves do not remember but imagine to be similar to what they themselves must have experienced.

Interventions

Bernard-Donals wrote that "we have paid too much attention in recent years to the way memories make present—or represent—a past, and have not paid enough attention to how aspects of memory intervene in and make possible a future."[47] The Kestenberg testimonies, acting as an intervention in the memory archive, show two ways of thinking about the process of witnessing. In one way, they demonstrate many of the pitfalls of the testimonial process, illustrating that the survivors have unwillingly become mediated versions of the child Holocaust survivor—asked to testify to something that they cannot remember, and forced to speak through other sources such as parents, photographs, and newspapers. Yet, this very same process provides a counterbalance to the popular culture version of the Holocaust as the Kestenberg testimonies interrupt, undermine, and exasperate the reading process; the reading of this kind of text seems necessary in a "contemporary culture [which] sweeps up difficult ideas with great ease and churns them into something smooth and palatable."[48] This reminds me of Michael Rothberg's entreaty for multidirectional memory, which he describes as a shift in perspective [from] "collective memory as *competitive* memory—as a zero sum struggle over scarce resources—[to] memory as *multidirectional*: as subject to ongoing negotiation, cross-referencing, and borrowing; as productive and not private." It is important to understand the potential of texts such as the Kestenberg archive to help us to understand the past, but also for how they potentially shape our future. In his book *Multidirectional Memory*, Rothenberg draws our attention to the potential of an intercultural dynamic where Holocaust texts, such as the Kestenberg archive, interact with other discourses, such as slavery and colonialism. Rather than blocking these other voices and events, as has been suggested by certain academics who believe that there can only be winners and losers in the struggle for identity formation, Rothberg champions the idea of using "the presence of widespread Holocaust consciousness as a platform to articulate," for example, "a vision of American racism past and present." Rather than simply articulating preestablished positions, the collective historical identities of these different groups might potentially "come into being through their dialogical interactions with others."[49]

I am reminded of how much has changed since the Kestenberg testimonies were taken in the 1980s: when these survivors were interviewed, the Berlin Wall had not fallen, most people could not find Rwanda on a map, and the Holocaust had not yet been extensively Hollywoodized. The twenty-first century-reader, however, lives in a post-Rwanda world, negotiates a post-9/11 political climate, and is able to watch YouTube transmissions of the most recent ISIS beheadings. This same reader also lives in a world of reality television with the likes of the Kardashians and a different kind of survivor—participating in the television show *Survivor*, a virtual world where the manipulation of narrative is not only recognizable but also celebrated in popular culture. The Holocaust, as an event, is now located somewhere between actual reality (what might be called historical reality) and reality as a popular cultural object. It is constantly being reproduced—in film, music, opera, and theater—and is part of the everyday environment, the daily discourse. Thus, if texts such as the Kestenberg archive are to expand their relevancy beyond the small circle of academic readers to a larger audience, we need to consider the changing nature and needs of contemporary readers and viewers of Holocaust narratives and continue to reinvent ways of keeping a passage open through the tightly closed borders of the memory archive.

At the end of their book, *Between Witness and Testimony: The Holocaust and the Limits of Representation*, Bernard-Donals and Glejzer discuss teaching and writing about the Shoah and call for a reexamination of the "relation between witness and testimony that can account for what exceeds the limit of knowledge."[50] Although this is the reexamination of an immense topic, in their book they explain in more detail that they are concerned with how, in the aftermath of a catastrophe, we can bear witness to what Maurice Blanchot referred to as the disaster—the "experience that is not a lived event," because "it exceeds the regularities of knowledge and the language that could contain it."[51] In other words, if we are always already engaged in an ethics of the impossibility of the representation of trauma, to move forward in our conceptualization of the Holocaust and other traumatic events we must recognize that "misperception is necessary for understanding"[52] Bernard-Donals and Glejzer urge us, as teachers and thinkers, to follow the lead of Berel Lang who perceptively suggested that we shift from the focus on "the limit of representation" to the "representation of limits."[53]

Bernard-Donals and Glejzer conclude by stating, "We need to teach that *what we are supposed to know we do not know*, that the most crucial—

hence most radically particular—learning is not to be found in the fabric of our lectures, tests, essays, understandings or knowledge of the event."[54] Students must be shown that the difficulty of learning about the Holocaust does not rest in "what we know, but the gulf that surrounds it."[55] We must pay attention to the silences, what is not said, and to the details that may be overlooked when we come to an event with some prior knowledge of it.. Although the focus here is not directly on pedagogy, I am concerned with instilling in our students (and by extension the general public) the intellectual desire to seek out the stories that may be outside the tightly controlled limits of popular culture—the world of easy reads and palatable tragedies—and to consider these outliers, such as the Kestenberg testimonies, as meaningful tools that teach us more about what we do not know, the silences, than what we do know. It is also imperative to keep showing that the testimonial process is a messy and inexact science. The Kestenberg archive recordings and transcripts are a powerful source for this kind of memory archive and are needed now more than ever because the Holocaust is in danger of becoming such a neatly packaged item that no one dare try to tear the wrapping.

Author

Stephenie Young is associate professor in the English department and faculty fellow of the Center for Holocaust and Genocide Studies at Salem State University, Massachusetts. Her research focuses on experimental testimony, the relationship between aesthetics and violence in contemporary images and narratives of war, and women's transnational writing. She is currently working on a book project about the relationship between collective memory, forensics, and visual culture in post-conflict Bosnia.

Notes

All interviews quoted in this chapter were held at the Oral History Division, Hebrew University of Jerusalem.

I would like to thank Sharon Kangisser Cohen and the Oral History Division of the Hebrew University of Jerusalem for inviting me to a workshop about the Kestenberg Archive in 2012. I am grateful to Adele Parker for invaluable suggestions during the preparation of this paper and the close attention of the anonymous reader of the manuscript. I would also like to acknowledge the work of William Connelly, Steven Vitto, and Krista

Hegburg at the United States Holocaust Memorial Museum, Washington, DC, for their assistance with survivor data.
1. Testimony of GE-JK, (257) 16-21, 6.
2. Derrida, *Archive Fever*, 36.
3. Huyssen, *Present Pasts*, 6.
4. The canon of work dedicated to witnessing and testimony about the Holocaust is vast. Some of the works that address the place of the Holocaust in contemporary culture and are most relevant to the questions brought up here are found in Novick, *Holocaust in American Life*; Mintz, *Popular Culture*; Shandler, *While America Watches*; Weissman, *Fantasies of Witnessing*; and Young, *The Texture of Memory*.
5. Laub, "An Event without a Witness," 75.
6. Bernard-Donals, "Conflations of Memory," 79.
7. Keenan and Weizman, *Mengele's Skull*, 11.
8. See Laub and Felman, *Testimony*.
9. Although today "Holocaust survivor" is just one identity group among many, the concept of the Holocaust survivor did not suddenly flood the newspapers in the United States in 1945. In fact, it is well known how undocumented the Holocaust was in the United States for many years. Alison Landsberg examines the absence of media about the Holocaust directly after the war in her book *Prosthetic Memory*: "In 1945, there was neither a *Newsweek* article on the liberation of the camps nor a single entry on Auschwitz or the Holocaust in the entire *Reader's Guide to Periodical Literature*. As an American event—even as an event in its own right—the Holocaust had yet to be articulated. Only one article, published in 1947 in the *New Republic* broached the subject of Auschwitz. Aptly titled 'Back-Page Story,' the opening caption declared, 'Today it takes a careful search of the news to find this chapter of Nazi Germany'" (114
10. Archive of Interviews with Child Survivors of Holocaust received by Oral History Division of Hebrew University's Harman Institute. The following two studies commissioned by The International Commission on Holocaust Era Insurance Claims (ICHEIC) in 2003 address this issue: the first, by Professor Sergio Della Pergola, is available at http://www.icheic.org/pdf/ICHEIC demography1.pdf and includes a country-by-country breakdown of the number of survivors; the second, by the Ukeles Associates is available at http://www.icheic.org/pdf/ICHEIC demography2.pdf. In addition, the UJA Federation of New York prepared a study of Holocaust survivors in the Greater New York area (the 5 boroughs and Westchester, Nassau and Suffolk counties) in 2002: http://www.bjpa.org/Publications/details.cfm?PublicationID=685. The Greater Miami Jewish Federation sponsored a demographic study of survivors in Miami in 2004 http://www.jewishdatabank.org/study.asp?sid=18420&tp=2. The *Registry of Holocaust Survivors* is a voluntary list of Holocaust survivors and their families. Although it is by no means a complete reckoning of all survivors, it is certainly the largest such name register of Holocaust survivors in the world.
11. See Suleiman, "The 1.5 Generation." As a definition of the 1.5 generation, Suleiman writes: "I mean child survivors of the Holocaust, too young to

have had an adult understanding of what was happening to them, but old enough to have *been there* during the Nazi persecution of Jews. Unlike the second generation, whose most common shared experience is that of belatedness [. . . my ellipses] the 1.5 generation's shared experience is that of premature bewilderment and helplessness." P. 277 *American Imago*

12. Hansen, "*Schindler's List* Is Not *Shoah*," 310.
13. Ibid., 310.
14. Ibid., 310.
15. Ibid., 310. Italics are in original.
16. Hoffman, *After Such Knowledge*, 172.
17. Bernard-Donals, "Conflations of Memory," 73.
18. This statement is based on Bernard-Donals's study that examines how visitors to the United States Holocaust Memorial Museum in Washington, DC, read the experience of their visit through a post9/11 world. See Bernard-Donals, "Conflations of Memory."
19. Testimony of GE, (257) 16-2, 1987.
20. Ibid., 2. GE says, "My father was a . . . coachman, you call it? He had horses and wagons and transportation."
21. Testimony of GE, (257) 16-2, 1.
22. Ibid.
23. Ibid.
24. Ibid., 11.
25. Ibid., 9.
26. Kestenberg, "Transposition Revisited: Clinical, Therapeutic, and Developmental Considerations." In *Healing their Wounds: Psychotherapy with Holocaust Survivors and Their Families*. 70, 78. "Transposition" is a complex psychological term defined by Barocas and Barocas "Wounds of Fathers," 331in the following way: "The children of survivors show symptoms which would be expected if they actually lived through the Holocaust. . . . The children come to feel that the Holocaust is the single most critical event that has affected their lives although it occurred before they were born" Kestenberg, "Transposition Revisited," 67. Kestenberg complicates Barocas and Barocas' concept about the inherited trauma of a child who lives in his or her parent's past. She explained that "the patient transpose[s] herself into her father's past via a mechanism similar to, but not identical with, the spiritualist's journey into the world of the dead." (ibid., 67). See Barocas and Barocas, "Wounds of Fathers," 331; Faimberg, "The Telescoping of Generations."
27. Kestenberg, "Transposition Revisited," 69.
28. Ibid.
29. According to the online *Psychology Dictionary*, a body memory is "the ability of the body to store memories unconsciously. It has a sensory recollection of traumatic experiences related to pain, discomfort, tension, and arousal. The hypothesis is that, despite infantile amnesia, the body itself experiences a sensorimotor encoding of each traumatic event."
30. Testimony of GE, (257) 16-2, 13–14.
31. Ibid., 4–5.

32. Ibid., 6.
33. Hirsch, "The Generation of Postmemory," 103.
34. Ibid., 115.
35. Testimony of GE. 15.
36. Testimony of DE, (257) 16-3, 1989. 11. For DE I was sent: DE-JC Box 16, Folder 16-3
37. Ibid., 1–2.
38. Ibid., 2
39. Ibid., 45–46.
40. Ibid., 5.
41. Ibid.
42. Ibid., 2.
43. Ibid.
44. Ibid., 38–39.
45. Ibid., 48–49.
46. Bernard-Donals, "Conflations of Memory," 49.
47. Ibid., 74
48. Hoffman, *After Such Knowledge*, 171.
49. Rothberg, *Multidirectional Memory*, 3, 5.
50. Bernard-Donals and Glejzer, *Between Witness and Testimony*, ix.
51. Ibid., ix.
52. Ibid., 183.
53. Lang quoted in ibid., 183.
54. Ibid., 174.
55. Ibid., 174.

References

Archive of Interviews with Child Survivors of Holocaust received by Oral History Division of Hebrew University's Harman Institute, The Hebrew University. http://www.huji.ac.il/cgi-bin/dovrut/dovrut_search_eng.pl?mesge130260695632688760

Barocas, Harvey, and Carol Barocas. "Wounds of Fathers: The Next Generation of Holocaust Victims." *International Review Psycho-Analysis* 6 no. 3 (1979): 331–340.

Bernard-Donals, Michael. "Conflations of Memory or, What They Saw at the Holocaust Museum after 9/11." *New Centennial Review* 5, no. 2 (Fall 2005): 73–106.

Bernard-Donals, Michael, and Richard Glejzer. *Between Witness and Testimony: The Holocaust and the Limits of Representation*. Albany: State University of New York Press, 2001.

de Rosnay, Tatiana, *Sarah's Key*. New York: St. Martin's Griffin, 2008.

Derrida, Jacques. *Archive Fever: A Freudian Impression*, translated by Eric Prenowitz. Chicago: University of Chicago Press, 1998.

Faimberg, Haydee. "The Telescoping of Generations." *Contemporary Psychoanalysis* 24, no. 1 (1988): 99–118.

Felman, Shoshana, and Dori Laub, eds. *Testimony: Crises of Witnessing in Literature, Psychoanalysis, and History.* Oxford: Taylor & Francis, 1992.

Hansen, Miriam Bratu. "*Schindler's List* Is Not *Shoah:* The Second Commandment, Popular Modernism, and Public Memory." *Critical Inquiry* 22 (Winter 1996): 292–312.

Hirsch, Marianne. "The Generation of Postmemory." *Poetics Today* 29, no. 1 (Spring 2008): 103–128.

Hoffman, Eva. *After Such Knowledge: Memory, History and the Legacy of the Holocaust.* New York: Public Affairs, 2004.

Huyssen, Andreas. *Present Pasts: Urban Palimpsests and the Politics of Memory.* Stanford, CA: Stanford University Press, 2003.

Keenan, Thomas, and Eyal Weizman. *Mengele's Skull: The Advent of a Forensic Aesthetics.* Berlin: Sternberg Press, 2012.

Kestenberg, Judith. "Transposition Revisited: Clinical, Therapeutic, and Developmental Considerations." In *Healing Their Wounds: Psychotherapy with Holocaust Survivors and Their Families,* edited by Paul Marcus and Alan Rosenberg, 67–82. New York, Westport, CT; London: Praeger, 1989.

Landsberg, Alison. *Prosthetic Memory: The Transformation of American Remembrance in the Age of Mass Culture.* New York: Columbia University Press, 2004.

Laub, Dori. "An Event without a Witness: Truth, Testimony and Survival." In *Testimony: Crises of Witnessing in Literature, Psychoanalysis, and History,* edited by Shoshana Felman and Dori Laub, 75–92. Oxford: Taylor & Francis, 1992.

Novick, Peter, *The Holocaust in American Life.* New York: Houghton Mifflin Company, 1999.

Rothberg, Michael. *Multidirectional Memory: Remembering the Holocaust in the Age of Decolonization.* Stanford, CA: Stanford University Press, 2009.

Shandler, Jeffrey, *While America Watches: Televising the Holocaust.* New York: Oxford University Press, 1999.

Suleiman, Susan Rubin. "The 1.5 Generation: Thinking about Child Survivors and the Holocaust." *American Imago* 59, no. 3 (Fall 2002): 277–295.

Tarantino, Quentin, dir. *Inglourious Basterds* (2009)

Young, James E., *The Texture of Memory: Holocaust Memorials and Meaning.* New Haven, CT: Yale University Press, 1993.

 6

Shadows of Memory and Intergenerational Legacies in Child Survivors' Testimonies from the Kestenberg Archive

Dana Mihăilescu

Toward the beginning of *The Truce*, Primo Levi's memoir about life in the wake of World War II, the well-known Holocaust survivor introduces the figure of Hurbinek, a young child who looks at most three years old, and whom he meets at Buna, the main camp of Auschwitz immediately after its liberation on January 27, 1945. Levi's description of the child's Holocaust-induced traumatic appeareance is both heart-wrenching and staggering: "His eyes, lost in his triangular and wasted face, flashed terribly alive, full of demand, assertion, of the will to break loose, to shatter the tomb of his dumbness. The speech he lacked, which no one had bothered to teach him, the need of speech charged his stare with explosive urgency."[1] Levi then ends his description of Hurbinek by emphasizing the little boy's extremely precarious and evanescent condition in contrast to adult survivors: "Hurbinek, who was three years old and perhaps had been born in Auschwitz and had never seen a tree; Hurbinek, who had fought like a man, to the last breath, to gain his entry into the world of men, from which a bestial power had excluded him; Hurbinek, the nameless, whose tiny forearm—even his—bore the tattoo of Auschwitz; Hurbinek died in the first days of March 1945, free but not redeemed. Nothing remains of him: he bears witness through these words of mine."[2]

In *Remnants of Auschwitz*, Italian philosopher Giorgio Agamben engages with Levi's presentation of Hurbinek and reads the above figure of the dying child as paradoxically both a possible epitome of the Holocaust witness—given the toddler's inability to speak, which suggests the unintelligible experience of the Holocaust—and the collapse of the witness position given the boy's senseless sounds that fail to bear witness.[3] I believe that Levi's forceful image of Hurbinek raises other equally fascinating questions about young child survivors, some of which this chapter will address. Most important among these, Hurbinek's urgent stare, which functions as an excruciatingly revealing judgment counterbalancing his lack of speech, offers an important research path: How did an upbringing within the traumatic situation of the Holocaust interfere with and impinge on children's channels of understanding during their developmental stages in comparison to adolescents and adults?

I will explore how young child survivors were affected by the Holocaust both during and after the war, given their particular mnemonic and identity-related structures, by focusing on those who were between zero and eight years old during World War II and living in a biological or foster family environment. Recent scholarly works on child survivors have particularly explored early testimonies usually given to historical commissions having ethnographic, memorial and juridical aims and to Zionist organizations taking care of those who were orphaned in view of relocating them to Palestine. The scholars have by and large examined child survivors' search for identity in the post–World War II period, especially foregrounding the problematic contours of their emotional make-up that made them susceptible to various ideological purposes of early interviewers and favoring the case of child survivors from Poland and Germany over other countries, in studies by Beate Müller, Boaz Cohen, or Rita Horváth.[4] In their 2012 article "The 1945 Bytom Notebook: Searching for the Lost Voices of Child Holocaust Survivors," Cohen and Müller have added the case of an unpublished Yiddish-language manuscript containing forty-two child survivors' testimonies collected in Polish Bytom in 1945 by the principal of the local Hebrew School, Shlomo Tsam, as representing a chronicle of their fate. This chapter supplements such concerns by my choice to consider child survivors' testimonies given to psychoanalysts in the 1980s and 1990s. In these later testimonies, child survivors' voices take center stage over the ideological or other agendas of interviewing bodies that were primary characteristic features of early testimonies. In these later testimonies, the child survivors' various ages during World War II emerge as a significant category of analysis. My study especially complements valuable findings like those of Nathan Durst whose 2003 article "Child-Survivors of the Holocaust" offered a systematic exploration of age-specific traumatization of child survivors by identifying five specific age stages: zero to three years, three to five years, five to eight years, eight to twelve years, and twelve to fifteen years.[5] For child survivors up to eight years old, Durst limited his analysis to Jewish war orphans or children separated from their families, while I will consider the particularities of memories for young child survivors who continued to live with birth or foster families, showing the equal significance of caring or dysfunctional biological family structures on children's memory and personality development.

In his eponymous book, psychologist Aaron Hass called the children of Holocaust survivors a generation growing up "in the shadow of the Holocaust," indirectly but inextricably marked by World War II events.[6] Using Hass's insight as a point of departure, I will show that young child survivors, at most aged eight when they and their families started to be directly affected by the Holocaust, occupied a liminal position between the first and second generations of survivors, given their shadows of memory. I examine testimonies from the Judith Kestenberg child survivor archive, focusing on those in which interviewers were asked to gear the conversation toward the survivors' specific examples of persecution and what they deemed as the most injurious circumstances undertaken: the type of memories they were likely to recall, their relation to discrimination, their future psychological state of mind, their feelings about rescuers, family, and friends, their relationships with their own children, their general view on their identity in relation to ethnic and religious coordinates, and whether or not they perceived themselves as survivors, refugees, and others.[7] I have chosen to focus on these five testimonies out of the dozen so-far digitized testimonies from the Kestenberg Archive of Testimonies of Child Holocaust Survivors belonging to child survivors in the younger age ranges because they most clearly and lucidly portray the patterns of life specific to each one of the three age stages I consider (zero to three years, three to five years, five to eight years). The same concerns are replicated in the other testimonies given by child survivors from the respective age ranges in the Kestenberg archive as well as in the case of child survivors of the same age who have become authors and presented similar patterns in their literary testimonies, which I analyze elsewhere.[8] This is why I believe they can be representative case studies for understanding the specifics of child survivors of young ages. They are equally relevant for highlighting the common and different characteristic features of the Polish and Romanian contexts in which they occurred and their impact on young child survivors' stances in the aftermath of the war.

My examination of these testimonies attempts to answer the following questions: What specific forms of memory can be detected from the testimonies of young child survivors, and to what extent do these memories take into consideration the age of the children during the Holocaust, their location, their gender, and whether they were still living with their biological parents? What are the effects of their specific forms of memory on their and subsequent generations' future life development, life view, and existence in relation to trauma? In order to answer these questions, I examine five English-language testimonies of child survivors from Romania and Poland found in the Kestenberg archive. My analysis of these testimonies uses as a basic criterion the children's ages on deportation or hiding, ranging from the case of a baby born in a camp and being five months old at the end of the war to children who were eight years old on deportation and eleven on liberation. These testimonies are further distinguished on the basis of their diverse patterns of family life, ranging from children who lived throughout the Holocaust alongside their biological family (with two prevailing patterns of either protective or dysfunctional parents) to those who lived without their biological parents, usually raised by Christian foster families.

These child survivors from Romania and Poland fall into two basic categories regarding when they first experienced anti-Semitic measures and the family pattern in which they were growing up during World War II. First, those from Romania were deported from Bukovina to Transnistrian Ghettos with their biological families in 1941, and started to return around March 1944 after the Soviet troops crossed the Bug River and ended the Axis-Romanian governance of the region; these children spent the war years with at least one parent by their side, the issue of protective or dysfunctional biological parents therefore being their dominant concern. As for the life of Romanian Jews during the Holocaust, Benjamin, Florian, and Ciuciu noted that children represented 22 percent of the Jews from Northern and Southern Bukovina, Bessarabia, Dorohoi and Hertza who were deported to Transnistria by the Romanian authorities from September 1941.[9] According to the Romanian authorities' deportation orders that were included in *The Black Book*, Matatias Carp's early report about the Holocaust in Romania, the Bessarabian Jews were deported first, on September 11, 1941,[10] followed by the Jews from Southern Bukovina on October 8 and 9, 1941,[11] and the Jews of Czernowitz and Northern Bukovina on October 10, 1941.[12] Since the three child survivors I analyze come from Bukovina, they were all deported in October 1941. Second and in contrast, the two child survivors from Poland were both sent by their parents to live in hiding with gentile families for the duration of the Holocaust. One reason for this specific choice of their parents was that, unlike Romania, which chose to officially join the Axis in November 1940 without a German invasion of its territory as a continuation of Marshall Ion Antonescu's already-implemented fascist dictatorship of the country, Poland had its territory invaded in September 1939 by both the Third Reich (western regions and districts around Warsaw, Cracow, Radom, and Lublin) and the Soviet Union (Eastern Polish territories). The German occupation lasted almost five years and was characterized by an aggressive Germanization policy, whereas the Soviet occupation ended in June 1941.[13] Both Polish child survivors I examined came from the Aryan-occupied territory of Poland, being native to the surrounding areas of Warsaw and Katowice. Joanna Michlic has noted that, unlike the Jewish children from Soviet-occupied Poland who spent the war alongside at least one of their parents, the common experience of the children from National Socialist– (or Nazi-) occupied Poland, as is also reflected in my two case studies, was separation from their parents, either by being sent to gentile families by their parents to give them a chance for survival, or by leaving the ghettos on their own, in the case of orphaned children whose parents had been killed or who had perished from hunger or disease.[14] In the case of the former, clashes between a disempowered biological family and a Christian foster family, as well as the age of the child on separation from his or her biological family, were important factors for the mnemonic structures that the Holocaust impacted on their future lives and for their level of understanding of what was happening and who they were.

Encamped Toddlers' Holocaust-Induced Mnemonic Structures: Between Postmemories, Somatic Memories, and the Impact of Being Reared in a Dysfunctional Family

Among the testimonies I examined, PC, born in January 1944 in the Balta labor camp, Transnistria, was the youngest. She belongs to the zero to three-year-old age group that, according to Durst, is characterized by passivity, emotional reactions to object-loss, and total dependence on a caregiver (usually the mother) for developing security and attachment.[15] PC was five months old on liberation in May 1944, and she demonstrates the extent to which strong sensation-related memories influence the way in which young child survivors relate to the Holocaust. PC's testimony thereby confirms the findings of psychoanalyst Paul Valent who emphasized the absence of sequential verbal memories in the case of young children, and hence the specific character of their memories as primarily nonverbal, nonsequential, and emotional.[16]

PC gave two separate testimonies to Kestenberg, one on May 16, 1988, in which she focused particularly on Holocaust memories and growing up in the aftermath, and the other on October 10, 1988, in which she emphasized her adult life and her relationship with her own children. In both interviews the issue of memory as intergenerational transmission takes center stage: in the former, PC concentrates on her relationship with her mother and grandmother, and in the latter, on her relationship with her own three children.

PC's mother and grandmother were in Transnistria from late 1941, and PC was born in the Balta labor camp in January 1944, thus she has relied on their recollections for her memories of the Holocaust: "Most of the things that I know ... from the Holocaust is from my mother and grandmother, because these are the people that I was in camp with."[17] Put differently, PC identifies herself as being primarily in possession of postmemories of the Shoah, a term coined by literary and memory studies scholar Marianne Hirsch to identify the indirect memories of children of Holocaust survivors. Hirsch defines posmemories as "the relationship that the 'generation after' bears to the personal, collective, and cultural trauma of those who came before—to experiences they 'remember' only by means of the stories, images, and behaviors among which they grew up."[18]

PC's testimony proves that she is, in fact, in possession of both intertwined postmemories and somatic or embodied sense memories. By relying on postmemories for the context of her birth, PC explains how at first her mother and father went into hiding near Balta with the partisans, until her mother realized she was pregnant with PC and let her husband move on by himself while she joined her own mother in the Balta camp in order to give herself a chance to give birth, since living in the camp had been described by others as an easy place to find "work" and "get food."[19] Such hopeful attitudes occurred in a context in which, PC explains, "the rumor was that the war was going to be over any minute."[20] Once in the camp, however, PC's mother learned differently and realized that as a pregnant woman she was especially at risk: "There were no children that she saw around. She heard that pregnant women were killed, just disappeared."[21] PC recounts in tears a terrible incident told to her by her mother: "She was telling about one incident, she said that the Germans one time found a baby in the fields and they came into the women and they asked whose baby that was and nobody answered and she said that in front of everybody they took the baby and they tore the baby apart and that was when she was pregnant."[22] PC's emotion at telling this story shows how deeply she has embedded the terrific physical and psychic vulnerability and helplessness of mothers and children during the Holocaust; later she actually refers to this vulnerability as her "heavy package" and "that victim within me."[23] Her adult life is thereby still structured by the frames of victimhood and precariousness that were hers and her mother's before she was even born. She also attributes her birth to her mother's skinny frame; nobody was aware she was pregnant because she wore "an old coat over her, and it [birth] happened at night and my grandmother was there and other women were there and she gave birth."[24]

PC goes on to discuss her mother's passivity and her grandmother's pivotal role in her survival, hiding her in the barrack wall and tying a rag around her mouth to prevent her from crying.[25] PC has a strong sense memory of physical weakness and subordination to an extremely strong, external controlling force: "If I do remember anything, it's just the covering of my mouth."[26] PC stresses the natural internalization of this feeling in her present life: "Even today, sometimes I wake up at night and I sleep with my hand covering my mouth, today."[27] This shows how the early embedded feelings of children become innate characteristics that function as formative life frames for the duration of their lives. Equally relevant, the strong roots of this embedded memory are suggested by a Proust-like associative memory technique: PC became aware of the role of these initial physiological memories in her life when, at thirty years old, PC, now a mother of three children, had to face "death again," went through a surgery, and found herself unable to breathe in the aftermath, since she had been once again applied a "covering" to her mouth.[28] This episode brought back the sensation of insecurity and helplessness at the start of her life and triggered a need for therapy. In recalling this moment, PC displays her most emotionally charged response of the two interviews; her hitherto rational control over past events seems to gradually collapse and meaning gets highly fragmented and incoherent, signaling a traumatic fixture that has not been worked through:

> And I couldn't . . . I couldn't breathe . . . I couldn't . . . . Something has happened to me. I could not have the strength to go back to life and I went to therapy and of course, that's when I discovered that the link that my breathing had to do with everything else . . . with facing death, with keeping quiet, not making any noise, because me making noise would put in danger of death everybody around me and the covering up and covering up . . . being quiet, being in a dark place, being still, being . . . and I have lived my life, I think, until the age of . . . with everything else that I did, I still kept very still . . . made sure everything is not, you know . . . .[29]

Drawing on Cathy Caruth's work on trauma and dissociation,[30] Ann E. Kaplan noted that trauma is "narration without narrativity—that is without the ordered sequence leading to a determined end to which we associate narratives," replacing linearity with an increased emotional intensity beyond rational control, which foregrounds paralysis, repetition, and circularity.[31] PC's confession represents the gradual restoration of her young self's traumatic memories by moving from an infant's viewpoint (namely the mediated rendering of a child's voice through the acquired knowledge of the child-turned-adult as theorized by Sue Vice),[32] as represented by adult PC's awareness of consequences ("because me making noise would put in danger of death everybody around me"), toward a recording of a child's voice via fragmented descriptions of embodied feelings that suggest a child's incomprehensible sense of threat, fear, and helplessness that PC internalized immediately after her birth. The most important aspect of these latter feelings is her inculcated belief that covering up and keeping silent are her only viable means of survival; they worked for her in the extreme circumstances at the start of life, and she tries to use them again and again whenever she feels in a bind. She augments this when discussing her feelings about her later depression at the age of thirty: "I want to cover up and hide. I don't feel that I want to go out and fight or do something."[33] Similarly, when the family left for Israel in 1948 and the custom guards in Romania tore open her rag doll to check for contraband, the four-year-old PC said nothing, later explaining, "I think I learned at an early age not to scream."[34] She thus identifies the main Holocaust mnemonic strain that was to burden her entire future life: the absolute control over feelings, and the redundancy of screams, cries, or any displays of emotion considered as essential survival mechanisms. Permanent vigilance and early maturity thus determined PC's cognitive development.

Regarding family structure, PC's revelations about the pivotal role played by her grandmother and a mother who failed to function both during and after the Holocaust indicate a dysfunctional family that was undoubtedly a further problematic aspect of PC's intellectual formation. There is, in addition, the father who PC never met and who died in Hungary as a soldier in the Russian army when she was two years old. PC carries his photo with her and shows it to Kestenberg along with pictures of her own children, suggesting how the early lack of a father figure has marked her, especially since she explains how she identifies with her father in view of their similar physical appearance and their shared "decent" attitude.[35] Meanwhile, she notes how she has never shared with her mother and grandmother just how much affected she was by the memory of her father, "because it's just too painful."[36] The strategy of total emotional control is once again at work here.

After immigrating to Israel, her mother remarried and her mother's new husband was a further point of estrangement for PC, since he was never kind to her and called her all sorts of derogatory names, all the while physically abusing her mother. It is particularly in the second interview that PC starts to openly expose her mother's flaws. She recalls that her mother sent her to work, even suggesting that PC seduce older men to help with the family upkeep, instead of encouraging her to get an education, so that she completed only elementary school. PC condemns her mother for her low moral standards and for being "manipulative and dishonest" with her affection, unlike her grandmother who was always honest and told her exactly what she thought.[37]

PC implies that she, unlike her mother, has provided her children with a different upbringing by, for example, encouraging them to go to college. Kestenberg, however, notes another characteristic feature of those who were children during the Holocaust: "As these young victims grew up, they repeated with their children not only what their parents and siblings had done to them, but also emulated the treatment they had received at the hands of the cruel, hostile persecution whose image merged both with the punishing and the protective parent."[38] In that sense, they often reenact the victim-related moments of their life and the faulty behavior of their parents in raising them. Likewise, in PC's case, there are elements of tension in her relationship with her youngest daughter, Patty, who had just been admitted to UCLA at the time of the interview. The tension concerns Patty's lack of honesty, which is similar to PC's problem with her own mother. In this case, PC had discovered that Patty had got an abortion at seventeen without telling her, and she had also found a pregnancy test that Patty had taken at the age of fifteen. PC is aware that the issue between the two of them is what she calls "her package," her Holocaust-inspired moral view regarding the sacredness of a baby's life (given the conditions in which she was born), with the added problem of too much sexual freedom that she associates with her own mother's manipulative ways.[39] PC recognizes her permanent vigilant stance and increased self-awareness as a child survivor but also her inability to move beyond deeply entrenched frames of reference in which she sees things in binary black-and-white tones in order to make things easier. Although her psychoanalyst tries to explain that Patty was born into another context, namely America, where her actions are nothing more than the regular behavior of an American adolescent girl, PC nonetheless feels betrayed.

Kestenberg lends significant nuance to PC's views in her interventions while taking PC's testimony on two grounds. First, she underscores that the choice to have an abortion is not necessarily a criterion to measure a woman's decency: "It's not indecent to have an abortion. I know for you the death of a baby . . . your mother could have had an abortion, but she didn't so you survived because of what your mother decided but it doesn't mean that she was such a decent person because of it."[40] Second, she explains that PC's daughter was merely following the rules of American society, the culture she had grown up in, and a context as deeply engrained in her as the Holocaust memories are in PC: "It's not indecent to get an abortion in today's culture."[41] "From her point of view, she didn't do anything wrong. All her girlfriends were doing the same things. Do you realize that?"[42] In other words, the first dysfunctional family that affected PC as a child during the Holocaust later impacts on a dysfunctional family that PC herself created as a result of the different understandings and experiences of life that separate mother and daughter.

Moreover, Kestenberg sees that PC is trying to transfer to her daughter the feeling that she does not dare to share with her own mother by drawing PC's attention to the fact that she transfers what she considers to be her mother's guilt to her daughter: "It's not fair to the child to get something that belongs to the grandmother."[43] Kestenberg manages to highlight the long-lasting effects of the family structure of a young child during the Holocaust on the family this same child later creates, and the inevitable pitfalls, such as PC trying to punish her daughter for an attitude that belonged more to her own mother. However, her mother's initial sacrifice of giving birth and keeping her daughter in the camp prevents PC from directly accusing her mother. Instead, she diverts her anger to the daughter who was born after the war and who becomes an indirect victim of the initial unpleasant Holocaust memories that molded PC in the first place.

Holocaust-Induced Mnemonic Structures of Hidden Toddlers and Children Aged Three to Five: The Impact of Being Hurled between Foster and Biological Families on Somatic Memories and Emergent Cognitive Memories

The testimony of GA, born to a nonreligious, assimilated Jewish family in Warsaw in 1939 and already in the ghetto at the age of nine months, is particularly relevant due to his many memories of early episodes despite his young age. As in PC's case, all of these early memories emphasize GA's physiological impressions (the taste of food or strong emotions such as his own fear, a neighbor's rage, or his joy when the foster grandmother taught him the importance of protecting the vulnerable by asking him to take care of an injured bird) and his need to permanently move around, following his parents' strategy of survival. Importantly, this latter dimension of existence served as an embodied memory well into GA's adulthood, which is characterized by an entrenched need to always be on the move, a lack of clear belonging, and a confused identity.

Jewish family choices in Poland were not like those in Bukovina, which was part of Romania during World War II, and thus the dynamics of GA's family structure during the Holocaust were very different from PC's family. Unlike PC who spent the Holocaust within the confines of her own family, not long after their move to the Warsaw Ghetto two-and-a-half-year-old GA and his ten-year-old sister were sent by their mother to live with a non-Jewish family called the Wapinskis. The siblings were soon separated, and from the age of three to six GA lived in Nowa Wieś, about twenty miles west of Warsaw with the Wapinskis's grandmother who became a fondly remembered grandmother figure affecting much of his later life. This detail of family separation and children sent into hiding in order to survive is a highly important factor in the identity confusion suffered by young child survivors for the rest of their lives. They particularly suffered this confusion, described by Alan L. Berger as "a complex psychosocial and theological legacy,"[44] in cases where they were brought up by non-Jewish families as non-Jews, and where they were fed negative interpretations of being Jewish either by their foster families or by the larger community.

Historian Debórah Dwork has distinguished between visible and invisible hiding, with visible hiding referring to children who went to live with another family, in a convent, or other social institutions where they usually hid their Jewish identity, and invisible hiding denoting children who literally hid in cabinets, caves, attics, cellars, sewers, and so on, and who had to conceal their physical existence.[45] GA falls into the category of visible hiding, characterized by the psychoanalyst Eva Fogelman as comprising the children's need to lead "double lives" by being "constantly reminded of one's new identity" and the simultaneous necessity to bracket one's real self.[46] This was particularly true of older children who were already aware of their family's Jewishness. Fogelman noted that "unless they were infants, hidden children lost their childhoods," in the sense that they had to become responsible for themselves, for other siblings, and for their parents, all the while undergoing a strict code of self-control. Nehama Tec, another hidden child survivor from Poland, added, "Giving up on our true identity created an emotional void and made us feel anxious, worried that we would never recapture our past."[47] Meanwhile, silence became a keyword for surviving, one that "became deeply engrained in all hidden children,"[48] and that, according to Alan Berger, took on a triple meaning: "silence about their Jewish identity; silence about their very presence in a particular hiding location; and silence in the form of controlling spontaneity, which is itself the defining trait of children."[49]

Very young children like GA, however, were too young to be aware of their Jewishness before moving in with foster families. The woman who took care of GA, for example, always reminded him that he had a mother to whom he would return but never mentioned his ethnicity, so until the age of six GA was unaware that he was Jewish. The testimonies of such children therefore add new insights to the particulars of hidden children who were separated from their families at very young ages. For them, a certain sense of anti-Semitism and Christian belonging, instilled in them by their foster families, became significant obstacles in their reunion with birth families at the end of the war and made them highly ambivalent regarding their identities.

I will divide GA's earliest "fragments of memories"[50] into memories from life with his biological parents in the Warsaw Ghetto and memories from life with his foster family. In his earliest memory of life with his own family he was about two and a half years old, sitting in their Warsaw apartment when the ghetto bombing started: "I remember seeing across the streets bricks falling and my mother wanted to go downstairs to the basement and I was afraid. I said I don't want to . . . I was afraid to go down to the basement, because I was afraid of getting shot. This is a vague memory that I have."[51] At this early stage, a sense of fear is predominant in the child who, from November 1940, at the age of thirteen months, was forced to live in the ghetto. A sense of his parents' insecurity seems also to have been transmitted to the infant who could not yet understand what death meant yet clearly felt that his early life alongside his parents was dominated by fear and vulnerability.

By comparison, the memories he has from living first with the Wapinskis, and then with the Wapinskis' grandmother in the countryside, evoke positive emotions. For the short period when he was living there together with his older sister, he remembers the good, warm soup he received in his crib.[52] Similarly, when he went to live with the Wapinskis' grandmother, his first memory is of the "very good potato soup" she used to cook.[53] A sense of heightened care as opposed to the previous image of insecurity related to GA's biological family takes center stage.

Another early memory from the time GA spent in the countryside took an interesting turn. This is an unpleasant memory recalling his fear that a neighbor's drunken husband, who had screamed and banged on their door, would get inside and hurt him. "I was petrified," GA recalls, but adds how the old lady kept him "in her lap."[54] The man did not manage to get in, and the next day, when he was sober, he actually repaired the door he had broken. The dominant characteristic of his mnemonic act is once again the sense of protection by a substitute mother figure in contrast to the image of his biological mother's helplessness within the ghetto.

GA also recalls how the old woman used to warn him not to go outside, "because if you go outside, you may be attacked by Jews and they will kill you and make matzoh out of your blood."[55] While it is not clear from GA's testimony whether the grandmother was aware that he was Jewish or whether she might, in fact, have given him this warning as a protective survival strategy, her statement undoubtedly imparted an anti-Semitic tendency in GA who was at the time unaware of his ethnicity.

GA's above-delineated earliest memories during the Holocaust fall into two distinct categories: first, the negative, unpleasant memories associated with his biological parents' sense of helplessness; and second, primarily pleasant memories of success against the odds with his foster family and deep feelings of a protective, kind, successful, and trustworthy foster grandmother. These feelings contribute to GA's ambivalence toward his biological family after liberation and his continued affection for the foster grandmother who his parents initially took as a nanny for the boy before fleeing to France in 1946 and then moving to the United States in 1952. GA remembers significantly how the reunion with his birth family did not invoke the emotional attachment and recognition he had anticipated, at least not toward his mother. Instead he notes, "I remember sitting at a table and my mother and my sister both walked into the room and they told me, I'm your mother and your sister. I looked at them and I didn't recognize them."[56]

Even more problematic for GA was finding out that he was Jewish; he was upset due to the anti-Semitic stories he had been fed and felt safe only at the side of the foster grandmother. He recalls, "Another thing on the first day I remember them telling me I was Jewish and I was terrible upset. Jews are these horrible people that make matzohs out of people blood, how could I be Jewish. So I remember being upset and then I didn't want that lady to leave us because to me, she was the closest person that I've had."[57]

Initial disidentification with his real but so far unknown identity and his continued attachment to the substitute mother were the postwar building blocks of GA's self. He was dismayed to let go of the grandmother when they left Poland, but as with older hidden children, he kept silently and passively accepting whatever befell him as predicaments beyond his control.

When GA was nine his father died in a work accident, and his mother had a nervous breakdown. He thus arrived in the United States without a real mother and was cared for more by his sister. As in the case of PC, here too the dysfunction of the biological family and the separation from the protective foster grandmother led to later feelings of ambivalence in the child survivor. On talking about the Holocaust years, though, GA does not generally feel as traumatized as others, which he attributes to the foster grandmother who was so protective: "I was lucky because the lady who took care of me was so good to me."[58]

These (post-)Holocaust memories are relevant because they show how pleasant memories, even from during the Holocaust, are often predominant for some young hidden children who were well cared for by foster families and who never knew about the real hardships of others at the time. In their case, however, the real traumatization came in the aftermath of the war with the failure to reconcile with their real, biological family and the unpleasant and insecure life they then endured. GA best sums up the condition of children like himself as feeling a "lack of roots."[59] He associates himself with various different identities at once: "I feel French but I'm not really French. I'm American but I'm not really American. I'm Polish but not really Polish and I'm Jewish but I don't have much experience. So I feel like a lack of identity in terms of roots."[60]

The testimony of A, born in 1939 near Katowice, Poland, endorses GA's memories and brings up the case of young girls brought up by Catholic families. At the age of three, A was taken in by a Catholic family. Her mother died in Auschwitz and her father survived the Holocaust and came back for her in 1945. A's memories of the Holocaust years are also fragmentary, including some especially colorful and emotional responses to Catholic rituals of the church where she was regularly taken in order to be able to successfully pass as a "good Christian girl."[61] A records her first assessment of her father, who appeared when she was six years old, with some "degree of mistrust or ingrained distrust for Jews such as for what they were, who they were."[62] In particular, her memories of an identity dilemma at the age of six in comparison to her physiological memories from a younger age capture the stages of child development proposed by Valent: the passage from predominantly sensational memories to cognitive-related memories that are likely to bring about children's feelings of guilt, shame, and fear.[63]

A's memories are also significant in terms of the persistence of trauma among young child survivors in post-Holocaust times. This is particularly pertinent in her decision not to tell her own children that her father's wife was actually her stepmother, her biological mother having died in Auschwitz. She makes this decision in order to avoid upsetting her father, as well as out of her own fear that her children may no longer consider her stepmother as their real grandmother. This is undoubtedly an outcome of A's own experience of growing up with foster parents, and as such, provides a covert commentary on her own feelings about being raised by the latter during the war and by a stepmother after the end of the war. She constantly refers to her postwar stepmother as "my mother" in contrast to her more strained concept of her wartime foster Catholic parents who she identifies as "my, whatever, father,"[64] in relation to their attempt to separate her from her biological father in 1945.[65]

A's case proves Dwork's point that a main determinant for the life trajectory of children in visible or invisible hiding was represented "by the physical situation in which they lived, and by the nature and culture of the host family."[66] Moreover, the difficulty of allowing a straightforward intergenerational transmission does not merely indicate the trauma of her surviving father and the stepmother's hardship of living with a husband who was a Holocaust survivor, but also the trauma of A herself as a young child survivor who fears producing a dysfunctional family. The intergenerational impact is thereby highlighted, especially to avoid traumatizing one's own children.

A's testimony most forcefully shows how young children between the ages of three and five brought up by Catholic families had to endure ambiguous identities and ethical dilemmas, while running the gambit between embodied memories and emergent cognitive-based memories. This tension is even more dominant among the next group of children who were aged five to eight during the Holocaust.

Holocaust-Induced Mnemonic Structures of Children between Five and Eight Years Old: Between Physiological and Cognitive Grids

CG was born in Czernowitz, Romania, in 1936 and was taken at the age of five to the Moghilev Ghetto in Transnistria where he remained with his family until liberation in April 1944, when he was eight years old. After returning to Romania, his mother divorced his father and emigrated with CG to Italy, hoping to get to Israel but finally emigrating to Australia. Despite his parents' separation, CG did not live in a dysfunctional family. He recalls that his father tried to get him back to Romania but his mother would not let him, so the father returned to Romania where he died at the age of fifty-eight.[67] But CG emphasizes that his mother soon met another man who became his stepfather and raised him from the age of ten, and of whom he only has good memories: "He was very nice, a lovely man."[68] No other mention of family discontinuity is mentioned in his testimony, nor is there any sense of dysfunctionality with regard to CG's relationship with his own son.

CG demonstrates the difference between child survivors' memories and adults' narrative factual memories. He explains how the memories of child survivors are basically a blur regarding what happened in the past. CG's 1993 testimony is therefore particularly valuable for the insight it provides into children's difficulty to remember. He suggests this by distinguishing between his "vivid" and "vague" memories of (pre-)Holocaust times as well as by his need to repeat that certain recollections have been "confirmed" by his mother or other Moghilev inmates.[69]

There are, in fact, seven such instances of confirmed remembrances: five are confirmed by his mother (crossing the Dniester River on page 3, the building near where they waited to be killed after their escape from a "starvation camp" on page 4, rationed food in Moghilev on page 6, a German officer hanging a Jewish man by his feet on page 7, a pre-Holocaust memory of his mother lighting the Sabbath candles and the two rooms of their apartment on page 20); and two are confirmed by Emanuel, another child survivor deported to Moghilev who CG later met in Australia (crossing the Dniester on page 4 and the moment of liberation on page 5). This strong sense of dependency on other people's recollections, especially those of his mother, suggests the vulnerability of child survivors toward their own Holocaust memories, their awareness of the difficulty of others to trust such memories as their own, and their tendency to permanently suspect their own internalization of public images and structures of the Holocaust to which they were exposed in their later lives. CG's clear emphasis on this uncertain character of his memories places not only toddlers but also older child survivors in a position that overlaps with that of the children of survivors. This is further supported by the way in which he associates to the Holocaust and his sense of disidentification with those experiences as if they had happened to somebody else: "Looking at it now, it's like seeing someone else, a child on a video or a movie, going through what I've been through. I must have been a spectator going through a happening."[70] Marianne Hirsch noted that the postmemory generation represented by the children of survivors emanates a similarly strange sense of being belated spectators of their parents' experiences without appropriating them. Child survivors seem to have taken on a similar role of spectators rather than participants during the Holocaust. However, in their case, as opposed to the children of survivors, there is a difference: no sense of belatedness is implied, they were on-the-spot spectators whose presence at the events in question has left them with some clearly discernible and ineffaceable marks. As a consequence, even in adulthood they continue to evince a strong sense of vulnerability and dependence on the moral and truth-setting guidance of their parents or others.

The memories that CG terms "vivid" fall predominantly into the category of sensational, physiological memories. However, they can also be seen through the five-year-old child's cognitive filter, in keeping with Durst's claim that between the ages of five and eight children are characterized by the "ripening of the cognitive abilities" and a growing awareness of justice and the forces of good and bad that provide them with "psychological defenses against remembering the unbearable" including dissociation, repression, or Freud's notions of "screen memories" or "concealing memories."[71] More precisely, the experience of persecution that CG "vividly" remembers from the times of the Holocaust is that of "starvation, hunger"[72] that he not only experienced but also started to understand and consciously struggle with: "I remember finding an apple, which my mother tells me now was frozen, but that kept us eating for a while. The camp we were in was not an extermination camp, it was a work camp and my mother and father were sent out to work. They were given certain rations, but certainly not enough. It was an open city so you could barter or trade or do extra work for someone and you would get extra money or bread."[73]

Two historically different layers of cognitive approach to his Holocaust experience in the Moghilev Ghetto can be distinguished in his words. One is clearly a retrospective look of the adult CG talking with Kestenberg in 1993 that corresponds to Sue Vice's idea of the viewpoint of a child who has learned in hindsight of the specifics of various Transnistrian ghettos, some of which were more open and not surrounded by barbed wire (the case of Moghilev) and some of which were closed and clearly delimited by barbed wire (e.g., Shargorod, and others).[74] The other layer, however, reads like Vice's idea of a child's "voice": the adult's attempt to reconstruct and record a child's emergent cognitive capacity of what hunger is and what causes it, demonstrated by CG's awareness of his parents' actions and the amount of food they actually brought back home, and by CG's recollection that he had to survive by his own wits at the time, because "mom and dad were working and I was left on my own devices."[75]

CG's testimony also validates the fact that the memories of child survivors lack stepwise organization that could facilitate their grasp of early experiences. On the margin of his memories, he notes, "There is not a time sequence. I don't know whether it happened in 1942 or 1943 or 1944. Beyond being liberated in 1944, I don't remember anything that has happened in between and at what times or what years."[76] It is all "a blur" that CG wishes to overcome: "I would like to be able to put everything into . . . to develop a sequence."[77] This difficulty to remember Holocaust experiences in narrative and sequel-based forms indicates more-deeply entrenched traumatic memories in the case of young children, especially given the absence of previous pleasurable experiences.

CG emphasizes in his interview that a characteristic feature of the life of young children in ghettos or camps during the Holocaust was the absence of any grid of comparison with life frames from previous times. The life situation was experienced without any alternative, not even in the realm of imagination (an idea also expressed in the autobiographical writings of another Romanian Jewish child survivor born in 1936 and taken to Moghilev at five years old).[78] On being asked if he felt persecuted, CG explains: "No, I didn't know . . . I had no comparison. As a child, I didn't know whether . . . I thought, well this is life and this is what happening."[79] Later on, the same sense of having had no normal childhood returned when he saw his own children growing up normally: "When I saw my children having a normal life and a normal upbringing in a normal environment with unlimited toys and time to play and not worrying about sole preservation."[80] The gap between the moment of losing childhood and the point of becoming aware of this (only after the Holocaust) explains how the absence of a grid of comparison to normal childhood and life frames affects the immediate life of child survivors and characterizes their future existence and development with permanent alertness and a distrust of metanarratives. In CG's case, however, the absence of a dysfunctional family has kept depression at bay and not hindered his communication with the next generation.

Screen Memories and the Crystallization of Cognitive Grids as Defining Traits of Eight-Year-Old Children's Holocaust-Induced Mnemonic Structures

SS was born in September 1933 in Wolschkowitz, Bukovina, Romania, within a traditional Orthodox family. He was taken to Transnistria in October 1941 at the age of eight and was liberated in June 1944. His father, who had enlisted in the Russian army, was killed when his train was attacked by the Germans. In his 1991 testimony, SS identifies a pre-Holocaust image as one of his earliest memories: his first day at the *heder* (the school for young Jewish boys), aged around three, and his pleasure at getting some beans prepared by Rabbi Usher's wife.[81] His pre-Holocaust home-based childhood memories relate to an affectionate internalization of the traditional Sabbath food preparation: "And I remember very well the oven in the winter time where they used to bake the challah and especially Thursday nights before Friday and Saturday and to prepare the *chulent*."[82] These recollections likely formed a protective shield that younger children who experienced the Holocaust did not possess.

Additionally, with his personality almost completely formed by the time of his family's deportation, SS's memories of the Holocaust years are more sequential than those of the younger children discussed previously. In light of this, he is usually able to sustain critical thinking, having understood most of what was going on. For instance, he remembers going as a five-year-old, in 1937 or 1938, with his parents to a neighbor's house that had electricity to listen to the radio and hearing about Germanys' intentions: "And we realized what it means. And I remember, as a child, how I became worried and I couldn't sleep that night and I felt as a child that it was dangerous."[83] Unlike the earlier memories of younger children in which the child is a mere observer and recorder of others' deeds, here SS places himself alongside the adults as a conscious experiencer of feelings, also choosing a cognitive word like "realize" to describe his and others' sense of fear. Meanwhile, his parents' strong moral precepts managed to keep up some sense of a normal, protective childhood for him, seen particularly by his mother's permanent provision of soap and kerosene to keep the family clean, his father and uncle's incessant praying,[84] and the boy's internalized moral lesson never to steal.[85]

Like the other child survivors examined, SS clearly emphasizes in his testimony the strong effects of his Holocaust experiences on his current life. For him, these effects represent his post-Holocaust strong reliance on multidirectional memory, especially as he relates his Holocaust memories to his postwar school experiences where he found it hard to "concentrate," all readings constantly making him think back on Transnistria,[86] and later to the 1967 Six Day War, and later still to the picture of his two-year-old grandchild wearing a gas mask during the bomb alerts in Tel Aviv. He notes that it is "very painful to see that we cannot run away, that we already thought we live in a different world."[87] "You can imagine that sometimes twice or three times a night, to wake up a baby and to put on the mask. So there are two ways . . . or she doesn't understand, then it's okay, but maybe from three years old or four years old . . . they were very scared because they also listening to the radio and the radio talks all the time and tells what the situation is."[88] Here he evidently connects the situation of his grandchild with his own direct experience and his earliest memory of the radio transmission about the Germans, drawing attention to the phenomenon of young children being exposed to trauma without it being recognized by others. He thus extrapolates: "I'm always at the same time thinking about many different things and sometimes, the difference or the distant between one thing to the other, could be years, places, I don't know."[89] Moreover, when he talks of his nightmares about people in uniforms following him, he highlights the blurry lines between reality and imagination that make up his dream: "I couldn't realize if I lived the reality or I see it like in a movie."[90]

This sense of partial involvement with Holocaust realities derives from being a child for whom imagined stories are understood on a par with real events and as being equally valid. His Holocaust memories as a child therefore correspond to Freud's claim that children's earliest memories most often represent "screen memories" that appear in their dreams and are acts of repression and simultaneous substitution of "essential elements of an experience" that has had a strong emotional effect on a child with "the inessential elements of the same experience" that covertly suggest it[91] and that I will later examine more thoroughly. These forms of multidirectional and highly imagination-based memory suggest the interweaving of a lingering sense of insecurity with defense mechanisms of detachment from threatening situations that can be seen as characteristic features of child survivors who had started to cognitively process their experiences during the Holocaust but did not have a clear-cut sense of their meaning.

SS is actually the well-known Israeli painter Shlomo Schwartz who, discussing some of his paintings with Milton and Judith Kestenberg, was trying to explain his traumatic child memories via his art work. The paintings discussed with the Kestenbergs broadly use the color red, which he associates with fire, blood, and red skies,[92] and depict a number of people clustered together in some closed environment and who have only each other to resist an all-encompassing and overwhelming sense of fear.[93] He also talks about a painting of a man in a blue suit, some form of observer whom he identifies as himself, while blue is the color of "morning hours," "between hope and between reality,"[94] perhaps the closest rendering he can give of a child's view of the Holocaust, mixing imagined and real events as part of his world experience. The significance of Schwartz's art as a locus of his earliest memory is demonstrated by the artist's description of the act of painting not as a consciously and closely controlled endeavor, but rather as a spilling out of ideas beyond his control, similar to the initial physiological imprints that define a child survivor's earliest Holocaust memories. He notes, "When I begin, when I paint, I feel that my hand is controlling me or my . . . in the background, in my brain, I mean I don't want to control what I do, I let it go."[95]

Schwartz relates his paintings to his early memories of deportation to Moghilev, perhaps the best means to show a child's view of the crossroads between feeling and representation:

> On the way to Moghilev, I wouldn't say so but I saw many people dying in their beautiful best dresses in the world. Like mink coats with gold watches and very fancy shoes with white [inaudible] and all this walking into the dirt and falling like leaves from a tree because there were people from houses, from very fancy rich houses with hundreds of servants around them and suddenly they found themselves that they had to take of themselves and they never did it before. So they were actually . . . it was like in a movie from Fellini. . . . And I was a child and I was looking . . . and this inspires me all my . . . you think all the grotesque figures what you are seeing in my paintings, these belong to the sinners.[96]

Lisa Farley demonstrated how child psychoanalyst D.W. Winnicott's "squiggle game" drawings—created in the aftermath of his treatment of British children placed with foster families in anticipation of German air raids during World War II—were an instance of visual images standing in for children's characteristic sites of memory and history-construction. Similarly, Schwartz's above discussions of his own drawings as those of a sensitive but somehow detached spectator show how the visual realm remembered by child survivors posits the unconscious as a visual site of memory that can offer "powerful clues of the psychic truth of the past."[97] Such drawings that go beyond mental processing are an indication that children's memories of difficult moments, such as those experienced during the Holocaust, indicate an important capacity of children's memories, one that "could not be faithful to the past 'as it really was,' but to the fantasies it engendered."[98] In this sense, Schwartz shows how for child survivors who used drawings in order to, at least partially, access their Holocaust experiences, the visual realm was a kindred phenomenon to Freud's idea of screen memories as daily residual anxieties that bypass a person's consciousness but find a creative distorted expression of reality.[99] These screen memories became central for child survivors dealing with a difficult past by functioning as a defense mechanism against the unknown and as a platform for developing their creativity. In *Psychopathology of Everyday Life*, Freud further noted how children's earliest recollections (that vary from one individual to another from as early as six months old to eight years old) seem to preserve the unimportant and accidental over affective impressions of the period, which he explained by the concept of "concealing memories," in other words "indifferent childhood memories" that are a "substitute for really significant impressions, whose reproduction is hindered by some resistance."[100] Most importantly, Freud explained that "visual pictures" usually represent one's earliest childhood memories, even in the case of those who later lack a visual element of recollection, concluding , "The visual memory, therefore, preserves the type of infantile recollections. Only my earliest childhood memories are of visual character; they represent plastic depicted scenes, comparable only to stage settings."[101] This does indeed correspond to the way in which SS presents his memories. Farley claimed that the work performed by such image making facilitated "impressions of the past [to] find expression, before they could be known."[102] This is particularly relevant for the child survivors who were less than eight years old during World War II that I have analyzed so far, since they lived through the Holocaust prior to developing a clearcut cognitive capacity; as a result, creative expression became a significant means for them to archive and store their experiences.

Conclusion

My study has attempted to unravel the dynamics of Holocaust survivors' memories both within the category of young child survivors and across generational lines. With regards to the zero to eight age group, my analysis reveals the dynamics of their memories ranging from predominantly sensational, physiological memories (prior to five years old) to an equal foregrounding of cognitive-related memories, analytical as well as screen memories (of five to eight year olds)—all deeply entrenched with traumatic undertones. In most cases, however, the recovery of embodied memories in adult life suggests how strong the initial corporeal, somatic painful memories are for lifelong identity and development, and the strained existence they impose on individuals whose formative years were spent within a context of unpleasant memories. For child survivors of these young ages, the experience seems to be similar for both genders.

My case studies have additionally shown that the family environment of Jewish child survivors from Bukovina, Romania, was different from that of Jewish child survivors from Poland; the family environment proves to have significantly influenced their types of memories and how they relate to their identity and their future families. The Romanian Jewish children remained with at least one parent during the Holocaust, the stability or instability of their identity being determined to a high degree by whether or not they were reared in a protective biological family (CG and SS) or a dysfunctional biological family (PC). The Polish Jewish children were characterized by being separated from their biological families (A and GA), being sent to live with gentile families before they were aware of their Jewishness, and being raised as non-Jews with an inculcated sense of anti-Semitism. Thus, after the war the ambiguity of identity and the difficulty of reconciling the inheritance from their disempowered biological families, on the one hand, and the more secure but ideologically problematic Christian foster families, on the other, became primary influences on their lives, especially on their feelings of insecurity and their permanent sense of vigilance.

Author

Dana Mihăilescu is associate professor of English/American Studies at the University of Bucharest where she received her doctorate in 2010. Her main research interests include Jewish American Studies, Holocaust survivor testimonies, trauma and witnessing, ethics, and memory. She has published articles in international journals such as *American Imago, European Review of History,* and *East European Jewish Affairs*. Her most recent projects are a co-organized visual exhibition entitled *Family Line-Ups: Trans-generational Encounters in Family Photography* (http://www.familylineups.com/), a coedited volume on *Mapping Generations of Traumatic Memory in American Narratives* (Cambridge Scholars Publishing, 2014) and an authored volume on *Regimes of Vulnerability in Jewish American Media and Literature* (University of Bucharest Press, 2015).

Acknowledgments

Research for this chapter was supported by a grant of the Romanian National Authority for Scientific Research, UEFISCDI, for PN-II-RU-TE-2014-4-0051 project no. 173 / 2015, *Intergenerational Dynamics of Vulnerability in American Trauma Narratives*.

Notes

> All interviews from the Kestenberg Archive quoted in this chapter are held at the Oral History Division, Hebrew University of Jerusalem.

1. Levi, *If This Is a Man / The Truce*, 197.
2. Ibid., 198.
3. Agamben, *Remnants of Auschwitz*, 37–39.
4. See the excellent comments on specifics of child survivors' testimonies taken by historical commissions in Cohen and Horváth, "Young Witnesses in the DP Camps," arguing for the importance of the immediate context in which these testimonies were given on their structure and content by focusing on the Aschau Children's DP Camp from Germany; in Müller, "Trauma, Historiography and Polyphony," and Cohen, "Representing Children's Holocaust," considering the case of the Central Jewish Historical Commission in Poland and the Central Historical Commission in Munich, respectively; in Cohen, "Children's Voices," looking at the input of the Zionist ideology that accompanied the interviewing process in the case of children's testimonies collected in 1946 by Benjamin Tenenbaum, a Polish-born Jewish author who emigrated from Warsaw to Palestine in 1937 and was a supporter of the left Zionist movement Hashomer Hatsair.
5. For my analysis of children's traumatization, by a child survivor's trauma of the Holocaust I understand the direct experiences of a child's gradually escalating persecution during World War II, persecution that often included their ghettoization, deportation, separation, or forced decision to live in hiding or on the run, whether or not the child was conscious of these experiences at the time when they happened. These simultaneously sudden and violent suspensions of normal life frames affected both the physical and the psychological states of the affected individual, becoming an unavoidable intrusion in the victim's relationship with any prior and subsequent life experience. Hence, the physical and psychological states experienced by these children correspond to the classical manifestation of trauma in the European and Western context as the result of a singular exceptional event that shatters all one's systems of representation and the possibility to be expressed within a narrative structure. For further details, see Cathy Caruth who asserted that trauma is nonsymbolizable and cannot be worked through because of the "collapse of witnessing [and] the impossibility of knowing what first constituted it" (Caruth, *Trauma*, 11), and Dominick LaCapra's more-nuanced ideas on this margin, especially his distinction between "structural trauma and historical trauma" (LaCapra, *Writing History*, 76).
6. Hass, *In the Shadow of the Holocaust*, 29.
7. Kestenberg, "Instructions for Interviewers," 4–6.
8. See Mihăilescu, "Being without Pleasurable Memories,""Traumatic Echoes of Memories in Child Survivors' Narratives of the Holocaust," "Holocaust Child Survivors' Memoirs."
9. Benjamin, Florian, and Ciuciu, *Cum a fost posibil?*, 162.
10. Carp, *The Black Book*, 406–408.
11. Ibid., 421–23.
12. Ibid., 429–30.
13. For a thorough presentation of the most significant moments of these two invasions and their effects on Polish Jews and Polish–Jewish relations

during World War II, see Michlic and Melchior, "Memory of the Holocaust in Post-1989 Poland," 405–11.
14. Michlic, "Who Am I?," 105.
15. Durst, "Child-Survivors of the Holocaust," 506.
16. Valent, "Transmission of Transgenerational Trauma," 2.
17. Testimony of PC, (257) 15-22, 1.
18. Hirsch, *Generation of Postmemory*, 5.
19. Testimony of PC, (257) 15-22, 3.
20. Ibid.
21. Ibid.
22. Ibid.
23. Ibid., 5.
24. Ibid., 3.
25. Ibid.
26. Ibid., 4.
27. Ibid.
28. Ibid., 5.
29. Ibid., 6.
30. Caruth, *Trauma*.
31. Kaplan, *Trauma Culture*, 63.
32. Vice, "Children's Voices and Viewpoints," 11–12.
33. Testimony of PC, (257) 15-22, 9.
34. Ibid., 11.
35. Ibid., 12.
36. Ibid., 13.
37. Ibid., 42.
38. Kestenberg, "Survivor-Parents and Their Children," 83–84.
39. Testimony of PC, (257) 15-22, 72–73.
40. Ibid., 74.
41. Ibid.
42. Ibid.
43. Ibid., 78.
44. Berger, "Hidden Children," 13.
45. Dwork, *Children with a Star*, xliii, 31–32, 68, 81.
46. Fogelman, "Psychology Behind Being a Hidden Child," 294.
47. Tec, "A Historical Perspective," 287.
48. Ibid.
49. Berger, "Hidden Children," 16.
50. Testimony of GA, (257) 14-13, 1.
51. Ibid.
52. Ibid., 4.
53. Ibid., 5.
54. Ibid., 6.
55. Ibid., 8.
56. Ibid., 11.
57. Ibid.
58. Ibid., 46.

59. Ibid., 58.
60. Ibid.
61. Testimony 1 of A, (257) 14-2, 2.
62. Ibid., 3.
63. Valent, "Transmission of Transgenerational Trauma."
64. Testimony 1 of A, (257) 14-2, 2.
65. Testimony 2 of A (257) 14-2, 5.
66. Dwork, *Children with a Star*, 88.
67. Testimony of CG, (257) 24-4, 12.
68. Ibid.
69. Ibid., 2, 3, 6.
70. Ibid., 11.
71. Durst, "Child-Survivors of the Holocaust," 509.
72. Testimony of CG, (257) 24-4, 2.
73. Ibid.
74. Vice, "Children's Voices and Viewpoints," 11.
75. Testimony of CG, (257) 24-4, 24.
76. Ibid., 23.
77. Ibid.
78. Writer Norman Manea deals with this issue, especially in his story "Proust's Tea." For a detailed analysis of this literary piece, see Mihăilescu "Being without Pleasurable Memories."
79. Testimony of CG, (257) 24-4, 7.
80. Ibid., 27.
81. Testimony of SS, (257) 21-20, 2.
82. Ibid., 2.
83. Ibid., 4.
84. Ibid., 9.
85. Ibid., 10.
86. Ibid., 11.
87. Ibid., 6.
88. Ibid., 21.
89. Ibid., 11.
90. Ibid., 12.
91. Freud, "Screen Memories," 306–307.
92. Testimony of SS, (257) 21-20, 15.
93. Ibid., 15–16.
94. Ibid., 17.
95. Ibid., 27.
96. Ibid., 29.
97. Farley, "Squiggle Evidence," 32.
98. Ibid., 31.
99. Freud, "Screen Memories," 319–20.
100. Freud, *Psychopathology of Everyday Life*, 58–59.
101. Ibid., 65.
102. Farley, "Squiggle Evidence," 16.

References

Agamben, Giorgio. *Remnants of Auschwitz: The Witness and the Archive*, translated by Daniel Heller-Roazen. New York: Zone Books, 1999.
Benjamin, Lya, Alexandru Florian, and Anca Ciuciu. *Cum a fost posibil? Evreii din România în perioada Holocaustului* [*How Was It Possible? Romania's Jews during the Holocaust*]. Bucharest: Elie Wiesel National Institute for the Study of the Holocaust, 2007.
Berger, Alan. L. "Hidden Children: The Literature of Hiding." In *Jewish American and Holocaust Literature. Representation in the Postmodern World*, edited by Alan L. Berger and Gloria Cronin, 13–30. Albany, NY: State University of New York Press, 2004.
Carp, Matatias. *The Black Book* [*Cartea Neagră. 1946–1948. Le Livre noir de la destruction des Juifs de Roumanie 1940–1944*], translated by Alexandra Laignel-Lavastine. Paris: DeNoël, 2009.
Caruth, Cathy, ed. *Trauma: Explorations in Memory*. Baltimore: Johns Hopkins University Press, 1995.
Cohen, Boaz. "The Children's Voices: Postwar Collection of Testimonies from Child Survivors of the Holocaust." *Holocaust and Genocide Studies* 21, no. 1 (Spring 2007): 73–95.
———. "Representing Children's Holocaust: Children's Survivor Testimonies Published in *Fun Lezten Hurban*, Munich 1946–1949." In *We Are here: New Approaches to Jewish Displaced Persons in Postwar Germany*, edited by Avinoam J. Patt and Michael Berkowitz, 75–96. Detroit, MI: Wayne State University Press, 2010.
Cohen, Boaz and Beate Müller. "The 1945 Bytom Notebook: Searching for the Lost Voices of Child Holocaust Survivors." In *Freilegungen: Überlebende—Erinnerungen—Transformationen* [*Exposures: Survivors—Memories—Transformations*], edited by R. Boeling, S. Urban, R. Bienert, 122–137. Göttingen: Wallstein, 2013.
Cohen, Boaz, and Rita Horváth. "Young Witnesses in the DP Camps: Children's Holocaust Testimony in Context." *Journal of Modern Jewish Studies* 11, no. 1 (March 2012): 103–125.
Durst, Nathan. "Child-Survivors of the Holocaust: Age-Specific Traumatization and the Consequences for Therapy." *American Journal of Psychotherapy* 57, no. 4 (2003): 499–518.
Dwork, Debórah. *Children with a Star. Jewish Youth in Nazi Europe*. New Haven, CT: Yale University Press, 1991.
Farley, Lisa. "Squiggle Evidence. The Child, the Canvas, and the 'Negative Labor' of History." *History and Memory* 23, no. 2 (Fall/Winter 2011): 5–39.
Fogelman, Eva. "The Psychology Behind Being a Hidden Child." In *The Secret Survivors of the Holocaust: The Hidden Children*, edited by Jane Marks, 292–307. New York: Bantam Books, 1993.
Freud, Sigmund. *Psychopathology of Everyday Life*, translated by A.A. Brill in 1914. Stilwell, KS: Digireads.com Publishing, 2005.
———. "Screen Memories (1899)." In *The Standard Edition of the Complete Psychological Works of Sigmund Freud. Volume III (1893–1899)*, translated by James Strachey, 299–322. Psychoanalytic Electronic, 2012.

Hass, Aaron. *In the Shadow of the Holocaust. The Second Generation.* New York: Cornell University Press, 1990.
Hirsch, Marianne. *The Generation of Postmemory. Writing and Visual Culture after the Holocaust.* New York: Columbia University Press, 2012.
Kaplan, Ann E. *Trauma Culture. The Politics of Terror and Loss in Media and Literature.* New Brunswick: Rutgers University Press, 2005.
Kestenberg, Judith. "Instructions for Interviewers." Judith Kestenberg Child Survivor Archive, The Oral History Division, Hebrew University of Jerusalem.
———. "Survivor-Parents and Their Children." In *Generations of the Holocaust*, edited by Martin S. Bergman and Milton E. Jucovy, 83–102. New York: Basic Books, 1982.
LaCapra, Dominick. *Writing History. Writing Trauma.* Baltimore: The Johns Hopkins University Press, 2001.
Levi, Primo. *If This Is a Man / The Truce*, translated by Stuart Woolf. London: Abacus, 1987.
Manea, Norman. "Proust's Tea." In *October Eight O'Clock*, by Norman Manea, 37–44. London: Quartet Books, 1992.
Michlic, Joanna B. "Who Am I? Jewish Children's Search for Identity in Postwar Poland 1945–1949." *Polin* 20 (2007): 98–121.
Michlic, Joanna Beata, and Margorzata Melchior. "The Memory of the Holocaust in Post-1989 Poland." In *Bringing the Dark Past to Light. The Reception of the Holocaust in Postcommunist Europe*, edited by John-Paul Himka and Joanna Beata Michlic, 403–450. Lincoln: University of Nebraska Press, 2013.
Mihăilescu, Dana. "Being without Pleasurable Memories: On the Predicament of the Shoah's Child Survivors in Norman Manea's 'Proust's Tea' and Kindred Narratives." *American Imago* 70, no. 1 (Spring 2013): 107–24.
———. "Traumatic Echoes of Memories in Child Survivors' Narratives of the Holocaust: The Polish Experiences of Michał Głowiński and Henryk Grynberg." *European Review of History/Revue européenne d'histoire* 21, no. 1 (February 2014): 73–90.
———. "Holocaust Child Survivors' Memoirs as Reflected in Appelfeld's *The Story of a Life*." *CLCWeb: Comparative Literature and Culture* 17, no. 3 (2015). <http://dx.doi.org/10.7771/1481-4374.2711>.
Müller Beate. "Trauma, Historiography and Polyphony: Adult Voices in the CJHC's Early PostWar Child Holocaust Testimonies." *History and Memory* 24, no. 2 (2012): 157–195.
Tec, Nehama. "A Historical Perspective: Tracing the History of the Hidden-Child Experience." In *The Secret Survivors of the Holocaust: The Hidden Children*, edited by Jane Marks, 273–291. New York: Bantam Books, 1993.
Valent, Paul. "Transmission of Transgenerational Trauma." Paper presented at the Symposium "Intergenerational Communication—Working with Holocaust Trauma's Legacy across Three Generations," Monash University, 12 June 2006. paulvalent.com/publications/.
Vice, Sue. "Children's Voices and Viewpoints in Holocaust Literature." *Holocaust Studies. A Journal of Culture and History* 11, no. 2 (Autumn 2005): 11–24.

 7

Symbolic Revenge in Holocaust Child Survivors

Nancy Isserman

Introduction

The attitudes of Holocaust survivors toward their persecutors present an intriguing subject for exploration. One component of the attitudes expressed is revenge. The concept of revenge is pervasive throughout literature, religious and legal writings, and history. Revenge is also considered a subset of political intolerance. Research on intolerance has been linked to age, education, and religious affiliation, among other demographic factors.[1] Political intolerance is associated with low education, older age, rural residence, and fundamentalist religious affiliation.[2] My recent qualitative research found a connection between family-of-origin relationships and intolerance.[3] Survivors who evidenced positive relationships with their family-of-origin caregivers also demonstrated tolerant attitudes toward the perpetrators of the genocide; conversely, survivors who had troubled relationships with their family-of-origin caregivers expressed intolerance toward the perpetrators.[4]

The *Oxford Dictionaries* online define revenge as both concrete and symbolic. The concrete definition incorporates physical behavior: "The action of inflicting hurt or harm on someone for an injury or wrong suffered at their hands."[5] Examples of concrete revenge are found in Holocaust survivor narratives during the later years of the war and immediately afterward.

The most famous example of concrete revenge is Abba Kovner, who believed that "the Jews must seek revenge, answering a crime that could not be answered."[6] In the spring of 1945 he declared, "Yes, the War is over, but no, not for the Germans; it is time for the Germans to suffer; the Germans, who killed the Jews, must now pay with their own lives,"[7] and quoted Psalm 94 in which God is called on to take revenge on the enemies of Israel. To seek revenge on the Germans he formed a brigade called the Avengers comprising approximately fifty Jews from the Vilna

Ghetto. Not satisfied with the international trials and military tribunals, Kovner wanted the Germans killed anonymously. He and his cohorts devised two plans: Plan A involved poisoning the water supplies of major German cities; Plan B entailed killing off Schutzstaffel (Protective Squadrons) guards held in American POW camps. In Plan A, false identifications allowed the members of the Avengers to disperse throughout cities of former concentration camps, get jobs in the city waterworks, learn how to turn off the pipes, and then fill them with poison. Plan B was to poison the bread that captured Schutzstaffel officers were eating as they awaited their trials in former concentration camps. Plan A failed when Kovner was arrested by the British. Plan B, however, worked, and a few thousand National Socialists (or Nazis) were poisoned, although no one knows how many were actually killed.[8]

In addition to Kovner's group, other individuals or small clusters of Jews in Europe pursued revenge at the end of World War II. Groups of individuals calling themselves the Din Assassins hunted down and executed several hundred Nazi war criminals. The Din assassins were British Jews, volunteers from Palestine, and Holocaust survivors. The word *din* is Hebrew for judgment, and symbolized the actions and justification for the actions behind these groups. After the war and the liberation of the camps, Jews and other survivors were sometimes given the opportunity by the Allied troops to take vengeance against the guards who had tortured them. Former victims tore guards to pieces or strangled Vichy collaborators. Rosenbaum wrote that most Jews accepted the notion that sporadic, improvised acts of vengeance were just and justifiable given the behavior of the Nazis and their collaborators.[9]

The second definition of revenge in the *Oxford Dictionaries* is of a symbolic nature: "the desire to inflict retribution."[10] Symbolic revenge operates on the level of fantasy or is not expressed directly to the perpetrators. This type of revenge after the war was exemplified by individuals who pursued revenge through less violent means, such as by controlling the administration of the displaced persons (DP) camps or by participating in the black market. The economic recovery of Jews while in the DP camps in Germany was itself seen as a form of revenge, although not via specific acts of violence. When given the opportunity, the DPs hired Germans as nursemaids and housekeepers.[11] Others responded by serving as witnesses at trials of former Nazis such as Demjanjuk, a former German guard, or by pursuing Nazis, as in the case of the famed Nazi hunters Simon Wiesenthal and Serge Klarsfeld. For these individuals seeking justice was a form of revenge for the evil acts committed by the Nazis. This distinction of seeking justice is in contrast to biblical notions of revenge. Rosenbaum stated that the word "justice" in the Bible always refers to the concept of revenge, which he posits is a symbolic vindication of justice.[12] Most individuals in the twentieth and twenty-first centuries are more comfortable with the concept of meting out justice than with revenge. After the Demjanjuk verdict in 2011, in a response meant to support the concept of justice and minimize the idea of revenge, a survivor stated, "I'm satisfied. It doesn't mean I can forget; it doesn't mean I can forgive."[13]

The concept of symbolic revenge toward the perpetrators of the final solution of the Jews was found in testimonies with Holocaust child survivors taken in the 1980s and 1990s as part of the Kestenberg Archive of Testimonies of Child Holocaust Survivors.[14] This chapter focuses on how the attitudes, behaviors, and feelings of child survivors illustrate symbolic revenge.

Review of the Literature

Vengeance has been called "a pervasive and perhaps inevitable response to injustice."[15] However, Schuman and Ross argued that acts of revenge are not necessarily automatic or universal responses to injustice. Acts of revenge may be minimized when external sources, governments or other systems, work to punish the perpetrators and thus provide some solace to their victims.[16] Supporting this view, some survivors stated that they did not believe in human justice since many of the Nazis and other perpetrators went unpunished.[17] They were found to incorporate acts of symbolic revenge against the Nazis in their descriptions of building their future, expressing anger, hatred, and the need for revenge.[18]

New research has further explored the concept of revenge, focusing in more detail on the idea of symbolic revenge among Holocaust survivors. A study based on twenty-nine interviews found a wide variation in aversion toward Germans and Germany.[19] Aversion in this study seems to be another name for symbolic revenge or intolerant attitudes toward the perpetrators of the Nazi genocide. In their study, Cherfas and his colleagues found the degree of aversion ranged from concentrating solely on those closest to the Nazi perpetrators to encompassing anyone with German ancestry or any situation or product linked to contemporary Germany. The study concluded, "This wide variation of aversion following horrific experiences in not easily explained by known psychological mechanisms and has important implications for understanding and ameliorating ethnopolitical conflict."[20]

The Kestenbergs asserted that revenge that was sought before liberation was transformed into a sense of justice rather than into personal revenge. They wrote that many of the child survivors would rather turn Nazis over to the authorities than punish them by themselves.[21] In an early research project, completed around the same time as many of the Judith Kestenberg interviews, Robinson found that the survivors spoke of symbolic revenge.[22] In a follow-up study several years later, the survivors continued to speak of revenge, more specifically fantasies of committing revenge against Germans.[23] Symbolic revenge may be one facet of the concept of intolerance. In my research, intolerant survivors expressed generalized hatred toward both the perpetrators of the Holocaust and ethnic, racial, and religious groups other than Jews, but it was no more than a small subset who actually participated in violent acts of revenge.[24]

The interviews in the Kestenberg archive describe the nature of symbolic revenge and its composition. This study explores the concept of symbolic revenge illustrated in the interviews and examines the viability of the factors that influenced individuals to express symbolic revenge.

Methodology

This study is a qualitative analysis of thirty-three interviews from the Kestenberg archive. The semistructured interviews chosen for this study were conducted in English. Given the fact that revenge, whether symbolic or concrete, can be described using many words, coding was conducted through the qualitative computer-coding program NVivo 7. Any statements about revenge, boycotting, avoidance of the German language or Germany; attitudes toward national, religious, racial, or ethnic groups other than Jews; or fantasies about revenge were tracked and coded.

For this pilot project the interviews that were reviewed for expressions of revenge were chosen randomly from the four hundred interviews in English that had been transcribed at the time of the study. These interviews had online abstracts available to the researcher. Two hundred interviews were randomly selected to be reviewed. Of the two hundred, the online abstracts of thirty-three indicated that they would be appropriate for the study. These thirty-three abstracts contained key words relating to prewar family life and attitudes toward perpetrators. Of the thirty-three interviews examined, twelve described attitudes toward perpetrators that conform to the *Oxford Dictionaries'* online definition of symbolic revenge. These interviews were then coded for such factors as age at onset of the war, war experiences, family losses due to the war, religious affiliation, and gender, to try to further understand the nature of symbolic revenge. Symbolic revenge is described as the desire to repay an injury or wrong and does not include physical acts of violence. The methodology in this study relied on grounded research theory, which is small scaled and focused, emphasizing the continuous exchange between analyzing the data and continuing to gather more data until enough data has been collected and analyzed that a theory fitting the data is created.[25]

Results

Who Were the Child Survivors?

Approximately one-third of the interviews mentioned revenge. All discussions of revenge in these interviews are symbolic acts of revenge. The responses of the twelve survivors profiled in this study to questions about their attitudes toward Germans and other European groups were unequivocal and not diminished by government or institutional actions.

While the hatred of some survivors was aimed specifically at Nazi Germans, the perpetrators from the World War II era, others identified Polish, Ukrainian, and other European ethnic groups as the source of their hatred and fantasies of revenge. The twelve survivors who discussed revenge in their interviews varied in age, war experience, and losses suffered. The oldest were born in 1926, and the youngest in 1942. The majority were under ten years old when World War II started. They were born in several European countries: Germany, Poland, Hungary, Czechoslovakia, Holland, and France. Four were born in Poland, making it the country with the largest representation of child survivors in this group, not surprising given the size of Poland's prewar Jewish population. Ten of the twelve survivors were female, making the gender factor the strongest demographic characteristic in this group. In the larger sample of thirty-three interviews, seventeen were female, three were male, and the gender of four was unidentified. Thus, while the percentage of females in the English language interviews in the archives is not known, the predominance of females in the larger sample reviewed for this study suggests that the majority of English language interviews in the archive are female. Nevertheless, without comparing the small sample analyzed for this study to a larger group of

English-speaking child survivor interviews, it is inconclusive whether gender is a factor that influences men and women to think differently about symbolic revenge.

The survivors' war experiences varied. Four of them spent the war in hiding, four in ghettos and camps, two used false papers and joined the partisans, and two escaped Europe just before the war began, having already experienced Nazi persecution. None of the twelve were the sole survivors of their families. Several survived with parents and siblings, and even those who lost parents survived with other relatives such as a sibling, uncles, aunts, or cousins. Their young ages at the time the war started precluded any analysis of the nature of the family-of-origin relationships. Most did not describe prewar family relationships or dynamics. Thus, any linkage between family-of-origin relationships and intolerance or aversion could not be explored. However, the concept of symbolic revenge found in these twelve interviews supports the Kestenbergs' observation that survivors would rather not punish the Germans themselves, but would rather turn them over to government authorities.

Symbolic Acts of Revenge

The words of the survivors in these interviews clearly shed light on the definition of symbolic revenge. When speaking about their attitudes toward perpetrators, they focused on symbolic acts of revenge comprising three types of behavior: (1) small-scale and individual behaviors of revenge, (2) intense feelings of hatred toward specific European national groups who they saw as anti-Semitic, and (3) thoughts of future acts of revenge. Small-scale behaviors are included in this group of symbolic revenge because, due to their size and nature, they do not impact the perpetrators' lives. Boycotts of goods or avoidance of speaking German are individual acts that may bring satisfaction to the child survivor but are not usually known to the perpetrators.

Individual Behaviors of Symbolic Revenge

Although the child survivors in this study did not engage in acts of violence toward their perpetrators, many engaged in personal acts of symbolic revenge including such actions as avoiding living in or traveling to Germany, boycotting German products and language, and avoiding contact with Germans. The key point of these symbolic acts was that they did not impact the perpetrators and were known only to the survivors.

156 • Chapter 7

HB was born in Hamburg in 1926 to a teacher and a housewife.[26] She survived with her father and brother by escaping on a train with the help of her family's maid and ultimately left Europe, departing on a boat from Italy in 1940. At the time of the interview, on May 20, 1986, she was a psychotherapist and had never married. HB stated, "I certainly couldn't see myself living in Germany. That's about the last place and I cannot understand how German Jews or Viennese Jews . . . . They say nothing will happen in Germany or anywhere. No one can live in such a place."

LC, another German survivor, also escaped from Europe in 1940 at the age of nine with her parents and sister on a boat to America with the help of her maid.[27] Married after the war and with two sons, LC was first an artist and then the director of a nonprofit agency. LC also expressed a strong antipathy toward people connected to Germany. She reported, for example, a very negative reaction to seeing skinheads near her at a racetrack in May 1994 in Las Vegas:

> In front of me was a guy and I saw on his arm a huge swastika and he looked like a biker and . . . I said right out loud . . . "They shouldn't let this pig in here, why are they letting this idiot bet; look at that Nazi!" and the guy ignored me. . . . I went to a different window and I mentioned it to some lady and I said: "Look at that guy over there, I wonder if he is a skinhead or biker . . . ," and she said: "Well let me get security." I said: "wait, it may be my wish but it's not illegal." LC then remarked to the interviewer, "Sometimes our freedom of speech here goes too far . . . when the Nazis almost marched in Skokie . . . I was ready to start a brawl if he [the skinhead] said: "yeah, I wish all you Jews just dropped dead," I could kill him . . . I get so furious. There I was and I could have had the whole place in a riot and I wanted to but I knew enough when she said she would get security, and I said: "no don't get security; it's not illegal for him to place a bet unless he comes in here naked."

Other survivors pursued revenge by making a stand against traveling to Germany, speaking German, or buying German products. EK was born in a small town in Hungary in 1927.[28] Her parents moved to Budapest to avoid persecution but ended up in jail. She survived with her brother and sister through false papers sent to her family by an uncle in Yugoslavia and through joining the partisans. At the time of the interview, EK was married with two children and living in the United States. She told her interviewer that she refused to speak German when visiting Germany on business with her husband. Regarding her attitude toward traveling in Germany she declared,

> I never wanted to and said, "Why should I give them my money? I can't stand them." He [her husband] said, "Look, I don't like them either, but it's business, so you can come along." So one day, I gave in and went to

Germany... I just refused to speak German. I kept walking up to people and saying, "Do you speak English?" if I wanted directions. And most of the people didn't, at the time. Finally, [one person] started speaking to me in German, giving me directions and I was listening and then he said something and I said [she spoke to him in German, the exact words not written into the transcript]. And he looked at me and said, "You speak German?" I... ran out of the store... such a feeling came over me that I just saw the SS [Schutzstaffel] marching and I saw... Hitler's picture hanging on the walls... in my imagination. And I said, "My God, what am I doing here?"... here I'm standing and nobody's telling me, "Dirty Jew,"... I could never forgive them for what they did.

PK was born during the war in 1942 in Slovakia.[29] He and his grandmother received false papers, while his parents joined the partisans. He ended up in Bergen-Belsen. After the war, his parents found him and they returned to Slovakia, eventually moving to Prague. PK married a non-Jew in Czechoslovakia and had one daughter with her. After living eight years in Israel and divorcing his first wife, PK moved to the United States with his second wife, an American he met in Israel. PK spoke of boycotting German products: "I still don't buy German products. You can't give me a Mercedes. I won't take it. And if I am in a department store and I... see something nice... first, I see if it's made in Germany. If it's made in Germany, I go to the bathroom and wash my hands... And unfortunately... when they opened the Berlin Wall... when I saw the happiness of the people, I wanted to throw up."

Another survivor, E, was born in Holland in 1939.[30] In 1943 she, her parents, and her two sisters went into hiding, each in several different places to avoid discovery. After the war E moved to Israel for six years and worked in a medical laboratory where she met her husband, an American citizen. E and their child returned with her husband to the United States where she gave birth to another daughter. E also avoided traveling to Germany: "I have never spent any vacation, although I have been in the airport in Germany. I have never deliberately made a trip to Germany; definitely not... I always have a hard time with Germans... First of all it depends on their age, if they are older, where were you? If they are younger, who are your parents? I always want to know... I certainly wouldn't go out of my way to choose a German for a friend."

LS, born in Poland in 1938, also hid with non-Jewish families in Poland during the war.[31] She survived with only her uncle, her mother's brother; they immigrated to the United States together when she was nine. As an adult she lived in New York City with her husband. LS noted that she was so young when the war started that her only memories of her family come from her uncle. She too stated that she avoided listening to or speaking German and hated traveling to Germany with her husband on business:

> I couldn't tolerate listening to the [German] language. When we came to the United States, my aunt used to listen to the radio . . . to opera. And there was a Jewish opera star who was from Germany, very famous, Schmidt . . . and . . . they used to play it on the radio. I either had to walk out of the room or shut the radio off . . . Years later, I married a German Jew. I was surrounded by German. But still, when my husband would refer to certain things and use the German for them, I would say: "Don't say that word! Use the English word for it!" . . . Of course, he travels to Germany quite a lot on business, and I've never wanted to go. I absolutely never wanted to go back. Until this past summer . . . I finally said . . . I better confront my fears . . . And I was angry because it was so beautiful . . . I was angry that the other countries didn't have as beautiful a countryside as Germany . . . I wanted to hate it and I didn't. I wanted to hate the people, and I didn't. Whoever I came in contact with . . . young people, I didn't hate them. I found them intelligent, I found them caring . . . , I found them concerned about what happened during the Second World War. However, anybody that I passed that was old enough to have done damage, the question went through my mind, where were you? And what did you do?

When asked by the interviewer, "Suppose you had a chance to kill, what would you do?," LS answered,[32] "You know something . . . I think I'm a very moral person [crying] but I'd kill any son of a bitch that did any harm to the Jews. I'd kill them all. Paying reparations in money is not paying for all the lives that were lost . . . I keep wondering whether I'm crying because being a moral person I would commit this sin and it would make me ashamed to do this but I sure as hell would. [crying begins to stop] Yes, I could kill. Thinking it out very cold bloodedly, not in passion, like somebody who gets angry and kills, and then realizes he has made a mistake, no. I could."

Some survivors revealed conflicting thoughts about revenge. FS, one of the older child survivors born in 1931 in Czechoslovakia, told the interviewer in vivid detail about the prewar anti-Semitic attacks she observed or that her family members underwent.[33] She survived in hiding thanks to the foresight of her father who prepared hiding places for his children. After the war FS moved to Australia with her family. In Australia she worked as a translator for medical school researchers, married an Australian, and had five children. FS told the following story: "They [the Allied troops] lined up the Germans and told the inmates they could do what they like with them. I remember there was a huge mountain of snow and the Germans had to stand on top and the Russians said: "Do what you like." They weren't touched, nobody touched them. I'm still not sure whether it was fear, whether we're not killers, or whether it was weakness. Whether we are not killers, this is what I would like to believe because nobody touched them . . . I wouldn't kill them." Yet she declared, "I feel very, very strongly that Nazis wherever they are that it's a horrible thing that they not be punished." The interviews did not disclose why FS did not want to be viewed as a killer, while other survivors expressed no difficulty with this concept.

The survivors who described the acts of revenge they committed against European groups, especially the Germans and Ukrainians, were born in different European countries. Their war experiences varied from escaping Europe, to hiding, and to living through the ghettos and camps. Their interviews did not reveal why they engaged in symbolic individual acts of revenge as opposed to the survivors who spoke of their hatred without participating in boycotts around travel, goods, or language.

In earlier research on revenge, four factors were found to influence the acts of revenge: (1) the persistence of anger, (2) the perceptions of the cost of revenge, (3) cultural and religious values regarding revenge, and (4) the presence of external systems that provided justice for the victims. It was concluded that there was a connection between victims who found religious support for revenge and their subsequent acts of revenge.[34] However, in the child interviews in this pilot study on revenge, no connection between religion and symbolic revenge was identified. Of the twelve interviewees only two identified themselves as religious Jews. The majority labeled themselves nonreligious or secular Jews. In addition, the relationship between the factors of anger, perceived costs of revenge, and values to symbolic revenge could not be discerned in the interviews because questions about these factors had not been asked in the original interviews. It is unknown if other considerations—such as moral values, worldview, or Western culture—influenced ideas of revenge because the original interviews did not solicit information about these factors either.

Targeting Hatred toward Specific European Ethnic Groups

Some survivors expressed strong feelings of hatred toward Germans, Poles, Ukrainians, and other European ethnic groups who persecuted the Jews during the war. TG, born in Lodz, Poland, in 1927 exemplifies the survivors who talked about revenge through labeling.[35] After living in the Lodz Ghetto from 1942 to 1944, she and her family were deported to Auschwitz where her parents and siblings were murdered. Her only surviving family member was an uncle. She immigrated to the United States with her German Jewish boyfriend who later became her husband. He worked as a tailor while she raised their three sons. TG expressed strong feelings of hatred toward the Polish people—not only those who lived during the war but also those she knew at the time she was interviewed. She stated, "I have a Polish girl working for me . . . I hate them. Even though she washes my floors and she's born after the war . . . I just hate them . . . I would never talk to her about it because I would talk of hatred, because they were the ones, really, to start all this . . . when they started among Polish Jews. Every Polish Jew will tell you it didn't start with Germany. It started with Poles, their hatred of the Jew, because the Jew could help themselves a little better than they could and that's how I feel. I always felt that way."

SI, a Polish survivor, also expressed hatred toward Polish people.[36] He saw his entire family, parents and sisters, shot in front of his eyes. He was in ghettos and camps, escaped into the woods from trains that were attacked, was captured by Germans and then rescued by Americans, one of whom was Jewish. SI moved to the United States and was single at the time of the interview. He remarked, "It's an old adage; the Pole doesn't like anybody, not even himself. He doesn't like the German, he doesn't like the Russian, he certainly doesn't like the Jew, and he fights with his children and beats his wife up anyway."

Other survivors vacillated between feelings of anger and hatred, on the one hand, and attempts to view Germans in a more positive light, on the other. SG, born in France in 1933 into an assimilated, financially comfortable Jewish family, remembered and described events she saw when the Germans invaded Paris.[37] She first hid in Limoges with her parents and then on her own in several farms and a convent. She was reunited with her parents and sister in the latter years of the war. After the war, she and her family returned to Paris. With her employer's help, SG immigrated to the United States, where she met her husband. At the time of the interview she had three children and worked as a teacher. She stated, "I hate Germany with a passion. [voice cracking] When the wall came down, I was . . . everybody, even Jews, were telling me: 'Oh, Germany is finally [...] democracy again,' and I was angry, I was angry. I hate Germany but then when I meet a German, I kind of deny my own feelings and I have to decide if that German is worthwhile befriending." She qualified her hatred further: "I've met Germans, non-Jew Germans and some of them are young . . . or they are my age and I have to tell myself that they were not responsible for what their parents did. So if their personalities [are] approachable, they are humans and we are compatible, then I will try to push aside you know the country that they came from. And I will try to judge them for themselves."

EK expressed similarly conflicting viewpoints.[38] When she was in Israel she saw many young Germans working on kibbutzim, and she saw that "they . . . were searching. They were trying to find . . . excuses for their parents' actions . . . There were a few good Germans . . . some that tried to help, but not enough and unfortunately, most of them, when you scratched them; it came out, the anti-Semitism. Very few really went out of their way to help, never mind risk their life."

PK expressed a far more positive opinion of the different European groups than of Germans during the war:[39] "I always admired the Danish, what they did . . . for the Jews, taking them to Sweden. I always admire . . . the Dutch that they are so ashamed. They did a lot for Jews . . . and they are ashamed they didn't do enough. . . . The French [are a] joke. They are [were] so eager to help. Even the Hungarians, they are anti-Semites, but more religious anti-Semitism. And really, until 1944, no Hungarian Jew was deported. The same with Italians. And look at the fascist Franco. He protected all the Jews."

Similarly, LS expressed both positive and negative attitudes.[40] LS's experiences differed from PK, and her positive attitude was related to her war experiences: "A lot of people have very ugly feelings for the Polish and cursed them and . . . the Russians . . . I only have good feelings. They saved my life. The Russians came in and saved my life. They wiped out the Germans. I mean, they may have done horrendous things in their own right, but . . . where I'm concerned, they saved my life. 1 don't have these negative feelings about the Polish people, or about the Russians." And she elaborated further: "Everybody hated the Ukrainians . . . Because they were the worst as far as Jew baiters, and Jew haters, and turning people in and even after the war, when the war ended."

Not everyone hated the Germans or was conflicted about how they viewed the European perpetrators. One survivor even expressed more positive feelings. NK was born to a Bundist father and traditional mother in 1929 in Lodz, Poland.[41] She survived a ghetto and work camp but lost her father, mother, and brother during the war. She immigrated to the United States where she married and raised a family. When asked by the interviewer if she hated the Germans, NK responded, "No." She went on to state, "I don't think I'm capable of hate. I don't hate anybody." She admitted that she had been afraid of the Polish police and that she had been aware that there was anti-Semitism in Poland and that Jews were not liked. It is not clear what factors influenced NK's more-positive attitude from her interview.

Imagining Future Acts of Revenge

There were survivors who imagined how they might engage in future acts of revenge. HB explained, "I would want to do everything I could to expose them and bring them to trial. I feel very, very strongly that Nazis wherever they are that it's a horrible thing that they not be punished."[42]

Another survivor discussed how the Germans should be punished. CK, born in 1926 in Czechoslovakia, was in a children's block in an unnamed death camp until 1944.[43] She also worked in a factory, was beaten, and survived bombings. After the war CK was reunited with her sister. She reported that post-liberation she was sick with tuberculosis for three years. CK married her husband, himself a survivor of camps, in Czechoslovakia before immigrating to the United States. CK expressed, "I would like to see every one of them [Germans] killed but not by me. I would like to see them punished because they don't deserve to live. But it's usually the ones who committed the worst atrocities that are free. They have power and money that people accept them . . . I would definitely have them arrested . . . In fact, I think I would even be able to shoot him. But I would want him to die a slow death not a fast one. But I, myself, can't do it." LC also fantasized about revenge:[44] "As a child, I was thinking, I want to find an SS [Schutzstaffel] man and I want to kill him . . . little by little. I want to pull out a fingernail and I was thinking these hateful thoughts and . . . if it's a bad person, I want to kill . . . the skinheads . . . I get so angry that if someone would say, if I give you a machine gun, do you want to infiltrate this group and help kill them, I would say yes I would."

PK expressed similar thoughts regarding punishment:

> They [the Germans] would destroy other lives . . . They really should be punished . . . Those are my feelings. . . . . You can live with it, even though you are missing a tooth and . . . you learn to live if you are one hand short . . . I learned to live with it also, but it is my private madness. I am . . . against Nazi hunting. No more. You don't punish the same person. You punish, actually, innocent people. The families, the children, they don't even know who the father was. And you catch the son-of-a-bitch, and you destroy the children's lives or grandchildren's, today. It is not right. But I am against camaraderie, also. Not to be friends with the Germans.

The nature of their war experience was not found to be relevant in influencing which child survivors discussed revenge. The twelve interviews spanned a variety of war experiences and yet no discernable pattern relating to the severity of war experiences arose in conjunction with the three particular facets of symbolic revenge identified in this study: targeting hatred, individual actions, or fantasizing about revenge.

Discussion

This study on revenge is a pilot project based on a small sample of semi-structured interviews in which the Holocaust child survivors discussed the concept of symbolic revenge in three different ways: boycotting of countries, language, or goods; expressing strong feelings of hatred toward certain European ethnic or national groups who had persecuted the Jews in World War II; and fantasizing about future acts of revenge. The analysis of the factors influencing the survivors to engage in one of these three types of symbolic revenge supports previous research findings for a few key factors while confirming that the other factors do not impact revenge in this study. The literature on intolerance and prejudice suggested that certain factors may play a role in the adoption of ideas of revenge by survivors of genocide. Conservative or liberal religious beliefs, pessimism versus optimism,[45] a view of the world as a threatening or benign place,[46] particularistic or universalistic political beliefs, altruism[47] or self-oriented behavior, and negative or positive family-of-origin relationships[48] have been identified as key influences on attitudes, behaviors, or thoughts of revenge. Due to the focus of the questions asked in the original Kestenberg study, information on several of these factors was not available. The one factor that is present in all the interviews is a description of the religious beliefs of the survivors. Beatty and Oliver postulated that religious theology, intolerant leadership cues, and a history of persecution for religious beliefs may interact to create distinctive denominational patterns of tolerance.[49] In some research, however, it has been found that high levels of religiosity are linked to greater levels of aversion.[50] Yet other studies do not find a connection between levels of religiosity and aversion or intolerance.[51] This study supports previous research that fundamentalist religious beliefs and attitudes, behaviors or thoughts of revenge are not linked.

Demographic factors vary in their level of influence on Holocaust child survivors. Because their war experiences varied, the severity of their persecution is not indicative of which survivors would be more likely to engage in symbolic revenge. This finding is confirmed by previous research.[52] The majority of the child survivors in this study were women. One reason for this finding may be that women, especially women who came of age in the middle of the twentieth century, would be more inclined to express thoughts of revenge rather than to participate in acts of physical revenge. The prevailing culture of that era did not encourage women to engage in physical acts of revenge, suggesting that they would be less successful than men in this arena.

The most salient finding of this study is that all the child survivors who spoke of symbolic revenge survived with at least one family member. This is a new finding not revealed in previous studies on revenge. Further research is needed to understand the connection between surviving with a family member and revenge.

Conclusion

This study looked at the concept of revenge in twelve child survivor interviews of the Kestenberg archive. All twelve interviews discussed notions of revenge toward Germans and others. The revenge expressed was symbolic in nature and could be classified into three types of behavior: (1) conducting small-scale and individual behaviors of revenge with no discernable impact on the targets, (2) intense feelings of hatred toward specific European national groups who they saw as anti-Semitic, and (3) thoughts of future acts of revenge. The survivors' words clearly illustrate each of the facets of symbolic revenge. However, the small number of interviews that discussed revenge in conjunction with the focus of the original study and the questions it asked did not allow for in-depth analysis of the underlying factors of symbolic revenge. The questions asked in these interviews did not lead to a disclosure of factors that may have influenced survivors to choose one form of symbolic revenge over another. Applying the ideas expressed about the nature of symbolic revenge to current survivors of genocide and probing for information about the influences on them could build on the material in the Kestenberg archive and give us a better understanding of symbolic revenge. This research is a pilot study about the nature of symbolic revenge and can be applied only to current child survivors of genocide. Oral and psychosocial life histories of child survivors of genocide need to include questions about revenge thus giving survivors the opportunity to both confront and express strong emotions about the perpetrators of the genocides. Validating survivors' statements about physical and symbolic descriptions of revenge is part of the healing process after persecution. In order to understand more about the underlying factors influencing who engages in physical acts of revenge as opposed to symbolic acts of revenge or no revenge, it is critical to ask survivors about key elements identified in the literature as possible influences on revenge. Some of these factors, such as the nature of the war experiences, family losses due to the war, religious affiliation, and gender, were tracked in this study. Future studies would also benefit from asking survivors who discuss revenge about their political beliefs and behaviors, levels of optimism, worldview, and family relationships and dynamics in their families of origin. The survivors' answers on these issues have the potential to give researchers a more in-depth understanding of who engages in symbolic revenge and why they do so.

Author

Nancy Isserman is Director of Operation Home and Healing: Services for Veterans and Their Families at the Council for Relationships in Philadelphia. Since 1993 she has been the co-director of the Transcending Trauma Project. She is the coauthor of *Transcending Trauma: Survival, Resilience, and Clinical Implications* and has coedited and authored articles, book reviews, and books on topics relating to trauma and Holocaust survivors, tolerance in survivors, marriage and family relationship education, and the contemporary Jewish experience. She received her doctorate from the Graduate Center of the City University of New York and was awarded the 2004–2005 Braham Dissertation Award for her doctoral thesis, "I Harbor No Hate: Tolerance and Intolerance in Holocaust Survivors."

Notes

1. Wilcox and Jelen, "Evangelicals and Political Tolerance," 42; Maykovich, "Correlates of Racial Prejudice," 1019; Alozie, "Political Tolerance Hypotheses," 1; Bobo and Licari, "Education and Political Tolerance," 303; Stouffer, *Communism, Conformity, and Civil Liberties*, 105; Karpov, "Political Tolerance in Poland and the United States," 1525.
2. Wilcox and Jelen, "Evangelicals and Political Tolerance," 42; Maykovich, "Correlates of Racial Prejudice," 1019; Alozie, "Political Tolerance Hypotheses," 1; Ellison and Musick, "Southern Intolerance," 393; Tuch, "Urbanism, Region and Tolerance Revisited," 509.
3. The research examined eighteen semistructured interviews of the Transcending Trauma Project (TTP), Council for Relationships that discussed tolerance or intolerance toward the perpetrators of the genocide against the Jews. The eighteen interviews were divided into three groups: tolerant, limited-intolerant, and intolerant individuals. Demographic findings revealed that no discernable pattern was found regarding education,

religion, country of origin, and socioeconomic status. The only demographic characteristic that differed in the three groups was gender, with males representing five out of six intolerant survivors and no tolerant survivors. In addition, the research explored the ways in which the quality of family relationships was found to be influential in creating tolerance in survivors toward both perpetrators and other groups in society through the TTP's Quality of Family Dynamics Paradigm, a five-factor continuum of behavior between the caregivers and the child that described the nature of the caregiver–child relationship. The five factors are closeness–distance, empathy–self-centeredness, validation–criticalness, expressive of positive emotion–expressive of negative emotion, and open communication–closed communication.

4. Isserman, "'If Someone Throws a Rock on You,'" 112.
5. http://www.oxforddictionaries.com/us/definition/american_english/revenge
6. Cohen, *The Avengers*, 136.
7. Cohen, "A Final Mission."
8. Ibid., 189; Greenberg, "The Avengers."
9. Rosenbaum, 17.
10. http://www.oxforddictionaries.com/us/definition/american_english/revenge
11. Grossman, *Jews, Germans, and Allies*, 109.
12. Rosenbaum, *Payback*, 24.
13. Ibid., 53.
14. All interviews quoted in this chapter were held at the Oral History Division, Hebrew University of Jerusalem.
15. Schumann and Ross, "The Benefits, Costs, and Paradox of Revenge," 1193.
16. Ibid., 1200.
17. Schumann and Ross, "The Benefits, Costs, and Paradox of Revenge," 1193; Greenberg, "The Avengers."
18. Mazor, Gampel, Enright, and Orenstein, "Holocaust Survivors."
19. Cherfas, Rozin, Cohen, Davidson, and McCauley," The Framing of Atrocities," 65.
20. Ibid.
21. Kestenberg and Kestenberg, "Organized Persecution of Children."
22. Robinson, Rapaport-Bar Server, and Metzer, *Echoes of the Holocaust*, 19.
23. Robinson and Metzer, "What Do Holocaust Survivors Feel Today?," 3.
24. Isserman, "Political Tolerance and Intolerance," 36.
25. Strauss and Corbin, *Basics of Qualitative Research*.
26. Testimony of HB-MK,(257) 10-4, 53.
27. Testimony of LC, (257) 15-20, 27.
28. Testimony of EK,(257) 18-31, 40–41.
29. Testimony of PK, (257)18-32, 21.
30. Testimony of E, (257) 18-34, 49.
31. Testimony of LS, (257) 21-26, 10–11.
32. This question is poorly worded and may have influenced the nature of the answer. Interview standards have changed since this original research

was conducted in the 1980s. Thus, there is not much discussion in the literature on qualitative research on questions like this one that appear to lead the interviewee to give responses that follow a specific direction. This is because currently research protocols are examined by Institutional Review Boards that eliminate questions like these. It is understood that values, beliefs, and life experiences influence the construction of research questions, data collection, and interpretation of findings (Hewitt, "Ethical Components," 1149) and need to be considered when constructing interview protocols.

33. Testimony of FS (257) 24-15:40)
34. Schumann and Ross, "The Benefits, Costs, and Paradox of Revenge," 1200.
35. Testimony of TG, (257) 16-33c, 74.
36. Testimony of SI, (257) 18-2, 14.
37. Testimony of SG, (257)10-38, 47.
38. Testimony of EK, (257)18-31, 42.
39. Testimony of PK, (257)18-32, 37.
40. Testimony of LS, (257) 21-26, 10.
41. Testimony of NK, (257) 18-35, 82.
42. Testimony of HB, (257)10-4, 62.
43. Testimony of CK, (257) 18-30, 7.
44. Testimony of LC, (257)15-20, 18.
45. Carmil and Breznitz, "Personal Trauma and World View," 403.
46. Beit-Hallahmi and Argyle, *Psychology of Religious Behaviour*, 220; Gibson, "Alternative Measures of Political Tolerance," 570; Gibson, "A Sober Second Thought," 833; Gibson, "Do Strong Group Identities Fuel Intolerance?," 27; Chanley, "Commitment to Political Tolerance," 344.
47. Sigal and Weinfeld, *Trauma and Rebirth* , 137; Monroe, *Heart of Altruism*, 200.
48. Isserman, "'If Someone Throws a Rock on You,'" 112.
49. Beatty and Walter, "Religious Preference and Practice," 327.
50. Cherfas et al., "Framing of Atrocities," 76; Corbett and Corbett, *Politics and Religion*, 290; McFarland, "Religious Orientations," 333; Moore, "Intolerance of 'Others,'" 304.
51. Grandin and Brinkerhoff, "Does Religiosity Encourage," 32; Kunovich and Hodson, "Conflict, Religious Identity," 643.
52. Isserman, "Political Tolerance and Intolerance," 42.

References

Alozie, Nicholas O. "Political Tolerance Hypotheses and White Opposition to a Martin Luther King Holiday in Arizona." *The Social Science Journal* 32, no. 1. (1995): 1–16.
Beatty, Kathleen Murphy, and Oliver Walter. "Religious Preference and Practice: Reevaluating Their Impact on Political Tolerance." *Political Opinion Quarterly* 48, no. 1 (Spring, 1984): 318–329.
Beit-Hallahmi, Benjamin, and Michael Argyle. *The Psychology of Religious Behaviour, Belief, and Experience*. London: Routledge, 1997.

Bobo, Lawrence, and Frederick C. Licari. "Education and Political Tolerance: Testing the Effects of Cognitive Sophistication and Target Group Effect." *Public Opinion Quarterly* 53, no. 3 (Autumn, 1989): 285–308.

Carmil, Devora, and Shlomo Breznitz. "Personal Trauma and World View—Are Extremely Stressful Experiences Related to Political Attitudes, Religious Beliefs, and Future Orientation?" *Journal of Traumatic Stress* 4, no. 3 (1991): 393–405.

Chanley, Virginia. "Commitment to Political Tolerance: Situational and Activity-Based Differences." *Political Behavior* 16, no. 3 (September, 1994): 343–363.

Cherfas, Lina, Rozin, Paul, Cohen, Adam B., Davidson, Amelie, and Clark McCauley. "The Framing of Atrocities: Documenting and Exploring Wide Variation in Aversion to Germans and German-related Activities among Holocaust Survivors", *Peace and Conflict: Journal of Peace Psychology* 12, no. 1 (2006): 65–80.

Cohen, Rich. *The Avengers: A Jewish War Story*. New York: Alfred A. Knopf, 2000.

Cohen, Rich (2000-09-11). "A Final Mission". *Newsweek*.

Corbett, Michael, and Julia Mitchell Corbett. *Politics and Religion in the United States*. New York: Garland, 1999.

Ellison, Christopher G., and Marc A. Musick. "Southern Intolerance: A Fundamentalist Effect?" *Social Forces* 72, no. 2 (December, 1993): 379–398.

Gibson, James L. "Alternative Measures of Political Tolerance: Must Tolerance Be 'Least-Liked'?" *American Journal of Political Science* 36 (May 1992): 560–577.

———. "Do Strong Group Identities Fuel Intolerance? Evidence from the South African Case." Unpublished paper (December 2004).

———. *Overcoming Apartheid: Can Truth Reconcile a Divided Nation?* Cape Town. Russell Sage Foundation. Institute for Justice and Reconciliation. 2004.

———. "The Political Consequences of Intolerance: Cultural Conformity and Political Freedom." *The American Political Science Review* 86 (June, 1992): 338–356.

———. "A Sober Second Thought: An Experiment in Persuading Russians to Tolerate." *American Journal of Political Science* 42, no. 3 (July, 1998): 819–850.

Grandin, Elaine, and Merlin B. Brinkerhoff. "Does Religiosity Encourage Racial and Ethnic Intolerance." *Canadian Ethnic Studies* 23, no. 3 (1991): 32–48.

Greenberg, David. "The Avengers: Is It Ever OK to Kill Serbs? Nazis?" *Slate*, August 4, 1999. http://www.slate.com/articles/news_and_politics/history_lesson/1999/08/the_avengers.single.html

Grossman, A. *Jews, Germans, and Allies: Close Encounters in Occupied Germany*. Princeton: Princeton University Press, 2007.

Hewitt, Jeanette. "Ethical Components of Researcher–Researched Relationships in Qualitative Interviewing." *Qualitative Health Research*. 17 (2007): 1149).

Isserman, Nancy. "'If Somebody Throws a Rock on You, You Throw Back Bread: The Impact of Family Dynamics on Tolerance and Intolerance in Survivors of Genocide." In *Transcending Trauma: Survival, Resilience, and Clinical Implications in Survivor Families*, by Bea Hollander-Goldfein, Nancy Isserman, and Jennifer Goldenberg (111–131). New York: Routledge, 2012.

———. "*I Harbor No Hate*": *The Study of Political Tolerance and Intolerance*. Unpublished doctoral dissertation, City University of New York, 2005.

———. "Political Tolerance and Intolerance: Using Qualitative Interviews to Understand the Attitudes of Holocaust Survivors," *Contemporary Jewry*, 29 (2009): 21–47.

Karpov, Vyacheslav. "Political Tolerance in Poland and the United States," *Social Forces* 77, no. 4 (June 1999): 1525.

———. "Religiosity and Political Tolerance in Poland." *Sociology of Religion* 60, no. 4 (Winter, 1999): 387–402.

Kestenberg, Judith and Milton Kestenberg. Organized Persecution of Children by Nazis, Summary of the Study's Results: Preliminary Findings. Paper presentation at the National Child Survivor Meeting in California at University of California, Los Angeles, 1987.

Kunovich, Robert M., and Randy Hodson. "Conflict, Religious Identity, and Ethnic Intolerance in Croatia." *Social Forces* 78, no. 2 (December, 1999): 643–668.

Lang, Berel. "Holocaust Memory and Revenge: The Presence of the Past." *Jewish Social Studies, New Series* 2, no. 2 (1996): 1–20.

McFarland, Sam G. "Religious Orientations and the Targets of Discrimination." *Journal for the Scientific Study of Religion* 28, no. 3 (1989): 324–336.

Mazor, A., Y. Gampel, R.D. Enright, and R. Orenstein. "Holocaust Survivors: Coping with Post-traumatic Memories in Childhood and 40 Years Later." *Journal of Traumatic Stress*, 3, no. 1 (1990): 1–14.

Maykovich, Minako K. "Correlates of Racial Prejudice." *Journal of Personality and Social Psychology* 32, no. 6 (1975): 1014–1020.

Monroe, Kristen. *The Heart of Altruism*. Princeton: Princeton University Press, 1996.

Moore, Dahlia. "Intolerance of 'Others' Among Palestinian and Jewish Students in Israel." *Sociological Inquiry* 70, no. 3 (Summer, 2000): 280–312.

Robinson, Shalom, Michal Rapaport-Bar Server, and Sara Metzer. "The Feelings of Holocaust Survivors Towards Their Persecutors." *Echoes of the Holocaust*, no. 3 (1994): 9–20.

Robinson, Shalom and Sara Metzer. "What Do Holocaust Survivors Feel Today Toward Their Perpetrators?" *Echoes of the Holocaust*, no. 6 (2000): 1–3.

Rosenbaum, Thane. *Payback: The Case for Revenge*. Chicago: University of Chicago Press, 2013.

Schumann, Karina and Michael Ross. "The Benefits, Costs, and Paradox of Revenge", *Social and Personality Psychology Compass*, 4, no. 12 (2010): 1193–1205.

Sigal, J.J., and Morton Weinfeld. *Trauma and Rebirth*. New York: Praeger. 1989.

Stouffer, Samuel A. *Communism, Conformity, and Civil Liberties*. Science ed. New York: John Wiley & Sons, 1967.

Strauss, A., and J. Corbin. *Basics of Qualitative Research*. Thousand Oaks, CA: Sage, 1998.

Tuch, Steven A. "Urbanism, Region, and Tolerance Revisited: The Case of Racial Prejudice." *American Sociological Review* 52 (August, 1987): 504–510.

Wilcox, Claude, and Ted Jelen. "Evangelicals and Political Tolerance." *American Politics Quarterly* 18, no. 1 (January, 1990): 25–46.

 8

Resilience in Child Survivors
History and Application of Coding of the International Study of Organized Persecution of Children

Helene Bass-Wichelhaus

I have been fortunate to be part of an ongoing research project, the International Study of Organized Persecution of Children (ISOPC), a division of Child Development Research begun in 1982 by the late Judith Kestenberg and her husband, Milton Kestenberg. Judith Kestenberg was a psychoanalyst who had a number of child survivors in her practice; Milton Kestenberg was an attorney involved in helping survivors apply for and receive Holocaust reparations from Germany. The Kestenbergs realized that the psychological impact of the Holocaust on children who had survived the persecution was different from the impact on adult survivors and thus required a different and broadened psychological understanding. They therefore founded the International Study of Organized Persecution of Children (ISOPC).

The project engaged mental health professionals from all over the world who began interviewing child survivors.[1] I was one of the early interviewers. As a child psychoanalyst, I was particularly interested in child development and the psychodynamics of trauma. From early on in the project, the resilience of child survivors in coping with extreme situations emerged as a major dynamic. Before her death, Judith Kestenberg requested that I continue the project, along with Eva Fogelman, a pioneer in studying and working with Holocaust survivors, child survivors, and the second generation.

On looking at the narratives of child survivors—as Eva Fogelman and I have been doing for many years—it is important to determine what factors entered into their resilience or what led to their lack of uniformity. What contributed to the resilience of the child who did well? What contributed to the lack of resilience and poor adjustment of the child who did not? Our study attempts to understand these factors and to postulate the underlying components that assisted their adjustment.

This chapter describes the cases of two female child survivors. They were chosen for their similarities: they were born in the same region, are roughly the same age, had similar backgrounds, and survived similar types of persecution. As I describe the lives of these two women, it will become evident that one fared well while the other did not. In addition, a review of the development for the coding will be described so as to define an underlying basis for the conclusion.

The Development of the Project

This study developed slowly. By seeking out child survivors of the Holocaust and taping our interviews (oral histories) with them, we were able to compile psychological and historical data for the study. From these interviews, we interviewers began to form ideas about how to find the psychological components that shaped their experiences and assess the impact these had on the children. The interviews were conducted by trained mental health specialists and were mostly tape recorded and then transcribed.

In addition, we determined how to move in specific directions in the interviewing process in order to obtain the material we were looking to research. Specifically, we were interested in learning about the personal history of the child survivors with an emphasis on the type of traumas they had endured: the impact of the trauma on their memory, and the long-term effect of the trauma on further development and adjustment in their later life. Various techniques enabled us to reach into preverbal and nonverbal memory derivatives of the interviewees and thus obtain material that added to our understanding of the development of resilience.

Keeping the interviews anonymous proved a major factor in encouraging the child survivors to share material with us. It enabled them to discuss aspects of their past that they might not want others to know. Often this included events that they were ashamed of and/or felt guilty about. We were thus able to obtain a greater range of material than those who interviewed using videos where the child survivor was easily identified. The protocol we developed for interviewing child survivors was incorporated into other research projects, including including the Institute for Visual History and Education, founded by Steven Spielberg in 1994 at the University of Southern California (USC) Shoah Foundation, that collected and indexed 52,000 survivor stories.

In the early 1990s Judith Kestenberg set up a study group that created a system that would code the demographic and psychological profile of each child survivor. This group met for many years to develop the codes that would enable us to focus on the components to allow for an overall understanding of every child survivor we interviewed. Through reading or listening to the narratives, we ascertained how similar experiences affected different children in different ways. The study group thus began to understand how a traumatic experience made its impact on the many child survivors interviewed. It became possible, due to the large number of child survivors interviewed, to compare the experiences of one specific child survivor with another. By comparing different children's narratives, we could clearly determine the factors that contributed to resilience and psychological stability—and those that did not. These factors were then turned into code that could be studied.

For more than twenty years, we delineated the areas of the child survivors' histories and the psychological consequences by assessing the material in the interviews. It is from these events and situations that resilience emerged that each child survivor had to deal with intrapsychically and in his or her own way. Many different issues emerged from the interviewing process. A wide range of topics was covered in our typical interviews, which varied in length from one to three hours each. Not every child survivor gave information on all of the topics, but the great majority did, and we were therefore able to create codes for this information.

Coding the Narrative of the Child Survivors

ISOPC's *Code Book* took shape in June 1997 and has not been changed since then. The indexing is divided into six areas:

1. Respondent Demographics

This includes basic information such as gender, date of birth, place of birth, number of siblings, and residence at the start of the persecution (which indicates whether the family had moved from the child's birthplace).

2. Prewar Background Variables

This is an attempt to understand the child survivors' psychosocial situation regarding their parents' socioeconomic status in the community, as well as the presence of significant relationships with people outside the nuclear family. Ties to Jewish practice and community are delineated, as well as primary Jewish affiliation and identity, ranging from Chassidic to Liberal, from Zionist to non-Jewish. Ties of the nuclear family to various aspects of Jewish life are also defined, since one parent might have been more affiliated than another. The child survivors' specific memories of prewar life are also indexed, including any prewar traumas such as the death of a family member or the presence of any abuse.

3. Wartime Experiences

In this section we coded the type of experiences described by the child survivors. These range from experiencing concentration camps, living in different ghettos, escaping from one country to another, joining the partisans, being on a *Kindertransport*, being one of the Teheran children, being on a death march, passing as a non-Jew, and being in hiding. The hiding experience is usually defined as being in a convent, orphanage, school, Christian home, protected house, forest, mountains, or outside houses such as in chicken coops, dams, or ditches. The experience of passing as a non-Jew is indexed for gender disguise or living a Christian lifestyle.

In addition, we coded the experience that had the greatest emotional impact on the child survivors, along with where they spent the greatest amount of time. The presence of social support, such as parents, siblings, relatives, or friends, is also noted. We attempt to understand the valence of the presence of this social support, especially of the mother. The age of the child survivor when actually with the mother is also considered an important factor to be indexed.

How the deaths of others—including deaths that they witnessed or caused—affected the child survivor was also measured. We also account for the emotions expressed during the recounting of these experiences.

The child survivors were questioned regarding to what or to whom their survival can be attributed. Their responses to this question were always revealing for understanding the psychology of the child survivor and were an important factor in our research. For instance, a child survivor might take sole responsibility for having survived. This will emerge as, "I survived because I could always change my identity and become what was expected of me." Some child survivors attribute survival to luck, chance, or God's will, and others to having been with someone who was able to save them.

The type of description given by child survivors is factored in as having an impact on the memory process and its relationship to trauma. This includes the clarity with which the persecutor is described, including specific details or images.

4. Immediate Postwar Adjustment and Mental Health

In this section we attempt to describe the child survivor's emotional functioning from 1945 to 1950—after the persecution. We refer to these years in order to determine the immediate impact of the persecution on the child survivor. This includes cases of poor functioning, including child survivors who have been hospitalized for both physical and mental disorders. The presence of a breakdown is considered to be both a result of the previous experiences and a negative prognosis for ongoing well-being. The influence of severe physical illness affects the child survivor's adjustment in all facets of life.

Regarding the indices for the components of good mental health, we factored in the existence of parenting in the postwar period. The possibilities included biological parents, foster parents including other relatives, adoptive parents, group homes, and orphanages. The option of the absence of all parenting experiences is, of course, also included. We also made an effort to factor in the competence of postwar parenting and its impact on the child survivors, as well as the parents' overall adjustment to postwar life. Child survivors were, at times, in the position of becoming a parenting figure to others, including their own parents or older relatives.

5. Long-Term Postwar Adjustment
(from 1950 to the time of the interview)

In this crucial section, we attempt to understand the impact of the Holocaust on the capacity of child survivors to live life to the fullest. We therefore rate the presence of ongoing, fulfilling relationships established by child survivors either within marriage or within other intimate relationships. We note the cases of divorce, separation, and loss of a partner or spouse. The number of children and the quality of the child survivors' relationships with their children is considered an ongoing factor in good postwar adjustment. Other social support systems are also mentioned, such as enduring friendships.

We also attempt to understand the ability of child survivors to participate in the workplace, in terms of a career, profession, or regular fulfilling employment. We note whether a woman has been a homemaker and how gratifying this has been for her. The highest level of education is also taken into account.

Our study also attempts to assess the child survivor's ongoing Jewish identity or lack thereof, using the following indices: strong, moderate, or weak Jewish connections with regular synagogue attendance and involvement in Jewish communal life; Jewish identification through

Holocaust-related organizations or groups; no connections to Jewish observance or communal life; and becoming non-Jewish. The valence effect toward the child survivor's Jewish identity is assessed as being positive, neutral, ambivalent, or negative.

The other postwar component evaluated is physical well-being, current physical health, and emotional health. Emotional health, an essential component of our study, is then measured by indices: (1) focusing on being a victim, (2) ongoing nightmares and/or flashbacks, (3) the presence of ongoing psychotropic medication and hospitalization, and (4) being plagued by guilt and regret.

The central theme of the child survivors' lives is assessed through their definition of the three things that are most important to their lives. These might include family, religious practice, control, financial success, helping others, or fighting for a particular cause. The degree to which child survivors have given an active and positive orientation to their lives, so as to get as much out of life as possible, is rated from positive to extremely poor. This ranges from active and assertive efforts to maintain a quality of life that rises above the trauma to a highly self-defeating and negative attitude in which nothing in life is ever worthwhile. In cases of extremely poor adjustment, there is the likelihood of severe emotional problems, including hospitalization.

We look for recurrent themes. In order to study the relationship between the uncovering of memories and repression of the ongoing trauma, we take careful note of the memories that have been exposed during the process. Often names of people and places will come up; occasionally a language spoken only in early childhood will emerge. The memory of a lost loved one is often solidified by deeper images.

The Case Studies: Rachel and Rosa

These two cases are sisters, aged two and four when they last saw their parents.

Rachel: Early Life

Rachel was interviewed in 1986 in Israel. She was born in March 1938 in Antwerp, Belgium, the first child of religious middle-class parents. "My father was a Cohan, and I must have seen him in the synagogue or something. . . . I know that we were religious from what my aunt tells me." Rachel remembers her parents wearing the yellow star. Her sister Rosa was born in November 1940, six months after persecution began in

Belgium. In 1942 the family fled the Jewish area of Antwerp for Brussels and were planning to go into hiding: "So they thought we'd be safe, you know, and get lost in Brussels. Anyway what happened, I remember this—next door to us was a Catholic family, and when the Germans came, my parents paid them money beforehand that they should take us in if anything should happen, if my parents should be taken." From her narrative it is evident that her parents could not conceal their Jewish identity and were discovered by the Germans. Rachel describes how she and her sister were saved. "My father wrapped my sister and me in mattresses and threw us over the wall. There was a yard at the back of the house. We had a yard and they had a yard. And they threw us over the wall, into the Catholic family, who took us." The children stayed for three days with the Catholic family who, on being visited by the Germans, claimed the sisters as their own. Rachel recalls that the experience was "like being an animal. I had an instinct. . . . Because I knew to be afraid of Germans. I knew that. And I remember that my sister was asleep. She was a year old and I remember that when the Germans came in and this woman said, 'These are my children.'"

Rachel remembers seeing her parents being taken "in the lorries" as they rode past the Catholic family's home, although she has no memory of parting from them. The children were then taken to a railway station. Rachel recalls the woman telling her, "'I'm taking you to a Jewish orphanage. I'm taking you there because I have a son, and if I keep you two, they're going to shoot my son.' . . . I remember that vividly. She would have been shot on the spot, if they realized we were Jewish children and she was helping us."

The girls were taken to a Jewish orphanage where Rachel stayed for about six months and Rosa remained for the duration of the war. Rachel was taken to live with a Catholic woman, Auntie Helen, who wanted to help a Jewish child. She was quite religious and Rachel recalls that she thought Rachel looked like the Virgin Mary. It was done secretly, despite the fact that Rachel spoke only Yiddish. She became assimilated into the woman's lifestyle and attended church twice daily. She had ongoing contact with her sister Rosa and visited her in the orphanage. She recounts that some suspicion was aroused in the Catholic community, and on being accused by another child of being a Jew, she recalls saying: "I am proud of being a Jew because Jesus Christ was a Jew. I believe in Jesus Christ." One of the nuns overheard this and Rachel was taken back to the orphanage for about six months, before being allowed to return to Auntie Helen with whom she spent most of the years from age four until seven. Rachel describes her attachment to the woman: "She was my mother as far as I was concerned." Auntie Helen was very good to her and Rachel remembers hating the six months back in the orphanage. She remained with Auntie Helen until the war ended and she and her sister were claimed by her paternal aunt who lived in England.

This English aunt was married with two daughters, with another daughter born soon after the sisters came. Rachel recalls that she presented herself as their mother: "I didn't recognize her, or know her, or anything. I knew nothing about her. All I knew was, suddenly my father's sister arrives and she's taking us to England." The girls were told that she was their mother, and that their background should be kept a secret because she wanted to tell everyone that they were one family. This was a factor that caused many identity issues for the two girls and their siblings. The aunt made a show of saying she loved all the girls the same. She adopted them legally and insisted that they call her mother. Neither girl felt comfortable with this, and it had repercussions later for both of them.

Rosa: Early Life

Rosa was interviewed in 1986 in Israel. She was born in November 1940 in Antwerp, Belgium, and moved to Brussels with her family after the start of the persecution in Belgium. She has no memories of her life before the orphanage and knows about it only through her sister's memories: "The first thing I remember is the orphanage." The interviewer tries to jog her memory with an attempt to focus on her toys or dolls, but she does not respond to that inquiry: "I remember the smell of going down into the dungeons, to the cellar under the orphanage whenever there was a raid. It's like the smell of boiled cabbage. Yeah, it was awful. And I remember looking out of the window of the orphanage into the gardens and soldiers running along the hedge in a crouched position. I see helmets and what do I feel, I see helmets and army uniforms. I feel that they feel scared and I, by thinking about, I also feel scared." Rosa was the youngest child in the orphanage. She was alone for much of the day when the others went to school. A young Jewish woman who was in charge of the orphanage took Rosa under her wing: "I remember being very close to this woman in charge of the cooking and housekeeping. I just remember always being in her arms." She adds: "I was like a daughter. I was 2 when she got me. She really loved me." This woman was in charge of the facility that was allegedly just keeping Jewish children of Belgium nationality until they were to be taken to the camps by the National Socialists (or Nazis): "The children were to be taken away at their [the Nazis'] discretion when the time was right. After they disclosed that, the young woman knew she could be taken away, but she was going to go with them. In fact, they actually did [round them up]. They rounded us up and put us into trucks to take us and she came with us, and she demanded to speak to the queen of Belgium. I mean she was a very forceful woman. Apparently, the queen dissented and somehow they took us back."

Rosa describes her experience in the orphanage as being surrounded by many other children and therefore not alone. She delineated her feelings of being within a group, in comparison to her sister "who was alone." Rosa also recalls that she did not miss her sister but just accepted the fact that Rachel lived elsewhere. She remembers being fetched by her aunt after the war: "When my aunt came to fetch me after the war, I didn't want to go. I was nearly six and I screamed and I didn't want to go. I mean, that was my home. It was the place I knew. I didn't associate her with anything. She was just a stranger to me. I don't know if I was happy, but that was my place. If you take a kid off the street who's been on the streets all his life, he won't be happy."

Post-Holocaust Experience

Both girls went to England to live with their aunt and uncle who formally adopted them and changed their last name. Their adoptive parents insisted that the girls never discuss their Holocaust experiences with anyone. Rosa says, "I still don't understand why they warned to suppress the fact that they had taken us in, and we were adopted kids. They . . . insisted that we don't talk about it with anybody and that we call them mom and dad, and they changed our name. It was like a big secret. I still don't know why. Maybe it was hurtful for them, but I would've thought she'd be proud to have done a thing like that [taking in these relatives]." Both girls felt that while their aunt tried to treat all the children the same, she clearly loved her own three birth children much more. Rosa recalls a good relationship with her adoptive father who she felt tried his best to involve her in activities. Rachel was additionally affected by the fact that they were observant Jews: "Well, here I was, suddenly thrown into a Jewish family. And they were religious. I remember going to bed, everyone laughs when I talk about it, and I laugh myself, and praying to Jesus that he would forgive me but I mustn't believe in him anymore." The girls also became involved in Zionist youth movements.

After high school, Rachel began to study to be a lab technician. She moved to Israel and lived on a kibbutz where she got engaged to a kibbutznik. He died suddenly and she returned to England. She became involved with another man, also a child survivor, whose mother constantly interfered with their relationship. At this point, Rachel suffered the first of many breakdowns that she describes painfully as having recurred every two years. At the time of the interview, she had been stable for many years and was optimistic that a combination of medication and therapy would prevent this terrible cycle of dysfunction from reoccurring. In her psychotic states Rachel had visions of Jesus and the Virgin Mary, as well as delusions and hallucinations.

Meanwhile, Rachel moved from Israel, to England, to South Africa, and finally back to Israel. At the time of the interview, she considered Israel to be her home and stated that she did not ever want to live anywhere else. She remained throughout able to enjoy her work, have relationships, and be a part of her sister's family. Therefore, in her initial adjustment and post-Holocaust adjustment, Rachel reflected a very poor level of resilience. After years of therapy and ongoing medication, she was able to maintain greater stability than in the immediate post-Holocaust years.

Rosa joined Rachel in Israel and lived on a nearby kibbutz. When Rachel went back to England, Rosa became engaged to a South African man. Their marriage coincided with the collapse of Rachel's second relationship. Rosa and her husband settled in South Africa where Rachel joined them. When Rosa and her family moved back to Israel, so did Rachel, and since that time both sisters have remained in Israel.

Rosa was a homemaker and mother to four children. In contrast to her sister, Rosa did not suffer any significant emotional upheavals. Her overall level of resilience appears indicative of having the strength and the ability to form good relationships with her husband and children. She mentions only one ongoing psychological issue, namely, that she has occasionally felt her mothering skills to be slightly lacking: "But then, now and again, I looked around at other people's parents and my [adoptive] mother wasn't a cuddly mother. And I always wanted a cuddly mother, as probably every child does. And I didn't know whether it's right to be a cuddly mother or wrong to be a cuddly mother. It all seems very mundane, but it puts one into a sort of a predicament. I couldn't be a natural mother because I didn't have the mother image. I just had this one. . . . She always maintained that she had five daughters and she was going to treat us all equally. . . . But she'd come in at night and say, thinking I'm asleep, "You know. Rita, I really love you the best." It was only when Rosa's own daughter, Sharon, suffered a severe breakdown that Rosa's early life came into focus. This occurred when Sharon was in her early twenties, soon after Rosa disclosed the facts of her childhood that she had been compelled to keep secret by her aunt. Sharon "shaved her head, starved herself, and believed she was in a Nazi concentration camp."

Sharon's breakdown enabled the family to open up further about the past. They all underwent therapy, and Rosa and her husband went back to Europe to search for various contacts, including the woman who had run the orphanage and cared for her. According to the interviewer who knew about the situation, Sharon "was hospitalized for several months and with the family's intense support, made a miraculous recovery."

Aspects of Adjustment and Resilience in Rachel and Rosa

This pair of sisters represents an understanding of resilience in child survivors and in the transposition of trauma from one generation to another. The following discussion is taken from the ideas emerging through an analysis of the coded interviews.

What is most striking is that the younger sister, Rosa, remained emotionally stable throughout her life, in contrast to the older sister, Rachel. It is interesting to examine why this should be so by looking at the basic dynamics. Rosa was younger at the time of the separation from her parents and was placed in an orphanage with fifty-five children and one main caretaker. It would seem that her ego was certainly weaker and the trauma of loss greater for her than for her sister Rachel. Rachel, two years older than her sister at the time of the separation, had a stronger ego that permitted her to retain clear memories of the situation. Rachel was given the undivided attention of a loving and devoted woman, Auntie Helen. She was allowed to be part of a community and did not live in the more isolated environment of the orphanage for most of the time. Both girls were silenced by their paternal aunt who made them suppress their Holocaust experiences.

It is my understanding that the resilience evidenced by Rosa throughout her life derives from the stability of structure, the presence of other children, and the support of a mothering person. The structure was the routine and relative isolation of the orphanage from the daily life and threats of the Gentile villagers. The presence and impact of other children in the face of trauma gave Rosa an identification with a group, some sense of strength in numbers. Her attachment to a person of strength who gave her protection was vital to Rosa. This young woman promised to keep her and the other children secure and managed this by actually saving them when they were already on a truck heading to the camps. Consequently, Rosa was not overexposed to the dangers that lay beyond the orphanage.

Rosa's attachment to structure more than to people seems to have contributed majorly to her sense of stability. Throughout her life, Rosa was able to find comfort in the structure of whichever organization or group she found herself in, particularly in the post-Holocaust years, as she moved from England, to Israel, to South Africa, and back to Israel. She always lived in structured situations, such as on a kibbutz or being a homemaker.

When she talks about herself, she confesses a lack of her own identity though: "I mean maybe my biggest fear is that somebody will take over my identity because I never had one. I'm just finding it, you know." This troubling aspect of herself was intensified by her aunt's demand that she deny her true background. However, Rosa was able to mitigate it by defining herself through the group or situation she was currently in. Regarding this connection with the outside world, she says, "I feel very sorry for people. . . . You just feel like . . . the inhumanity of the world, and you don't realize why. You just know that you feel it. . . . You don't realize that you're feeling your own sorry. Not theirs, but you're putting yourself onto them. I used to say I wanted to go and be a missionary in India. I didn't realize why I used to identify with the person I was angry with. You can't imagine the pain." The past was suppressed for her aunt's convenience, while the present was projected onto the suffering in the world at large. While this enabled Rosa to achieve stability, it denied her the option of speaking the truth. Some of her past trauma may have been alleviated through a certain level of identification with her sister's breakdowns, but Rosa could not ultimately suppress enough of her past. This formed the context for the transposition of her trauma to her daughter, who had the breakdown.

The transposition of trauma is a psychological mechanism in which the unspoken trauma is unconsciously transposed or transmitted to the following generation. It permits the first generation to detach from the impact of the trauma. It is not surprising that Rosa was able to do this; indeed, she was almost encouraged to do so by her English family. Because Rosa had the ability to attach more readily to structure than to feelings, she could remove this aspect of another past from her life. The later emotional breakdown of her daughter provided the entire family, including the English adoptive parents and Rachel, with the opportunity to own their specific identities. The interviewer of the two sisters states in his notes that Sharon's (Rosa's daughter) breakdown opened up years of suppressed secrecy for the entire family.

In reviewing the components of Rosa's resilience, I have identified that belonging to a group, identifying with other children, and having protection against overexposure to the impact of annihilation anxiety were the major factors in producing her relatively good adjustment.

The opposite components were evidenced by Rachel who was further along developmentally at the time of the loss of the parents. Rachel was denied the opportunity to be with many other children. She tried to identify with her Catholic community but was not given the necessary help. Therefore, she neither had a stable peer group experience nor could she identify with those she was in contact with when in hiding. In addition, Rachel, as the only Jewish child in a hostile Gentile village, was not protected against the impact of annihilation anxiety by Auntie Helen. Her adult life, with its emotional breakdowns and hospitalizations, indicate a fragility in coping that resulted from her traumatic childhood.

Both girls were profoundly affected by their aunt's ideas of secrecy, which ultimately became a blight on the next generation. It was also the next generation who fortunately enabled them to be truthful with each other. The component of annihilation anxiety was ever-present for both sisters. However, the closeness of a mothering figure and other children in the orphanage gave Rosa greater emotional strength, while Rachel experienced greater exposure to trauma through her life with Auntie Helen.

This examination of the cases of Rachel and Rosa will hopefully lead to an understanding of how the measure of resilience is coded in our project. In reviewing their cases, it becomes evident that the dynamic of being with one's peers is a major factor in the development of ego strength and identity stability. These can subsequently influence lifelong character traits that contribute to resiliency. For these child survivors, continuity of structure, such as a Jewish upbringing and identity, can also contribute to resiliency. The component of emotional distancing, somewhat like detachment, served to keep Rosa loyal to the family structure.

An understanding of these influences on development can provide the opportunity to help the many children who have been exposed to trauma in our troubled world in their current adjustment.

Author

Helene Bass-Wichelhaus is a child, adolescent, and adult psychoanalyst in private practice in Manhattan. She is co-chair of the International Study of Organized Persecution of Children, a project of Child Development Research. She is on the editorial board of *The Psychoanalytic Review*. In addition, she is a senior member of the National Psychological Association for Psychoanalysis and has served as a faculty member of the National Psychological Association for Psychoanalysis, the Institute for Expressive Analysis, and Adelphi University. She has written various articles on annihilation anxiety, anti-Semitism, human development, and child survivors of the Holocaust.

Note

1. All interviews quoted in this chapter were held at the Oral History Division, Hebrew University of Jerusalem.

References

Testimony of RK (257) 27-32, Judith Kestenberg Child Survivor Archive, The Oral History Division, Hebrew University of Jerusalem.

Testimony of RW (257) 37-76, Judith Kestenberg Child Survivor Archive, The Oral History Division, Hebrew University of Jerusalem.

PART FOUR

NON-JEWISH VICTIMS OF WAR AND NAZISM

 9

"They Were Jews, but They Were Very Kind People"

Polish Language Testimonies in the Kestenberg Archive

Katarzyna Person

> I remember that this girl was red-haired, freckled and so hopeless, she was four years old, and I was older. I always defended her because the children teased her a lot. When I later found out that they took her to the ghetto, I took it very badly, I cried after that girl, I wanted my mum to let me go to the border of the ghetto, so that maybe I would see her, bring her bread, but those were just childish dreams.[1]

This chapter will discuss a group of more than two hundred interviews among Jewish and non-Jewish Poles living in Poland contained in the Kestenberg Archive of Testimonies of Child Holocaust Survivors, a collection of documents of children's experiences under the National Socialists (or Nazis) that were gathered in the late 1980s and early 1990s.[2] The vast majority of those interviewed had been children during the war, ranging in age from newborns to teenagers.[3] There are interviews with people who had been in charge of the children, and those who had witnessed the persecution of the children, such as doctors, nurses, and even camp overseers. Though there are exceptions—such as an interview with Irena Sendler, a renowned Polish social worker who rescued 2,500 Jewish children from the Warsaw Ghetto[4]—the majority of the Polish-language interviewees were testifying to their wartime experiences for the first time. While they were not openly discouraged from sharing their experiences earlier on, there was not much interest in their stories, and they often suppressed their need to share memories, identifying them as insignificant or as a hindrance to moving on and organizing their postwar lives. As Sharon Kangisser Cohen wrote in reference to child survivors of the Holocaust, "Child survivors themselves, like adult survivors, realized that, in order to 'belong,' they needed to direct their energies into rebuilding their lives; they needed to look forward and not back. Therefore, they themselves needed to silence their past."[5] The same can be applied to non-Jewish child survivors of camps and forced labor camps who were interviewed for this collection.

The Kestenberg archive allows us to access testimonies that even today remain peripheral to Holocaust scholarship—first because they come from those who experienced the war as children and remained silent about their experiences,[6] and second because they come from those who remained in Poland after the war and were not reached by the documentation projects carried out in Israel and the United States.[7]

Interviews with Non-Jewish Poles

The non-Jewish Poles interviewed for the archive about their wartime experiences reflect a social and geographical cross section of Polish society. It is not clear how they were chosen to participate in the project because very often their links to the Holocaust are tenuous. The vast majority of those interviewed were children during the war, and thus they are not representatives of the Poles most often interviewed in documentation projects, namely those who were active in the underground aid initiatives.[8] They also rarely experienced the same concentration or forced labor camps as did the Jewish interviewees. Because the bulk of each interview is taken up by interviewees' individual stories, with the interviewer attempting to ascertain what influence wartime trauma might have had on their postwar lives, the testimonies speak primarily of Polish wartime experiences of prison, concentration camps, and forced labor camps, as well as of the wartime experience of children taking on the role of adults in their quest for survival. In the vast majority of the testimonies the persecution of Jews serves only as a backdrop to their own traumatic experiences. This comes across particularly clearly in a large collection of testimonies of former inmates of a concentration camp for Polish children and youth in Lodz (Polenjugendverwahrlager der Sicherheitspolizei in Litzmannstadt), which was established in 1942 within the borders of the Litzmannstadt Ghetto in Lodz. Those imprisoned in the camp were non-Jewish Poles and the camp was separated from the ghetto by a high wooden fence. According to the testimony of its former inmates, the sounds and sometimes brief sight of the ghetto created the setting for their own suffering. "One could hear cries, screams . . . cries of those children, inhumane screams. It was terrifying," recalls JZ.[9] However, the topic of the persecution of the Jews is often introduced only in the last part of the interview when the interviewer specifically asks about the interviewee's knowledge about the Holocaust, about Polish–Jewish relations in their locality before the Holocaust, or about their own attitude toward anti-Semitism. In some interviews the Holocaust is not even mentioned at all. "People were more concerned with their own matters," explains HK candidly.[10]

Yet in all these stories and silences, one can still attempt to find a common thread. As Joanna Michlic pointed out in her study of child Holocaust survivors, "In spite of a multitude of individual children's wartime biographies, it is possible to detect certain clear patterns and commonalities in the children's micro-universes of wartime experience and interaction with the adult world, whereby one can conjure up a history of a generation or generations of children and youth."[11] It is my claim that the experience of bearing witness to the Holocaust among non-Jewish Polish child survivors of World War II also show certain commonalities that I will discuss below.

Due to the age of the interviewees, testimonies from the Kestenberg archive rarely speak at length of the prewar Jewish community in Poland. The picture of prewar Poland that emerges from the archive is one of peaceful Polish–Jewish coexistence. The interviewees clearly attempted to dispel the image of prewar Polish anti-Semitism, though their rhetoric often uncovers more of their attitude or, considering their age at the time, their parents' attitude, than they may have intended. While attempting to clarify the relationship between Poles and Jews in their locality, EB explains, "They were Jews, but they were very kind people. . . . What I'm trying to say is that they did not have hatred against Catholics."[12] Only some interviewees when speaking of that period mention individual Jews, usually neighbors, parents' friends, or school acquaintances who they recall specifically in relation to their later fate during the Holocaust.

And it is these prewar acquaintances who are the first cases of Nazi persecution that they witness as Polish children. A common image in their testimonies is of Jewish neighbors being forcibly removed from their homes. One witness, MO from Poznań who was eight years old at the outbreak of the war, remembers the violence against her neighbor and his family: "How horribly those Hitlerites tormented that Jew, his wife and their children. They threw them down the stairs like sacks, kicked them, hit them with rifle-butts. I saw all of them covered in blood."[13] More often, however, the first instance of anti-Jewish violence they recall involved their peers. A detailed description of this type comes from JR, six years old at the outbreak of the war. A native of Warsaw, JR spent the early years of the war living by the ghetto wall. She recalls this event:

As children do, we were playing in the courtyard, and one time we went outside the entrance and this little girl, I later found out that this girl's name was Roza, tiny, delicate, skinny girl crawled through those openings, there were those semi-circle openings under the [ghetto] wall, I remember, and as this child crawled from under the [ghetto] wall, a soldier came with a badge on his chest and he said something to this child, [and] the child threw herself down on her knees, threw herself, rather than kneeled down. I remember those words "Her[r] bitte" [Mister, please] with hands outstretched she was crawling to that kraut, and he was aiming at her little fingers. To this day I cannot forget it. Horrible things.[14]

Even when the violence they witnessed was directed against other children, it seems that the Holocaust was something that children saw as belonging to the world of the adults. The fact that they were forced to leave the town or relocate to the ghetto, in addition to any specific experiences, moved the Jewish children outside of the interviewees' familiar sphere.[15] This was reinforced as the persecution progressed, and several respondents testified that news of the Holocaust was kept from them by their parents or other adults for fear of upsetting or scaring them. HP, who was eight years old at the start of the war and spent the war in Lodz, recalls Jewish children visiting their house, begging for food:

A few times us, and some other Poles . . . were visited by a young Jew, he was maybe 13–14 years old. He walked around and asked for help, bread, potatoes, anything to eat. Once he even stayed overnight. He lived on the other side of the street, I remembered his parents. He spoke of such horrible things that my dad made me leave so that I would not listen to it, but I heard a lot anyway, as I had good hearing and you could hear the conversation in another room. He said that in the ghetto there is no water even to drink, not to speak of washing and doing laundry. He spoke of an unimaginable hunger, that people, in particular children, die of hunger on the streets, that there is nobody to bury them because often children have no parents or relatives left. Special carts were going there to pick up the dead ones from the street. My mum always gave him something, even though we too found it difficult.[16]

Another interviewee who witnessed the Holocaust against her parents' wishes was IW from Warsaw, eleven years old at the start of the war. In her testimony she speaks of trips that, unbeknownst to her parents, she undertook with other children to the railway siding located on the ghetto border. She recalls, "We were going to Dworzec Gdański [train station], and there was a rail ramp, and we were watching, as children who get anywhere do, from that railway station we were watching, how they load them and take them away."[17] When asked if she knew where the Jews were being taken, she answers, "Everyone had some assumptions, but it was not certain."[18] All doubts disappeared with the start of the Warsaw Ghetto uprising in April 1943. "Warsaw was covered in smoke as everything was burning, shooting, that shooting day and night, those explosions you could hear," recalls IW. She is asked by the interviewer, "And you knew what it was?" and she confirms, "We knew what it was."

BB, aged twelve, watched the suppression of the Warsaw Ghetto uprising in secret from the roof of her apartment block situated by the ghetto wall: "We lived in a five storey house, I went up to the roof with other children. My mother strongly forbade me, but did my mother know everything? So I went up to the roof and there we could see the whole [Jewish] quarter from the fifth floor, you could hear the shots, you could see fire, you could hear screams, the echoes carried."[19]

An exception here was ten-year-old KW who also watched the suppression of the ghetto uprising from a building next to the ghetto wall but who was encouraged to do so by her father who wanted her to remember what had happened in Warsaw. She recalls: "Our windows were covered with those black blinds, we made little holes in them and I saw this horrible moment, you know how a child is always curious, that a house was already burning on the second floor and on the third floor stood a Jewish woman with two children and she pushed out those children and then jumped herself. I remember this awful moment."[20]

The interviewees emphasize the trauma they experienced from witnessing such events at a very young age and express to the interviewer their empathy with the suffering of the Jews, in particular the children. However, in their recollections they draw a very clear line between us (Poles) and them (Jews). Crossing this line by reaching out to the Jews was associated with immediate danger, a point made very clear to them by the adults around them. EB was four years old when the war started, and he remembers walking past the Warsaw Ghetto: "I remember some sort of sewage, a type of sewer grate and children stretching their hands through them from the other side of the wall. And I know that my mother handed them over something, oranges and something, whatever she had to eat and that she was very scared."[21] While EB speaks only of his mother's fear, the majority of those testifying emphasize the danger Poles were facing as a whole. In the most poignant part of her testimony, HP remembers taking a tram through the Litzmannstadt Ghetto: "In the beginning of 1944 I rode on a tram through the ghetto with my dad. I don't remember why we went there. I saw horrifying images, cadaverous Jews, dirty children in rags were looking at the tram, as if they expected help from there. Through the open window some woman threw a piece of bread. Children, like little animals, threw themselves at this bread. A gendarme saw it and after we passed the ghetto, he got the woman off the tram and took her with him. I remember that aiding the Jews was threatened with death."[22]

HP further underlines her point by speaking about known cases of Poles who were arrested for extending help to Jews. The aim of her narrative was not self-justification; she was only a child at the time and a victim of Nazi persecution herself. At the time of this incident she was working in a German factory where she suffered hunger and brutal beatings, all of which significantly affected her postwar life. She was unable to help those in the ghetto. As in her quote that opens this chapter, helping Jews was for her nothing more than just a "childish dream."[23] As with many others Poles whose testimonies appear in the archive, HP understands that bearing witness is, in Erica Lehrer's words, "a kind of moral remembering."[24] HP perceives it as her moral duty, when facing the interviewer who was a representative of a foreign organization, to clarify the behavior of Poles during the Holocaust, and place it appropriately on the hierarchy of suffering. Others understand moral remembering as remaining silent. In the vast majority of testimonies, prewar Jewish acquaintances were reduced to anonymous shadows on the streets of the ghetto, sometimes reappearing to ask for help, sometimes mentioned in a conversation. And one day those shadows simply disappeared. As one of the respondents put it, "Suddenly you just stopped seeing them."[25]

Testimonies of Jewish Polish Child Survivors

The second group of testimonies to be discussed are those of Jewish Polish survivors of the Holocaust. While the non-Jewish Poles interviewed for the Kestenberg archive can be seen as representatives of Polish child victims of Nazism, the Jewish Poles cannot be seen as representative of either their prewar communities or of survivors of the Holocaust. They form a very particular group of people who decided to stay in Poland following the war.[26] Their identity narrative, therefore, opposed the mainstream narrative of Jewish identity after the Holocaust, which was "predicated on the erasure of its links to the Polish past."[27] Having been forcibly removed from their prewar communities, the majority of Polish Jewish survivors decided not to return there after the war. Those who chose to remain in Poland were very different from those who left, and their postwar fates fully confirm Lawrence Langer's claim that there as many coping mechanisms for the trauma of survival as there were ways of surviving.[28] For this group, silence became a significant way of coping to survive.

A group often associated with postwar silence is Jewish hidden children, especially those who remained with their Polish guardians after the war. EB is an example of this group of survivors.[29] She was born in 1942 in the Warsaw Ghetto and was smuggled out at the age of five months when her parents hid her under a pile of bricks in a cart. On the Aryan side of the wall she was taken in by a Polish family who had her baptized and raised her as their daughter. At the time of the interview, the adult EB expresses awareness of the emotional sacrifice that her birth family must have undergone in order to hand her over to the Aryan side. In her testimony she recalls being told that her grandfather prepared a christening outfit for her that he handed over to the nanny employed by her Polish foster family. She recalls, "[The nanny] told me later [when EB was a teenager] that he prepared everything for the christening: a white robe, white shoes and even a golden cross and that he was crying when he handed it to her, saying that [EB] is not ours anymore. Nanny told me that he had red hair and that he cried."[30] Nonetheless, EB makes it very clear to the interviewer that she considers her Polish family her "real" family. When referring to her "mother," she speaks of her Polish foster mother, and she often talks of the difficulties her foster mother had to endure in order to keep her safe during the war and to provide her with a happy and carefree childhood after the war. She tells about representatives of a Jewish organization that came looking for her after the war at the request of her surviving family members and does not blame her Polish foster mother for hiding her and refusing to hand her over.

EB did not discover her Jewish identity and that "my mother is not my mother"[31] until she was a teenager. This discovery was made harder by the fact that by then she had internalized the surrounding society's view of Jews. In the interview she states, "I began to reflect on this whole Jewishness. I had no idea about it. It always had a negative meaning for me. I always associated the term Jew with something bad, I didn't know what exactly, but I knew that there was something not right with Jews. When I couldn't deal with it on my own anymore, I confided in my teacher at school. I stayed behind after the class, went up to him and asked him: 'Sir, who exactly are Jews?' I think he realized what the matter was, and he spoke to me very kindly and for a long time and said that they too are normal people."[32]

Despite her discovery, EB remained silent. Unlike many other child survivors, her silence was not imposed on her during the war as she was too young to have any memories of her birth family; instead, her self-imposed silence came out of consideration for the feelings of her Polish foster mother and the desire not to add to her burden: "It turned out that for my mother it was a great tragedy that I found out that she was not my mother and I decided never to return to this topic. I saw how much she was hurt by every conversation and there were no more conversations on this topic. We never spoke of it anymore. . . . Maybe it's because it was easier for me this way. I preferred to return to my previous identity, I still had a loving mother and I was an only child. This lasted until I gave birth to my own daughter."[33]

The seminal moment for her, as for many others of her generation, came during the 1968 government-sponsored anti-Semitic campaign that resulted in the forced emigration of approximately fifteen thousand Jews.[34] Only then did EB speak out. In her testimony she says, "When in 1968 someone asked me 'Are you a Jew ?' I answered: 'I am. I am and nobody will be throwing me out of my country.'"[35]

Even those who grew up confident with their Jewish identity saw silence as preferable in everyday life in postwar Poland. One such person was HL.[36] HL, twenty-two years old at the outbreak of the war, came from a traditional Jewish family. She escaped from the ghetto in Lvov and spent the war in Warsaw under an assumed Polish identity. In postwar Poland she became a teacher of mathematics. Despite the repeated questions regarding her faith, she refuses to admit if and when she converted, though this is clearly implied by the interviewer. In her testimony HL refers to a difficult relationship with her mother and difficulty in forming emotional attachments. She compares this with her reluctance to categorize her identity and, we can assume, to speak out about her Jewishness. Until directly confronted with a question regarding her identity, HL is very careful not to define herself as either Polish or Jewish and does not use the word "Jewish" even once. She explains to the interviewer that she would prefer to describe herself as a citizen of the world rather than as a Pole of Jewish origin. "I wish everyone well, which means that when in a foreign country I would never act in a way which would not suit people of that nationality. Being here [in Poland] I could never belong to a party or anything. This is out of question. Putting aside whether I have such or such convictions, I could never involve myself. It is the nation that chooses. I feel a little bit, as if I was, well, simply a guest. Wishing [everyone] well and hoping for what people hope."[37]

It is only following further questioning that HL admits to knowing Hebrew and expresses that, should the opportunity arise, she would seriously consider a future in Israel. This is not, however, something that she is happy to discuss openly within her close environment.

Postwar silence was also adopted by DD, even though she was the only one of the three interviewees to actually participate in Jewish communal life in postwar Poland.[38] Fourteen years old at the outbreak of the war, DD came from a Zionist family in Lodz and survived the Częstochowa Ghetto. After the war she witnessed numerous cases of anti-Semitism and fully intended to leave Poland and emigrate to Israel but stayed behind at the insistence of her husband. DD says in her interview that even before the war she had considered herself a "second class citizen." However, she recalls, "I did not care about it at all. Maybe because I was already born into it and I was simply used to it."[39] DD describes Polish anti-Semitism as "inbred" and consequently saw silence as the safest choice for those Jews who decided to stay in Poland. When speaking of her wish to protect her son, who despite her encouragement did not choose to leave the country, settling instead in the Polish countryside, she says, "I always said to P to omit those things. . . . I always said—don't speak about that topic, try to avoid those things somehow. . . . You will be living here after all, so that this does not follow you and your family."[40] While DD speaks openly of her regret at not leaving Poland, she concludes her testimony by saying, "I regret a lot, but on the other hand, Jews have a great love for this country, a truly great love. This is the so-called *hassliebe*. It's love through hate, yes. Just as in the past there was this one-sided love of Jews for the Germans. And now there is this great love for Poland. Many people don't want to come here, but this colossal love remains, because there is no other topic of conversation there. People keep coming back to it."[41]

Conclusion

A recent exhibition in the United States Holocaust Memorial Museum on collaboration and complicity during the Holocaust displayed a quote by the theologian David Gushee: "From a moral point of view there may be no such thing as a bystander. If one is present, one is taking part."[42] The Kestenberg archive, which allows us a rare glimpse at the testimony of those witnessing the Holocaust, fully endorses this quote. Poles who appear in studies of the Holocaust are usually either rescuers and aid-givers, or accomplices to murder. Those presented here simply observed. Yet, it is precisely this quality of being an "ordinary" witness to the Holocaust that makes the testimony of Poles interviewed for the archive so unique and this documentation project so valuable. We thus see the Holocaust through the eyes of a child watching his neighbors leave their apartment, or sitting on a tram going through the ghetto, or watching a deportation train roll past. Discussing Polish reactions to the Holocaust, the historian Michael Steinlauf wrote, "To witness murder on such a scale, at such close range, for such a long time, cannot lead to simple responses. To inquire about the Polish reaction to the Holocaust is to investigate the effects of mass psychic and moral trauma unprecedented in history."[43] The Kestenberg archive proves that the response was and still is silence. This silence also influenced the testimony of the Holocaust survivors who remained in Poland. When asked whether she ever talked about the Holocaust, DD simply states, "I have nobody to talk to."[44] For a myriad of reasons many Jewish and non-Jewish Poles remained silent after the war. The archive offered at least some of them the opportunity to speak out.

Author

Katarzyna Person is assistant professor at the Jewish Historical Institute in Warsaw. She is a historian of Eastern European Jewish history and has held postdoctoral fellowships at Yad Vashem's International Institute for Holocaust Research, the Center for Jewish History in New York, and La Fondation pour la Mémoire de la Shoah. She has written a number of articles on the Holocaust and its aftermath in occupied Europe, and has edited four volumes of documents from the underground archive of the Warsaw Ghetto. Her book, *Assimilated Jews in the Warsaw Ghetto 1940–1943*, was published in 2014 by Syracuse University Press.

Notes

1. Testimony of HP, (257) 20-79.
2. All interviews quoted in this chapter were held at the Oral History Division, Hebrew University of Jerusalem.
3. According to the guidelines that were given to the interviewers, child survivors were defined as those who were thirteen years of age or younger at the beginning of the persecution (thus at most nineteen at the time of liberation). No age limits were imposed on those who were interviewed as children who witnessed persecution.
4. Testimony of IS, (257) 29-85, 1985.
5. Kangisser Cohen, "The Silence of Hidden Child Survivors," 192.
6. For early collections of children's testimonies see Cohen, "The Children's Voice." For children's experiences during the war, see Stargardt, *Witnesses of War*; and Nicholas, *Cruel World*. For information on Jewish children, see Hochberg-Mariańska and Grüss, *The Children Accuse*; and Dwork, *Children with a Star*.

7. For information on Polish Jewry in immediate postwar Poland, see Hurwic Nowakowska's research conducted between 1947 and 1950 among survivors settled in Poland (*A Social Analysis of Postwar Polish Jewry*).
8. On Polish aid initiatives see, inter alia, Tec, *When Light Pierced the Darkness;* and Pawlikowski, "Polish Catholics and the Jews."
9. Testimony of JZ, (257) 29–37, 1990. As many of those interviewed about the camp refer in their testimonies to others who were interviewed for the archive, it seems that the contact was often passed by word of mouth. A number of interviews on this topic were conducted by one particular interviewer, Józef Witkowski, the author of the camp's monograph (*Hitlerowski obóz koncentracyjny*) and a former inmate in the camp himself. It is clear that the interviewees knew Witkowski from when he was conducting research for the monograph.
10. Testimony of HK, (257) 29–74, 1986.
11. Michlic, "'The War Began for Me After the War,'" 485.
12. Testimony of EB, (257) 29–58, 1988.
13. Testimony of MO, (257) 29–77, 1990.
14. Testimony of JR, (257) 30-1, 1986.
15. On the same issue from the point of view of child survivors of the Holocaust who felt alienated from children who were not persecuted, see Kestenberg and Kestenberg, "The Sense of Belonging."
16. Testimony of HP, (257) 29–79, 1990.
17. Testimony of IW, (257) 29-86, 1990.
18. Ibid.
19. Testimony of BB, (257) 29-70, 1988.
20. Testimony of KW, (257) 30-11, 1988.
21. Testimony of EB, (257) 29-62, 1990.
22. Testimony of HP, (257) 20-79, 1990.
23. Ibid.
24. Lehrer, "'Jewish Like an Adjective,'" 162.
25. Testimony of JL, (257) 29-92.
26. On reasons for leaving or staying in Poland in the immediate postwar years, see Hurwic Nowakowska, *A Social Analysis*, 53–65.
27. Glowacka and Zylinska, "Introduction. Imaginary Neighbors," 7.
28. Langer, *Holocaust Testimonies*, 205.
29. Testimony of EB (257) 29-59, 1985. On hidden children, see Marks, *Hidden Children*; and Bogner, *At the Mercy of Strangers*. On secondary silencing—the silence of hidden child survivors in their postwar environment—see Kangisser Cohen, "Silence of Hidden Child Survivors," 171–202.
30. Testimony of EB, (257) 29-59, 1985.
31. Ibid.
32. Ibid.
33. Ibid.
34. On the 1968 anti-Semitic campaign in Poland and its aftermath, see Gluchowski and Polonsky, *Polin*. On the impact of 1968 on Jewish youth in Poland, see a collection of interviews by Joanna Wiszniewicz (Wiszniewicz, *Życie przecięte* [in Polish]).

35. Testimony of EB, (257) 29-59, 1985.
36. Testimony of HL, (257) 29-76, 1987.
37. Ibid.
38. Testimony of DD, (257) 29-4, no date.
39. Ibid.
40. Ibid.
41. Ibid.
42. "The Exhibition Experience," 13.
43. Steinlauf, *Bondage to the Dead*, ix.
44. Testimony of DD, (257) 29-4, no date.

References

Bogner, Nahum. *At the Mercy of Strangers. The Rescue of Jewish Children with Assumed Identities in Poland*. Jerusalem: Yad Vashem, 2009.

Cohen, Boaz. "The Children's Voice: Postwar Collection of Testimonies from Child Survivors of the Holocaust." *Holocaust and Genocide Studies* 21, no. 1 (Spring 2007): 73–95.

Dwork, Debórah. *Children with a Star: Jewish Youth in Nazi Europe*. New Haven, CT: Yale University Press, 1991.

"The Exhibition Experience." *Memory & Action* Spring 2013, 13. https://www.ushmm.org/m/pdfs/20140509-spring-2013-memory-action.pdf

Hochberg-Mariańska, Maria, and Noe Gruss, eds. *Dzieci Oskarżają* [Children Accuse]. Kraków: Centralna Żydowska Komisja Historyczna w Polsce, 1947. (*The Children Accuse*, translated by Bill Johnston. London: Vallentine-Mitchell, 1996.)

Glowacka, Dorota, and Joanna Zylinska. "Introduction. Imaginary Neighbors: Toward an Ethical Community." In *Imaginary Neighbors: Mediating Polish-Jewish Relations after the Holocaust*, edited by D. Glowacka and J. Zylinska, 1–18. Lincoln: University of Nebraska Press, 2007.

Gluchowski, Leszek, and Antony Polonsky, eds. *Polin: Studies in Polish Jewry*, vol. 21, *1968: Forty Years After*. Oxford: The Littman Library of Jewish Civilization, 2008.

Hurwic Nowakowska, Irena. *A Social Analysis of Postwar Polish Jewry*. Tel Aviv: Zalman Shazar Center for Jewish History, 1986.

Kangisser Cohen, Sharon. "The Silence of Hidden Child Survivors of the Holocaust." *Yad Vashem Studies* 33 (2005): 171–202.

Kestenberg, Milton, and Judith S. Kestenberg. "The Sense of Belonging and Altruism in Children Who Survived the Holocaust." *Psychoanalytic Review*, 75, no. 4 (1988): 533–560.

Langer, Lawrence. *Holocaust Testimonies. The Ruins of Memory*. New Haven, CT: Yale University Press, 1991.

Lehrer, Erica. "'Jewish Like an Adjective'—Confronting Jewish Identities in Contemporary Poland." In *Boundaries of Jewish Identity*, edited by S.A. Glenn and N.B. Sokoloff, 161–187. Seattle: University of Washington Press, 2010.

Marks, Jane. *The Hidden Children: The Secret Survivors of the Holocaust*. London: Piatkus, 1993.
Michlic, Joanna. "'The War Began for Me after the War:' Jewish Children in Poland, 1945–1949." In *The Routledge History of the Holocaust*, edited by Jonathan Friedman, 482–497. London/Oxford: Routledge, 2011.
Nicholas, Lynn H. *Cruel World: The Children of Europe in the Nazi Web*. New York: Alfred A. Knopf, 2005.
Pawlikowski, John T. "Polish Catholics and the Jews during the Holocaust." In *Contested Memories: Poles and Jews During the Holocaust and Its Aftermath*, edited by Joshua D. Zimmerman, 107–123. New Brunswick: Rutgers University Press, 2003.
Stargardt, Nicholas. *Witnesses of War: Children's Lives under the Nazis*. London: Jonathan Cape, 2005.
Steinlauf, Michael C. *Bondage to the Dead: Poland and the Memory of the Holocaust*. Syracuse, NY: Syracuse University Press, 1997.
Tec, Nechama. *When Light Pierced the Darkness: Christian Rescue of Jews in Nazi-Occupied Poland*. Oxford: Oxford University Press, 1987.
Wiszniewicz, Joanna. *Życie przecięte. Opowieści pokolenia Marca* [Life Cut in Two. Stories from the March Generation]. Wołowiec: Wydawnictwo Czarne, 2009.
Witkowski, Józef. *Hitlerowski obóz koncentracyjny dla małoletnich w Łodzi* [Hitlerite Concentration Camp for Youth in Lodz]. Wrocław: Zakład Narodowy im. Ossolińskich, 1975.

 10

WAR CHILDREN IN NAZI GERMANY AND WORLD WAR II

Ilka Quindeau, Katrin Einert, and Nadine Teuber

> I would have become a Nazi if it had continued. I was so enthusiastic about it. To fight and worship heroes was valued in our society. So, I became what they wanted the young people to be, namely "quick as a flash, tough as leather and hard as steel." That's how we wanted to be.[1]

The War Child Project, now part of the Kestenberg Archive of Testimonies of Child Holocaust Survivors at the Hebrew University,[2] comprises oral histories of Germans who were children when they experienced National Socialism and World War II. Their accounts of World War II include experiences such as being bombed, experiencing hunger, and being evacuated. It is evident from their narratives that the socialization of these war children was impacted by their parents' childrearing practices and their education in accordance with National Socialist ideology. The majority of these children were raised in an authoritarian fashion with minimal consideration for their individual needs.

This chapter is based on twenty-six interviews with war children conducted from 2009 to 2012 in Frankfurt, Germany. Their wartime experiences included relationships in the family and in school, and their multigenerational relationship to National Socialism.

In the 2000s many of these war children, now elderly, suffered repercussions from the traumatic experiences of their childhood and youth. As elderly people many of them started to feel abrupt and violent reactions that they struggled to understand: sudden anxiety attacks, restlessness, and inexplicable physical symptoms. Age-related physical weakening, illness, and the need for help as well as changes such as the loss of a partner or friend or the move to a nursing home can weaken psychological defense mechanisms, and thus allow the delayed release of threatening memories of the past.

Background

Many scientific studies have been conducted in the years since the war in order to understand the painful experiences of war children and to provide them with the appropriate professional help.[3] It is the acts of war to which these children were exposed at a very young age—bombing, flight and displacement, and the loss of relatives, for example—that are viewed as the cause for their anxiety in later life. While it was previously estimated that between a third and half of the generation of war children still carry this burden of traumatization up to the present day,[4] newer epidemiological and population studies have shown significantly lower figures: around 4 percent of the older generation has been diagnosed with posttraumatic stress disorder (PTSD), with 12 percent displaying varying symptoms.[5]

Within the research conducted among war children, the impact of National Socialism has either been largely ignored or only superficially acknowledged, and it is therefore not regarded as a central factor in the current psychological state of this generation. While it is fair to assume that socialization within National Socialism left behind traces in the psychological well-being of the war children, many of their psychological problems remain in old age but are generally (mis)interpreted as a consequence of war events without addressing the specific context of National Socialism. The diagnosis of trauma and treatment of individuals who were children during World War II needs to be embedded in their sociohistorical context, as it is claimed by various trauma experts.[6] The public discourse and collective memory of the past influences the understanding of the war children's psychological challenges. War children are not a group who took an active part in war or in crimes of the National Socialists and their suffering has gained more public attention in the past ten years. Although the suffering of war children is commonly addressed and recognized today, the recent developments in discourse on children of war in National Socialist Germany is, however, not without controversy.

At the Nuremberg Rally in 1935 Hitler presented his ideas about the educational goals for German youth, ideas that were implemented in subsequent years in different educational institutes. Children and youth were to be socialized to be tough and disciplined, and to internalize the ideals of National Socialism. Some war children believe that National Socialist ideology has left noticeable traces on their personality to this very day.

Contention between persecuted victims of National Socialism, on the on hand, and nonpersecuted displaced persons, on the other, can be observed in German memory culture. The theme of war children has been regarded as a variation of German victim discourse, whereby the Germans, who were not persecuted, try to place themselves within the group of victims and thereby profoundly change German memory culture.[7] In research and public discourse this theme has been taken out of its historical context, and instead has been connected to other discourse on victims in general. The term "war children" with its inherent association of childhood innocence plays an important role in contributing to a further cover-up of the German past, especially when the focus of research is mainly on war and not on National Socialism.[8] The discourse on the war children seems especially convenient for assuaging German guilt over their National Socialist past and its consequences, but may thereby actually neglect to address the real suffering of this group of people.

David Becker, a noted German psychologist who specializes in trauma studies, criticized the current research on psychological trauma as a denial of culture. He demanded a change in theory and practice due to its disregard for sociopolitical backgrounds in the analysis of trauma.[9] Contextual differences and culturally specific dimensions must, he claims, be taken into account in understanding the war children of National Socialism and World War II. According to Becker, because trauma cannot be defined universally, it must be defined by the individual, intrapsychic, and social dimensions of each specific context. José Brunner, a leading historian at Tel Aviv University, described trauma as a social construction and suggested that trauma is not just a psychological, clinical concept, but that it also has a moral dimension.[10] The comparison of war children as victims just like Jewish Holocaust child survivors are victims without addressing individual and, more importantly, cultural differences such as the impact of persecution for Holocaust child survivors, or the role of National Socialist education in families of bystanders or National Socialist sympathizers creates moral problems. Clinical conceptualizations of trauma need continuous analysis and open discussion. The difficulties in this particular historical case lie in different and very specific cultural perspectives that need to be addressed.[11]

In this chapter we demonstrate that it was not just the recurring nights of bombings, escapes, or displacement that had a stressful and traumatic impact, but also traumatic experiences within family relationships. Childrearing during the Third Reich and the attitudes of parents toward their own children as well as the transgenerational transfer of ideology and ideals of National Socialism must therefore be regarded as important aspects in understanding (latent) suffering of the war children.

Childhood during World War II and National Socialism

Research on war children began as early as 1941, when Anna Freud and Dorothy Burlingham studied children who were evacuated from the inner city of wartime London and placed in the children's homes of Hampstead Nurseries. The children had suffered experiences such as air raids, nights in bomb shelters, and separation from their fathers. They arrived either accompanied by their mothers or alone. Freud and Burlingham discovered that children who had arrived with their mothers could cope much better with their wartime experiences than those who were separated from their mothers during evacuation. The ability of the mothers to manage their own fears as well as the fears of their children and to provide stability in the face of the external threat has been found to be an important resilience factor.[12] For decades after the liberation there was no systematic research on the long-term effects of World War II on German war children. Since the late 1980s, however, studies have focused on the psychological consequences for the descendants of National Socialist (or Nazi) perpetrators.[13] Some of these studies addressed the strong sense of loyalty toward the Nazi perpetrators and followers, transgenerational transfer of guilt, feelings of shame, identification with Nazi ideals and anti-Semitism, and narcissistic bonds within the family. Even after 1945 the rationale of National Socialist ideology was still present in German families and influenced relationships between parents and children. As Werner Bohleber described, "The dynamic of hate and debasement raged frequently within the family."[14] He continued, "Own weaknesses and failures, gnawing doubt and feelings of guilt were projected onto the child, deposited there and despised."[15] Parents thus misused their children in order to maintain a narcissistic balance. Out of loyalty to their parents, the children unconsciously (and unwillingly) adhered to National Socialist ideals of greatness and power. In the current German research discourse, studies on war children are, however, not linked to former research on children of Nazi perpetrators, which were mostly conducted in the 1990s. It is possible to regard this as a process of an unconscious split. Over the past ten years, the long-term effects of direct encounters with war during childhood have been examined intensively. Violence, separation, and loss of an important attachment person, as well as flight and displacement, have been emphasized as traumatic experiences that result in vulnerability to psychological damage, anxiety, depression, somatoform disorders, interpersonal conflict, and PTSD, among other.[16] However, effects of traumatic experiences can be mitigated by a stable and secure mother–child relationship, presence of a large family, or an important substitute person to help cope with the loss of a father. In a study that examined trauma after the great fire in Hamburg, differences in coping style were also found between men and women. The Hamburg Firestorm Project revealed that women were three times more likely to report depression as a result of experiences of aerial warfare. In addition, women were more likely to address negative impact on their well-being, family relationships, career choices, and sexuality.[17]

Education during National Socialism

The meaning of National Socialist education has until recently played only a small role in the research of war children. From 1933 to 1945 Nazi education was aimed as a "total education."[18] It aimed to cover all areas of children's lives: preschool, school, and extracurricular activities.

This authoritarian form of education has its roots in the nineteenth century and was further developed according to the maxims of Nazi ideology. A central role was played by the guidebooks for mothers—*Die deutsche Mutter und ihr erstes Kind* (The German mother and her first child)[19]—that was first published in 1934 and describes how a child from birth onward should be raised and educated to become an "obedient" person.[20] The books were closely related to National Socialist ideology and were the main guidelines for education during this time. They were widely distributed in the Nazis' "mother schooling courses" in which a fifth of all women over the age of twenty had participated by 1937.[21] By 1943 as many as 3 million young women had participated. Even as late as the 1970s, different editions of the book were still present in almost every household in Germany.[22] The main features of the educational ideals were discipline, submission, and hygiene. Any empathy toward children was regarded as weakness. When the child cried and a pacifier failed to soothe, women were instructed, "Then, dear mother, become hard! Don't take the child out of the bed, to carry it, to hold it on your lap or even breast-feed it."[23] Crying and screaming children were to be "neutralized" and taken into another room.

After infancy the main aim and content of education consisted of absolute obedience, discipline, and the willingness to make sacrifices. Children were "specifically encouraged to take part in competitions, to march and to act out scenes of war."[24] A nursery school at the time described it this way: "One can already see that Rolf is a born leader. He marches along the front line like a captain. . . . Now they are no longer playing at soldiers, they are soldiers. . . . The activities are good . . . because they give the child insight on war at the front line and at home."[25] The focus of education was on physical training, through the encouragement of "breeding of healthy bodies . . . determination, motivation and aggression and the 'ability to cope with trials and tribulations.'"[26]

Teaching of the *Führerkult* (leader cult) differed in each nursery. Besides images on walls, there were picture books, stories, verses, and prayers that were used to instill an emotional bond with Hitler. Racist and anti-Semitic education played a central role. Children were indoctrinated with the *Blut und Boden* (blood and soil) ideology and to hate everything foreign and non-German and, in particular, to hate Jews. This intensified with the outbreak of World War II. Children were prepared for war with games, songs, and picture books that glorified warfare and played down the dangers of war.

Gender education during National Socialism was based on the portrayal of men as fighters and women as mothers: "How lovingly little Gretchen looks after her doll children at home. Meanwhile little Hänschen is sneaking up on a sparrow sitting in front of the door in order to kill it with a stone. Here the future defender of the homeland, there the future loving housewife."[27]

Method

Between 2009 and 2012 video interviews were conducted with twenty-four German adults (twelve women and twelve men) who were born between 1930 and 1945 and had experienced National Socialism and World War II as children. The first session consisted of an open nonstructured narrative interview format in which the interviewees were invited to address their personal war experiences and biography. The second interview was conducted in a semistructured format and focused specifically on family relations because the first interviews revealed confusing and often horrifying reports of how some parents treated their children. In addition, after each interview the interviewer was asked to record his or her own impressions and feelings about the interview.

In the interviews the war children recalled their experiences as children and adolescents during National Socialism and how they coped with these experiences in later life, until the present day.[28] On the basis of these narratives, the following questions were addressed: How did National Socialist education and the war get weaved into their stories of childhood? What is the individual meaning of war for their personal life story? Which physical, psychological, and social damages have they experienced? In which contexts—family, social, or cultural—did these experiences occur? The identified hypotheses addressed the aftereffects of early traumatization during war and National Socialism. Coping styles and factors of resilience were also taken into account. In a process of expert-validation, a panel of experienced trauma experts and psychotherapists discussed the hypotheses on the experiences of the war children and their long-term consequences.[29] Additional data were collected in a sample of 103 people who were born between 1930 and 1945 and who describe themselves as war children.[30] This sample answered standardized clinical questionnaires concerning war experiences, family relationships and their psychological adaptation.[31]

Interviews

Most interviewees contacted the project after reading a small newspaper article about the war children interview project. They were highly motivated to participate in the interviews and could be characterized by high reliability, punctuality, and commitment. Due to the confusing and sometimes terrifying reports in the first interviews of how adults—specifically how the parents had treated the children—it was decided to conduct a second interview session with each interviewee. Besides narratives of war experiences, the reports of severe punishment and generally stressful incidents in family relationships were recounted in a casual manner.

KH Interview

KH was born in Germany in 1937 and raised in the countryside near a large town as the only child of an affluent family.[32] Her father was a self-employed master craftsman who initially resisted taking part in the war, but after 1942 repaired vehicles for the German army in Russia. According to KH, he was not involved in fighting. After returning home from a three-month period in a French war prison, he quickly found work and became successful in his job. Her mother worked in a creative profession, which she gave up after the war. KH herself was awarded a degree from a technical college, and later she also became an artist and won recognition for her work at home and abroad. She is now retired but still works as an artist. She lives on her own, having been divorced twice, and has children and grandchildren. She describes her relationships with her children as difficult and strained.

KH contacted us by telephone after reading the newspaper article about the war children interview project. Even at first contact on the telephone she was eager to talk and gave a full account of her father. She arrived at the interview a few minutes early. She appeared eager and interested in participating. In the applied questionnaire, KH described her wartime experiences as traumatic. The war and postwar period had affected her childhood and youth. From 1944 until 1945 she was evacuated with her mother and grandmother. She recalls suffering hunger and poverty from 1943 to 1945, stressing repeatedly that she should not have had to go hungry. She was never able to talk to her parents about her experiences during wartime; in the questionnaire she stated that the atrocities committed by the Nazis were never discussed in her family. She did not respond to questions regarding her parents' possible membership in the National Socialist Party.

She started the interview by describing in detail the countryside and surroundings of her childhood—the beautiful garden, the pond behind the house: "I had a beautiful childhood," she states in her first sentence. She commences with a lively narrative about her father, his many talents, and his professional success. But after he was drafted into the army "everything became worse." The idealized father from the beginning of the interview changes with the ongoing narrative. Later on in the interview she mentions that she had never been "particularly proud" of her father's occupation and that he in turn would have preferred to have a son but was "satisfied" with her.

After a time KH talks about her relationship with her mother. While her mother cared for her daughter's physical needs, she never had time for her and was barely there for her emotionally, sometimes even displaying callousness toward her. KH describes both of her parents as very strict; they punished her severely, both physically and emotionally, and rarely showed affection. KH is ambivalent about having been a very curious, bright, and lively child. On the one hand, she seems to be proud of it, but on the other it was these characteristics that often led to her parents punishing her harshly. For example, when she refused to do as she was told, she was sent to bed at lunchtime without food until the following day. She indirectly defends her mother by letting the interviewer know that she had been a very headstrong child.

For the most part KH presents idyllic memories of childhood. When asked about siblings, she does not respond directly to the question. Instead, she shares an experience of baking bread with her grandmother in the winter. Later in the interview, however, KH comes back to the question of siblings and recalls her pregnant mother climbing onto the roof to repair it after an air raid and losing the baby after she fell. Her mother suffered because of this, she remembers, but never spoke about it. She simply told KH that the baby would not be coming and had to die. KH describes her own sadness and to this very day bemoans not having a brother or sister. KH recalls her eagerness to forge new friendships after learning about the miscarriage. Understanding this loss explains the loneliness and defenselessness, which echoed throughout the entire interview.

During the interview KH regularly stresses that her mother "never had time for her"—she uses this to indirectly explain her own career choices: "My mother had very little time. . . . By the way, I'm an artist. . . . People are creative in times of trouble." She describes various episodes in which she felt abandoned or unprotected by her mother: "For example I can remember that every month my mother aired the bedding. At that time we only had feather bedding and nothing else and they had to be aired and there was a bomb alert and she was taking in the bedding and I stood there with my teddy bear and screamed loudly, full of despair and cried while calling— "My Daddy should come! My Daddy should come!"—and she remained busy with the bedding and I was alone—I felt terribly alone." KH had hoped for protection from her absent father as her mother was physically and emotionally unavailable. She casually talks about how her mother once lost her after she had fallen off the luggage rack of her mother's bicycle: "Yes and I was tired because I mean, one was just a child, and I was tired and as I said I fell off the bicycle and she didn't even notice—then she was—yes, that's how she lost me and thank God nothing happened to me but still to fall from a bicycle, that's high, isn't it? And when as a child you fall asleep and fall off it that isn't very nice. She didn't . . . notice anything at all."

In an effort to defend her mother, she adds that her mother was overburdened. Due to her middle-class background her mother always tried to maintain a sense of normality in which everything was perfect, even during the war. Some anger can be heard when KH recalls that she had always had time for the complex embroidering of clothes and doilies: "She still managed to do that." However, she had no time for her daughter. KH recounts another difficult episode: "If I tell you this, I don't know if I can. I really will tell you now—yes—I have to continue talking about the war—anyway after the end of the war we didn't know which zone we would end up in and my mother, yes, she had a terrible fear of the Russians, even though my father . . . and we had a bridge over the river and one Sunday she went with . . . she went with me onto the bridge and said: 'And we'll jump in if the Russians come!' because . . . and then I held her hand and asked . . . said: 'Yes Mummy and what will Daddy say to that?' . . . I was terribly afraid." At this point the interviewer asks if she was actually able to swim at this age, and KH explains that she was not supposed to swim but to die; her mother had wanted to kill herself and her daughter by jumping into the water. The initial reaction of the interviewer, who identified with the frightened child who cannot understand her mother's plan, is dismay and anger.[33] After seeing the interviewer's horrified reaction, KH added, "And I thought it was awful, too. And I have to say that when I grew up it was an experience which actually . . . but we haven't spoken about that. . . . I never felt safe with my mother, I still remember that."

It seems that the recognition of her feelings as a child through the eyes of someone else (i.e., the interviewer) enables in KH this emphatic perspective on her situation. Only then does she feel justified in thinking and feeling this way. Following her description of this terrible scene, KH tries once again to justify her mother's actions, asserting that her mother was "an amazing woman."[34] This positive description of her mother, however, is only expressed in a single scene in the entire interview. KH recounts an episode one Christmas when her mother hid sweets for her. She ends the story with the sentence, "Yes, everyone tried to make an effort," bringing the account into perspective. Her emphasis on how "amazing" her mother was seems to be an effort to convince not only the interviewer but also herself. She describes how as a child she came to the conclusion that her mother did not really love her. Nevertheless, she narrates at the end of the interview how she and her mother had a "reconciliation" later on her mother's sickbed before she died. KH concludes that she actually had "a fantastic mother who cared for her and her family." Her desire for a reconciliation of the conflicting images of her mother and the loyalty to her seem to drive this harmonizing perspective at the end of the interview. In the end, she seems to have been able to overcome the contradictions between the "fantastic" and the cold, chastising mother that emerged during the interview. But at the same time she recalls that she could have never talked about her difficult experiences with her mother and their problematic relationship: "I had a lot of time to say goodbye to her strangely enough, then, therefore . . . before she died and . . . we didn't talk about that and I didn't want to make life more difficult for her—yes, I didn't want that.—But it was like this, I don't know if my mother could have fathomed certain things.—I believe . . . no, because my mother was always withdrawn and then she just never responded in a conversation." KH herself does not always respond to questions, but she does not withdraw herself. Instead she charges on at a fast pace and thereby makes it hard for the interviewer to ask questions that could help clarification. KH talks quickly and excessively and long over the allotted time. Her sentences are complicated, and she jumps from one theme to the next, which she herself eventually notices and comments on, and she frequently loses her train of thought. This was described by the interviewer as having a hypnotic effect,[35] making it difficult for the interviewer to concentrate and keep track of the interview. The interviewer can hardly get a word in and later reports feeling "overwhelmed" and "beaten to death." When KH talks about what individual family members "did during the war" and where they were at different times, she becomes vague and her language is often incomprehensible, such as when she discusses her grandfather and his high position in a war-related business. There is no chance in this interview, in contrast to other interviews, for the interviewer to pursue questions regarding her awareness of Nazi atrocities, the possible involvement of her family, and her coping mechanisms. When such questions do arise, the interviewer is reluctant to persist for fear of triggering an angry reaction. In her briefing after the interview, the interviewer discussed her own feelings of guilt as if she had pushed the interviewee or tried to break through her wall of defense. The interviewee is in her eighties and the interviewer a young woman in her thirties. A common reaction between the generations is, "You cannot possibly understand. You weren't there." This sentence serves as one of the most common excuses in postwar Germany to interrupt a conversation about the war and National Socialism. The interviewer noticed a difference in the way KH talks about her war experiences as opposed to her family relations: When she speaks of the war, her language is well-structured and easy to understand but lacks emotion. When, however, she speaks of her parents, her language is disjointed, halting, and confused. The interviewer reported the impression that this was the first time that KH really confronted her ambivalence toward her mother, while she had clearly talked about her war experiences before.

KH emphasizes several times during the interview that she is very different from her mother. This differentiation appears to be important for KH. She does admit at one point, however, that she, like her mother, had raised her own children strictly and that they in turn had also resented her for this. During the interview it often happened that roles became confused between KH's mother and herself, or between KH as a mother and KH as a daughter, and also between KH and her own daughter. It is not always clear who she is addressing.

To this day, it is obviously painful for KH to admit to the insult and injury caused by her mother. Feelings of guilt immediately set in that suppress the anger and sadness and lead her to make attempts to compensate. On a rational level, she tries to recognize her mother's accomplishments, but cannot fully achieve this due to her unconscious negative feelings and thus, likewise, she cannot achieve her desired reconciliation with her mother. In the course of the interview KH tries to overcome all of the terrible experiences by conveying a harmonious picture of her childhood, but during the process this idyll develops more and more cracks that she then tries to patch up. Her feelings of loneliness and defenselessness recur throughout the narrative. She draws a picture of a mother who does not emphatically perceive or show interest in the needs of her child.

The idea of suicide in perpetrator families at the end of the war is not uncommon. The literature on the children of Nazi perpetrators has described the phenomenon of extended suicide. Müller-Hohagen reported a similar case of a child with a "fear of being murdered by his own mother when 'the Russians' come."[36] Similarly, Bar-On described a case in which a boy overheard his father telling his mother that he may kill himself and the family if the war is lost and the mother convincing him to let the children live. For years afterward the son was plagued by fears that his mother wanted to poison him, and he thus refused to eat at home. Even in boarding school, he was not freed from these fears.[37] The reasons why the mother wanted to kill herself and her child are less important in this case; what is more significant is how the child perceives the mother's desire for murder-suicide. As demonstrated in trauma research, when the threat comes from a beloved parent on whom the child is dependent for protection, the results are extremely dramatic. The child's perception of safety is fundamentally shattered. (It may be even more dramatic when the threat comes in the form of protection, and the child has no way to express shock and insecurity.) This can lead to feelings of guilt in children as well as the delusion that by "being good" they can preserve the bond with the parents.[38] Such efforts to be obedient and to be all things to all people can be clearly identified in KH.

The interview with KH supports the hypothesis that the relationship to close others—who is in most cases the mother—strongly influences and interacts with the perception, coping, and impact of traumatic war experiences in children.

EK Interview

Unlike KH, EK exemplifies growing up in a more loving and cohesive family. She grew up as an only child and lived during the war with her mother and grandparents in a house in the city.[39] At a certain point, she was evacuated to the surrounding area to avoid the continuous bombings in the city. Her mother struggled to get by with temporary jobs, repeatedly looking for new places of work in order to provide for her daughter's needs. Her father, who was a tradesman, was drafted into the army late in 1942 and spent some time in France as a prisoner of war. He returned home suffering from malaria when EK was seven years old. EK reports that, due to lucky external circumstances, her father was hardly involved in the war. Despite a mention in her preinterview questionnaire, during the interview EK does not comment on his National Socialist membership. EK describes her relationship with her mother as very good despite the external hardship. In fact, she connects her mother's present living situation to her reason for getting involved in the war children project. Her mother lives in a nursing home and EK would like to get more involved in the treatment of residents "who experienced the war." She wants to talk about their experiences and enable a better understanding of their burdens. Her son and daughter-in-law are currently living with her after returning from living abroad, and she describes a good and rewarding relationship with them.

On being asked about her first childhood memory, she first recalls a scene in a bomb shelter when she was two and a half years old. Due to the continual air raids, her street had been completely destroyed with only her house spared:

> Yes, that was actually the time in which I would be carried off to the bomb shelter by my family. Back then my family was my grandfather who never went with us into the cellar. He could always be found up on the roof trying to gather up the bombs. And there we all sat, all of the older ladies, just there. From the house, that was a house with five, six tenants and we sat close to each other and on the floor there was wooden grating and we had put up chairs. It was dark and you had to go down a sinister sandstone staircase. I still remember that my mother had a beautiful fox fur, which she put around my head and somehow took me up in her arms. And then we sat there. Such a small child, how old would I have been, two, two and a half, I think. We sat there and the time was endlessly long and a child looks at everything and I could still describe the room today and the people in it. . . . Yes they were with me a long time and nothing happened. But, hmm . . . I remember the time in the cellar that was somehow I wouldn't say fearful, I was protected and guarded by my mother, but a child senses the situation and the fear of the people and they always reacted if any kinds of noise became louder. That was actually my earliest memory. . . . I was safe, but I noticed something in the faces of the other people around me. And a child sits there and notices things but doesn't know what to make of them.

Even though she vividly describes a child's inability to understand the frightened faces of the adults, the interviewer is presented with a picture of closeness and protection conveyed through the soft fox fur in which the mother protectively wrapped the child (EK) in the cellar. The protective fur, seen by the interviewer as a transitional object, symbolizes the mother's efforts to shield her daughter from the cold, the terrors of the war, and the danger of the cellar. Likewise, EK gives the interviewer the impression that despite the terrible situation, she never felt alone or overwhelmed. EK has kept the fox fur to this day. She shows the interviewer a childhood photograph. Her mother is dressed for a Sunday stroll and is pushing her young daughter in a pram. The fur is wrapped around the mother's neck.

In another recollection, EK describes a traumatic incident in which a shockwave caused by a bombing hits her apartment, and her mother and grandparents cannot find her:

> The door was open and I was pulled by the suction across the hall of the stairwell and I sat at the door of the neighbor's apartment and didn't say a word. That's why I couldn't be found. After they discovered me I had lost my speech and couldn't speak anymore. My mother was very worried and brought me to the doctor. And the doctor, who was very sensible, told her to leave the child in peace and that it was an unusual experience for a child and that it was caused by shock and the ability to speak would return through another unusual emotional experience, maybe through a happy experience. And that happened half a year later. My father came back from the war on home leave and then I saw him and started to babble dadadadada. And after that happened, my father made sure that we were—that was after 1943—evacuated, then we were all together in a small town in the surrounding countryside.

EK describes this highly traumatic scene in her own way. The small child's fear and loss of speech are clearly dramatic consequences as the girl, whose language is just beginning to develop, regresses to an earlier stage of development. However, EK emphasizes the people who helped and calmed her, and reassures the interviewer, who reacts with worry, that such a response was not abnormal in light of the traumatic experience and that her mother, father, and the doctor were reassuring and tried to help her to cope with the traumatic event of the bombing, as well as to protect her from future harm by moving to the countryside together.

It is after this incident that EK and her mother move to her aunt's house in the countryside. EK recalls that her mother had to do heavy physical work, which meant she had little time to look after her daughter. EK's mother took charge and organized an apartment for herself and her child. Neighbors looked after EK, while her mother found employment in a medical facility and on a nearby farm, which led to improved food supplies. She describes a subsequent move to a small house with a "beautiful garden with cats and kittens." In order to heat this house in the winter, her mother and a friend went into the nearby forest during the night to cut down small trees for firewood: "And in one of these nights I woke up and left the apartment in my nightdress in winter to look for my mother and I went for a walk in the forest. I knew where she was and I shouted and somewhere she heard me and from then on her friend's sister looked after me when the women had to go into the forest at night, someone was always there. . . . She always tried to bring me somewhere where I would be looked after." Despite difficult moments of loneliness and fear, EK felt always surrounded by adults who responded to her fears. In the midst of horrific war-related events and hardship, EK describes the evacuation with her mother as "a carefree childhood," a time when she could "play barefoot, without shoes," with "no cars driving by," and as a time when, using her courage and stamina, she could assert herself against the boys in the neighborhood and was eventually allowed to play football with them. She recalls a generous neighbor making ice cream and giving it to all the children. EK has positive recollections of the neighbors as helpful people: "Everyone knew each other, the neighbor was someone you had to look out for, was he doing well or badly, could you help him."

Thus, apart from the dangers of the war, the hunger and "being left to her own devices," it is apparent that EK experienced her surroundings as secure and protective. Not only her mother and grandparents but also the neighbors were eager to help. She interprets her mother's and her own resourcefulness as successful and sees herself and those around as being capable of survival. This narrative depicts a clear picture of positive coexistence within the family leading to a strong sense of self-efficacy in the child.

Results

The interviews with war children revealed that when children grew up during the Third Reich they were affected not only by experiences of war, but also by socialization that was steeped in the ideology of National Socialism.

Most of the war children reported being subjected to severe physical punishments. Difficult parental relationships were expressed in almost all of the interviews. It was, however, surprising how often these scenes were described in a casual way. The interviewer was often confused and shocked, while the interviewee seemed to display little discomfort.

It can be assumed that this form of distant narrative was an attempt to cope with these negative experiences and thus separate and alienate them from personal meaning. The warm, loving, and protecting parenting exemplified by EK's upbringing was the exception rather than the norm.

Through the interview process a developing connection was found between the experiences of war and the severity of parental adherence to Nazi educational values. The war children who suffered physical punishment at the hands of detached, unsympathetic parents with rigid rules and unquestionable obedience to authority tended to exhibit more-severe PTSD symptoms than war children whose parents were less committed to Nazi education. The interview process itself revealed that memories of bombings or other acts of war often served as "screen memories,"[40] meaning memories that act as substitutes for underlying suppressed pain. It may be easier, for example, to talk about the external horrors of war and incidents that occurred to others rather than about the individual cruelty within one's own family. War children were often not properly protected and cared for by their parents. But these children, now elderly, do not perceive this as neglect or maltreatment. Therefore, they do not contemplate this treatment as the cause of their suffering and blame it on the war instead.

The chronological sequences of the narratives illustrate the desire of the interviewees to show their parents as good people. Many interviews thus began with the portrayal of a harmonious childhood. However, toward the end of the interviews the interviewees expressed a chain of traumatic experiences. Often the stories of war were woven together with memories of negative relationships with parents or other caregivers and teachers. In the interviews a careful step-by-step approach toward the traumatic painful memories was facilitated through the understanding of the underlying meaning of the screen memories. It is very painful psychologically to connect a representation of loving parents with memories of incidents in which the child feels threatened, hurt, or betrayed by those same parents. In order to leave a child's world intact for the sake of a harmonious relationship with the caregivers, the most oppressive scenes are distanced from their consciousness and replaced by images of "good" parents. This often happens at the expense of recognizing one's own vulnerability and disappointment, which can cause lifelong psychological stress. Therefore, these memories of the caregivers need to be analyzed in connection with the child's war experiences.

The internal feeling of not being protected by the adults may influence the descriptions of war experiences, such as bombings and escape.

While external stressors may, on their own, have been traumatizing for children during the period of National Socialism, these also interact with interpersonal relationship stressors such as parental educational styles. Thus, children who grew up in a protective and loving environment perceive the war as less threatening and cope better, expressing fewer problems in facing their memories of war later in life. It became apparent through the interviews that terror attributed to the war as an external event may actually have been connected to parental behavior and thus become a lifelong trauma. Even if parents' actions during National Socialism and World War II may be retroactively understood in light of the need to adapt to the system, the excessive demands and problems of a state of war, personal anxieties, and fears, the child's experiences during that time nonetheless affect their adaptive development. In addition, most war children could never speak to their parents about their painful experiences either during or after the war.

There are different forms of identification with National Socialist ideology. Due to the young age of the interviewees at the time of National Socialism most of these identifications do not stem from cognitive political beliefs but instead can be regarded as an unconscious adherence to greatness and power, the subliminal illusion of belonging to the superior master race. Through an early identification process this became an integral part of the person rather than the ideological structure in the older generation. This can be seen in the interview with WE, born in 1932, who recalls a scene from 1942:[41]

> Then of course this worshiping of uniforms! I knew all the ranks inside out and I was just ten years old. From the *Bannführer* [paramilitary rank of the Hitler Youth] to . . . I would have been a Nazi. Yes, that was also, I mean, also the parades and the Hitler marches. Yes, that was so sparkling for all of us and then those, there were so formative for me, those *Musikfähnleinzüge* [marching band with swastika flags], and when they appeared, with traras and drums and when they joined the parades, first flag in the front, then another flag, then the second and in the end another one, that's how we marched through town. That really was something! So, not just the uniforms, that we were all wearing, also the music, that they were playing. Yes. I would have been a Nazi.

The illusions of being superior serve as introjections—feelings or convictions that are unconsciously incorporated into the self—and are a part of the unconscious memory. Through a psychological splitting mechanism, the introjections are no longer experienced by the person but exist in isolation from other psychological dynamics. They remained unconscious after 1945 and were thus not accessible to any developments or changes. The splitting mechanism serves as a psychological defense to alleviate guilt, anger, or shame toward one's parents or oneself. In old age this psychological defense organization wanes. Through changes in personal history, such as the death of a parent or the end of an occupation, the defense is weakened and painful feelings emerge from the unconscious. Current losses intensify past traumas and increase painful feelings rather than keep such emotions at bay. The illusion of superiority is confronted with the reality of old age. The perceived changes of old age bring new problems for this generation that has been trained to hold weakness in contempt. This confrontation, with its traces of National Socialist ideology buried within the self, leads to violent, defensive reactions and to an almost unbearable sense of shame. The fantasies of greatness turn into the fear of being a "nobody."

The interviews reveal that when elderly war children feel vulnerable, they unconsciously identify with the victims of the Third Reich who were considered *Lebensunwertes Leben* (life unworthy of life)—the physically deformed, mentally challenged, and emotionally disturbed. The interviewees often demonstrated, as a defense mechanism, a harshness against themselves combined with a contempt for weakness. In this context the deep scars left by the parental relationship, which have led to a cumulative traumatic debasement, is accompanied by a sense of shame and a belief by the war children that they should not get help but must cope alone, even in cases of illness and age-related impairment.

Individual experiences, suffered not only within the family but also in nursery and elementary school, may have also had an abusive character. Feelings of inadequacy, as well as a sense of guilt and shame, play a huge part in the self-perception of this generation. While it is often assumed that these feelings are connected with National Socialist atrocities, they can also be explained psychologically in terms of these narcissistic fantasies of greatness and power that had to be repressed after the collapse and failure of National Socialism in 1945.

Our interviews reveal that there were rarely discussions in the families about their personal participation in the criminal regime or their choice to be bystanders. The nationwide denial, however, was not related only to the Holocaust, but also to the personal fascination with and enthusiasm for National Socialism,[42] a phenomenon that is evident in the interview with WE.

An interesting difference emerges in how men and women relate to their National Socialist past. Some of the men interviewed were able to live out their fantasies of power during their working life but on retirement suffered more than women did. Ambivalence notwithstanding, women often have a closer relationship with their mothers, which can impede individuation, even in old age. In terms of attachment theory, this characteristic of an ambivalent bonding derives from a rigid National Socialist upbringing. In an effort to compensate, women often feel a need to care exhaustively for their elderly mothers and fear that they can never do enough for them. This was particularly apparent in the interview with KH.

Conclusion

In recording the history and psychology of war children, two dimensions coexist. The war experiences of the children were interwoven with the socialization they were subjected to by their parents, caregivers, teachers, and social groups. Unfortunately, until recently research and public discourse has reproduced the same splitting mechanisms used by war children as resistance to the experiences of painful relationships. Their experiences with National Socialism and especially with the often brutal educational methods of parents are mostly separated and their meaning only revealed by addressing the interpersonal relationships. For war children it is important to conduct this confrontation in a protected setting without exceeding the individual processing capacity. However, if only external war experiences are focused on in the interviews, as has happened in many studies in this field, the denial and misinterpretation of history is perpetuated.

A social platform needs to be created where children of National Socialist perpetrators and bystanders can verbalize their painful relationships along with the suffering caused by the war. This is also relevant when looking at the transgenerational transmission. The psychological consequences of the war have affected the war children as individuals, as well as in their interpersonal relationships. In addition, early internalized and unconscious fragments of National Socialist ideology—power, superiority, strength, and a lack of empathy—may create narcissistic wounds and feelings of shame and guilt that can also affect the ensuing generations and must be addressed individually as well as societally.

In relation to European and German cultural memory and the history of politics, the sociohistorical contextualization is of great importance. While discourse on war children is possible without reference to National Socialism, contextual embedding is necessary in order to differentiate between the effects of National Socialism and World War II on completely different groups of people. If trauma is observed as a purely clinical category, as often happens in the literature,[43] then the fundamental differences between the Jewish child survivors who were persecuted by the National Socialists and the war children who were not persecuted cannot be conceptualized. With regards to their experiences of trauma and their coping mechanisms, these are two completely different groups. If the focus is primarily on the common aspects of different groups of war children, then the process ignores specific sensitivities of the subjects, obscures existing differences, and impedes an adequate positioning and recognition within the sociocultural context.

This study of war children under National Socialism and World War II can serve as a basis for studies of war children elsewhere when accompanied by the individual, cultural, and historical contexts.

Authors

Ilka Quindeau is full professor of clinical psychology and psychoanalysis at the University of Applied Sciences, Frankfurt, and associate professor at Goethe University, Frankfurt. She is president of the Sigmund Freud Foundation and is a psychoanalyst in private practice. She is, in addition, a training and supervising analyst at the German Psychoanalytical Society (IPA). Her research interests include studies on memory, trauma, and sexuality. She is the author of a number of titles, including *Seduction and Desire: The Psychoanalytic Theory of Sexuality Since Freud* (Karnac Books, 2013). She is currently working on a book to be titled *Traumatization in Older Age: Psychic Aftermath of War and Persecution in Early Childhood*.

Katrin Einert was an academic researcher in the SILQUA-FH project Trauma in Old Age. She was the recipient of a dissertation scholarship from the Ernst-Ludwig-Ehrlich Foundation. Her research interests include National Socialist education and upbringing, transgenerational transmission in the families of Nazi perpetrators and bystanders, and trauma.

Nadine Teuber is a psychoanalyst at the German Psychoanalytical Society (IPA) and lecturer in the faculty of psychoanalysis at Goethe University, Frankfurt. She worked as an academic researcher in the SILQUA-FH Project Trauma in Old Age. Her research interests include gender, depression, and trauma. She is a member of an interdisciplinary research group on trauma, transgenerational transmission, and anti-Semitism at the Sigmund-Freud-Institut, Frankfurt.

Notes

1. Testimony of WE, (257) 50-1.
2. All interviews quoted in this chapter are to be held at the Oral History Division, Hebrew University of Jerusalem.
3. Schulz, Radebold, and Reulecke, *Söhne ohne Väter*; Lamparter, Holstein, Apel, Thießen, Wierling, Möller, and Wiegand-Grefe, "Die familiäre Weitergabe"; Glaesmer and Brähler, "Die Langzeitfolgen."
4. Radebold, *Kindheiten im Zweiten Weltkrieg*.
5. Glaesmer and Brähler," Die Langzeitfolgen," 347; Glaesmer, Gunzelmann, Brähler, Forstmeier, and Maercker, "Traumatic Experiences."
6. Becker, *Die Erfindung des Traumas*; Brunner, "Die Politik der Traumatisierung"; Fischer and Riedesser, *Lehrbuch der Psychotraumatologie*.
7. Klundt, Salzborn, Schwietring, and Wiegel, *Erinnern, verdrängen, vergessen*, 17ff.
8. Kötscher, "Verdeckte Spuren deutscher Geschichte."
9. Becker, *Die Erfindung des Traumas*. Becker's goal is to include a postcolonial perspective in concepts of trauma.
10. Brunner, "Die Politik der Traumatisierung."
11. Becker, *Die Erfindung des Traumas*, 177ff.
12. Freud and Burlingham, *War and Children*.
13. Bar-On and Schmidt, *Die Last des Schweigens*; Bergmann, *Kinder der Opfer*; Müller-Hohagen, *Geschichte in uns.*; Rosenthal, *Der Holocaust im Leben*.
14. Bohleber, "Das Fortwirken des Nationalsozialismus," 78, author's translation.
15. Bohleber, "Transgenerationelles Trauma," 261, author's translation.
16. Radebold, "Während des Alterns."
17. Lamparter, Holstein, Thießen, Wierling, Wiegand-Grefe, and Möller, "65 Jahre später."
18. Keim, *Erziehung unter der Nazi-Diktatur*. The claim of total education has fortunately not been completely implemented. Evidently, not every child was raised according to these guidelines, and there were also differences in educational practices. Due to the young age of our interviewees we focused on education in early childhood and primary schooling. Organizations like Hitler Youth or League of German Girls barely played a role for this age group but probably served as an example for these younger children.
19. Haarer, *Die deutsche Mutter*.
20. Later Haarer also published *Unsere kleinen Kinder* and *"Mutter, erzähl' von Adolf Hitler!"*
21. Klinsiek, *Die Frau im NS-Staat*.
22. Dill, *Nationalsozialistische Säuglingspflege*.
23. Haarer, *Die deutsche Mutter*, 158, author's translation.
24. Berger, "Heil Hitler Dir!," author's translation.
25. From the trade journal *Kindergarten* ("Deutscher Volksverlag," 83, author's translation).
26. Ibid.
27. R. Benzing 1941, quoted in Konrad, *Der Kindergarten*, 169, author's translation.
28. Straub, *Historisch-psychologische Biographieforschung*; Quindeau, *Trauma und Geschichte*.

29. We would like to thank the psychotherapists of the expert panel for their validation: Janine Cunea; Kurt Grünberg, PhD; Christiane Lüders, PhD; and Dr. med. Friedrich Markert.
30. The number of self-ratings at having experienced a traumatic event both during the war and postwar was remarkable. Fifty-six (54.4%) people reported having experienced a traumatic experience themselves, whereas thirty-two (31.1%) reported no personal traumatic experience. Sixty-two (60.2%) reported having suffered deprivation (hunger, cold, poverty) and seventy-three (70.9%) reported the absence of their father. Only nineteen (18.4%) subjects described no experience of a lengthy paternal absence. A further noteworthy result was the limited willingness to answer questionnaire categories that addressed involvement of the family in National Socialism. Although twenty-five (24.3%) people answered that their mothers or fathers had been members of a National Socialist organization, fifty-six reported no association and twenty-two (21.4%) gave no information at all (no other category in the questionnaire had such a high rate of omitted answers). The statistical analysis is not fully completed.
31. Schlesinger-Kipp, *Kindheit im Krieg.*
32. Testimony of KH, (257) 50-2.
33. Probably the most well-known in a series of such murder-suicide incidents is the Goebbels family who killed themselves and their children on May 1, 1945. Magda Goebbels justified this to her oldest son as follows: "Our wonderful idea is perishing and all that goes with it, all that I have known in my life that is beautiful and admirable. The world that comes after the leader and National Socialism is not worth living in and that's why I have also taken the children with me. . . . The children are wonderful, they never complain or cry. . . . We only have one goal: Loyalty to the leader up until death. Be proud of us" (Fest, *Der Untergang,* 169).
34. Marks states that the derealization, in addition to the coldness and idealization, was part of the National Socialist objectives that had an effect on the upbringing of children. In interviews this often led to a clash between the different "worlds of emotion" of the interviewees and the interviewers (Marks, *Warum folgen,* 140ff).
35. A "profusion of verbalization," complicated sentences, talking "nineteen to the dozen," and vague terminology have, according to Marks, a hypnotic effect on the listener. Some interviewees spoke with childlike voices and language, and some even gushed like small children (Marks, *Warum folgen,* 49).
36. Müller-Hohagen, *Geschichte in uns,* 171.
37. Bar-On, "Aus dem gebrochenen Schweigen," 298.
38. Riedesser, Schulte-Markwort, and Walter, "Entwicklungspsychologische und psychodynamische," 19f.
39. Testimony of EK, (257) 50-3
40. Freud, *Standard Edition of the Complete Psychological Works* 299–322.
41. Testimony of WE, (257) 50-1.
42. Mitscherlich and Mitscherlich, *Die Unfähigkeit zu trauern.*
43. See Becker, *Die Erfindung des Traumas.*

References

Bar-On, D. "Aus dem gebrochenen Schweigen werden soziale Bindungen." In *Unverlierbare Zeit. Psychosoziale Spätfolgen des Nationalsozialismus Bei Nachkommen von Opfern Und Tätern, Psychoanalytische Beiträge*, edited by K. Grünberg and J. Straub, 281–327. Tübingen: Edition Diskord, 2001.

Bar-On, D., and C. Schmidt. *Die Last des Schweigens. Gespräche mit Kindern von Nazi-Tätern*. Frankfurt am Main and New York: Campus, 1993.

Becker, D. *Die Erfindung des Traumas—verflochtene Geschichten*. Freiburg: Edition Freiburg, 2006.

Berger, M. "Heil Hitler Dir! Du bist und bleibst der beste Freund von mir". Zur Kindergartenpädagogik im Nazi-Deutschland (1933–1945). Unter besonderer Berücksichtigung der Fachzeitschrift Kindergarten (1933–1942)." In *Kindergartenpädagogik. Online-Handbuch*, edited by M. Textor. www.kindergartenpaedagogik.de/1258.html (last update: 08-25-2016).

Bergmann, M., ed., *Kinder der Opfer, Kinder der Täter. Psychoanalyse und Holocaust*. Frankfurt am Main: Fischer, 1995.

Bohleber, W. "Das Fortwirken des Nationalsozialismus in der zweiten und dritten Generation nach Auschwitz." *Babylon* 4:7 (1990): 78.

———. "Transgenerationelles Trauma, Identifizierung und Geschichtsbewusstsein." In *Die dunkle Spur der Vergangenheit. Psychoanalytische Zugänge zum Geschichtsbewußtsein*, edited by J. Rüsen, and J. Straub. Frankfurt am Main: Suhrkamp, 1998.

Brunner, J. "Die Politik der Traumatisierung. Zur Geschichte des verletzbaren Individuums." *WestEnd: Neue Zeitschrift für Sozialforschung* 1 (2004): 7–24.

Dill, G. *Nationalsozialistische Säuglingspflege. Eine frühe Erziehung zum Massenmenschen*. Stuttgart: Enke, 1999.

Fest, Joachim, *Der Untergang. Hitler und das Ende des Dritten Reichs*. Berlin: Verlag Alexander Fest, 2002.

Fischer, G., P. Riedesser: *Lehrbuch der Psychotraumatologie*. Stuttgart: UTB, 2009.

Freud, A., and D. Burlingham. *War and Children*. New York: Ernst Willard, 1943.

Freud, S. (1899). *The Standard Edition of the Complete Psychological Works of Sigmund Freud, Volume III (1893–1899): Early Psycho-Analytic Publications*. London: The Hogart Press.

Glaesmer, H., and E. Brähler. "Die Langzeitfolgen des Zweiten Weltkrieges in der deutschen Bevölkerung: Epidemiologische Befunde und deren klinische Bedeutung." *Psychotherapeutenjournal* 4 (2011): 346–353.

Glaesmer, H., T. Gunzelmann, E. Brähler, S. Forstmeier, and A. Maercker. "Traumatic Experiences and Post-traumatic Stress Disorder among Elderly Germans: Results of a Representative Population-based Survey." *International Psychogeriatrics* 22, no. 4 (2010): 661–670.

Haarer, J. *Die deutsche Mutter und ihr erstes Kind*. Munich: J.F. Lehmann, 1934.

———. *"Mutter, erzähl' von Adolf Hitler!" Ein Buch zum Vorlesen, Nacherzählen und Selbstlesen für kleinere und größere Kinder*. Munich: J.F. Lehmann, 1939.

———. *Unsere kleinen Kinder*. Munich: J.F. Lehmann, 1936.

Keim, W., *Erziehung unter der Nazi-Diktatur*. 2 Bände, *Antidemokratische Potentiale, Machtantritt und Machtdurchsetzung; Kriegsvorbereitung, Krieg und Holocaust*. 2. Auflage. Wissenschaftliche Buchgesellschaft, Darmstadt 2005.

Klinsiek, D., *Die Frau im NS-Staat*. Stuttgart: Deutsche Verlags-Anstalt, 1982.
Klundt, Michael, Samuel Salzborn, Marc Schwietring, and Gerd Wiegel. *Erinnern, verdrängen, vergessen. Geschichtspolitische Wege ins 21. Jahrhundert*. Giessen: NBKK, 2007.
Konrad, Franz Michael. *Der Kindergarten. Seine Geschichte von den Anfängen bis in die Gegenwart*. Freiburg im Breisgau: Lambertus, 2004.
Kötscher, D. "Verdeckte Spuren deutscher Geschichte—verdeckende Psychoanalyse." *Forum der Psychoanalyse* 28 (2012): 277–297.
Lamparter, U., C. Holstein, L. Apel, M. Thießen, D. Wierling, B. Möller, and S. Wiegand-Grefe. "Die familiäre Weitergabe von Kriegserfahrungen als Gegenstand interdisziplinärer Forschung." *Zeitschrift für Psychotraumatologie, Psychotherapiewissenschaft, Psychologische Medizin* 8, no. 1 (2010): 9–23.
Lamparter, U., C. Holstein, M. Thießen, D. Wierling, S. Wiegand-Grefe, and B. Möller. "65 Jahre später. Zeitzeugen des 'Hamburger Feuersturms (1943)' im lebensgeschichtlichen Interview." *Forum Psychoanal* 26 (2010): 365–387.
Marks, Stefan. *Warum folgen sie Hitler. Die Psychologie des Nationalsozialismus*. Düsseldorf: Patmos, 2011.
Mitscherlich, A., and M. Mitscherlich. *Die Unfähigkeit zu trauern. Grundlagen kollektiven Verhaltens*. Munich: R. Piper, 1967.
Müller-Hohagen, J., *Geschichte in uns. Psychogramme aus dem Alltag*. Munich: Knesebeck, 1994.
Quindeau, I. *Trauma und Geschichte. Interpretationen autobiographischer Erzählungen von Überlebenden des Holocaust*. Frankfurt am Main: Brandes & Apsel, 1995.
Radebold, H. *Kindheiten im Zweiten Weltkrieg. Kriegserfahrungen und deren Folgen aus psychohistorischer Perspektive* Weinheim und Munich: Juventa, 2006.
———. "Während des Alterns anzutreffende Folgen: aktueller Kenntnisstand." In *Kindheiten im Zweiten Weltkrieg. Kriegserfahrungen und deren Folgen aus psychohistorischer Perspektive*, edited by H. Radebold, 139–148. Weinheim und Munich: Juventa, 2006.
Riedesser, P., M. Schulte-Markwort, and J. Walter. "Entwicklungspsychologische und psychodynamische Aspekte psychischer Traumatisierungen von Kindern und Jugendlichen." In *Entwicklung nach früher Traumatisierung*, edited by L. Koch-Kneidl and J. Wiesse. Göttingen: Vandenhoeck & Ruprecht, 2003.
Rosenthal, G., ed. *Der Holocaust im Leben von drei Generationen. Familien von Überlebenden der Shoah und von Nazi-Tätern*. Gießen: Psychosozial, 1997.
Schlesinger-Kipp, G. *Kindheit im Krieg und Nationalsozialismus*. Gießen: Psychosozial, 2012.
Schneider, Christian, Cordelia Stillke, and Bernd Leineweber. *Das Erbe der Napola. Versuch einer Generationengeschichte des Nationalsozialismus*. Hamburg: HIS, 1996.
Schulz, H., H. Radebold, and J. Reulecke. *Söhne ohne Väter. Erfahrungen der Kriegsgeneration*. Berlin: Ch. Links-Verlag, 2004.
Straub, J. *Historisch-psychologische Biographieforschung. Theoretische, methodologische und methodische Argumentationen in systematischer Absicht*. (Heidelberg: Asanger, 1989.

 11

Insights into the German Interviews of the Kestenberg Archive
Children of Perpetrators and How They Dealt with Their Parents' Actions

Christina Isabel Brüning

Introduction

The Kestenberg Archive of Testimonies of Child Holocaust Survivors contains interviews with more than 1,500 child survivors of the Holocaust but also, and rather strangely considering the title of the collection, interviews with children from non-Jewish German families.[1] These include interviews with children of high-ranking National Socialists (or Nazis) such as the son of Hans Frank, governor-general of Poland. The sample used for this chapter is not representative and each interview, its context, and the biography of the interviewee must be examined individually.[2] Although the four interviews with children of Nazis that I found in the archive comprise an extremely small sample, they are highly interesting for a number of reasons. First, they are a very special sort of source because the interviews were mostly conducted by psychoanalysts with therapeutic intentions. Second, they offer a rare insight into reflections on German guilt after the era of National Socialism and into the way that German society dealt with the testimonies of these children. These social strategies for coming to terms with the Nazi past[3] shape the narratives of the interviewees and also influence their personalities and states of mind. With Halbwachs and Welzer in mind, I relate to the interviews here not only as individual narratives, but also as models for the viewpoints of groups.[4]

As a researcher with a background in gender studies,[5] I am trained to start papers or lectures with self-positioning. At first glance, this might seem unnecessary when researching the Holocaust. However, especially in my case, it is important to disclose any personal involvement in the topic. My mother's father was too young to be an active soldier in World War II, but because he had been born in Berlin in 1930, he neither learned the concept of democracy at school nor did he get a good education. He was parentless and lived in children's homes as well as on the streets. There he grew up with the inhumane racial ideology of the Nazis. Still today, he is deeply anti-Semitic and racist. Thus, being the third generation of German perpetrators, I grew up with a lot of questions and believed that something had to be wrong when my grandfather again and again started quoting from one of the 1940s books that he kept in our cellar. Maybe some of these early childhood experiences sparked my interest in what is today my field of research. And maybe I have been studying history for all this time just to prove my grandfather wrong. This is the reason why it was at times very hard for me to read the accounts of the German interviewees in the Kestenberg archive. I found it difficult *not* to judge them, particularly when the interviewees did not seem to distance themselves from the ideology of the regime. Consequently, I am sure that some of my interpretations in this chapter can be read as quite harsh or judgmental. However, the legacy of racial ideology in German society is something that deeply concerns me, especially in these recent times with right-wing parties gaining influence, multiple demonstrations against asylum seekers, and a growing number of violent attacks.[6]

In this chapter I will try to explore how German society came to terms with Nazi perpetrators by focusing on interviews with two children of Nazi parents: a son of a very famous and high-ranking Nazi and a daughter of a soldier and NSDAP party member who volunteered for the Schutzstaffel (SS). As historians working with the extraordinary collection that comprises the Kestenberg archive, we must keep two things in mind: First, the archive founders (Milton and Judith Kestenberg) and most of the interviewers were interested in psychological questions such as trauma, nightmares, and family relations. Second, the purpose of the archive was not initially as a collection for educational purposes or publication. We, the researchers, thus have to be aware that these interviews are psychological and not historical. Their structure differs immensely from the oral history transcripts or video interviews that historians usually work with. However, these interviews can be used as a source of history especially under the leading research questions of how the second generation of perpetrators dealt with their family's past and how society reacted.

I am not a psychoanalyst, and thus I do not try to analyze any deep or hidden psychological structures but rather work with the interview text itself and its communicative content. It is therefore important for me to stress what and *how* things are said by the interviewees, and to try to contextualize and contrast their utterances and narratives with cultural codes and transparencies of commemoration used in West Germany at the time of the interviews.

The twelve years of the Nazi regime brought destruction and international condemnation upon the German nation-state and fostered decades-long mistrust toward national narratives. In both East and West Germany, Nazism and later the Holocaust became a negative founding myth that marked Germans with a moral stigma to which they responded in different ways.[7] In examining how the children of perpetrators approached this burden of the so-called Third Reich, I first identify two contrasting ways of dealing with the past in the two distinct narratives. On the one hand, there are those who spoke openly or even published books about their parents' deeds. These people were often seen as *Nestbeschmutzer* (those who foul their own nest) and have been criticized by many Germans for doing a terrible thing to their families. Another common strategy was the reversing of facts and roles, thus victimizing or excusing the parents and with them the whole of German society. These children of perpetrators became history revisionists as they participated in the rewriting of history.

Second, I show that the interviewees' different reactions to the historical and familial burden of Nazism are embedded in interfering and interacting levels of the production and reception of narratives: the micro level of the individuals themselves—and on a meso level their families—and the macro level of German society during the time of the interviews or the time when the children were dealing with their past.

One transcript that I discuss in detail is an interview with a woman (Frau Z) whose father was a member of the Schutzstaffel (SS) and became an alcoholic after the war. In analyzing her interview, it is useful to look at the transmission of Nazi ideology. From her utterances, it is evident that she retains Nazi gender concepts and racial stereotypes, frequently using words taken from Nazi terminology. She also idealizes members of the family who she claims were resistant to the regime, although this was clearly not the case. Great care must be taken with positive narrations in which these children idealize their parents because their stories can easily become part of history revisionism.

The other interview that I examine is with Niklas Frank. He is the son of Hans Frank, the former governor-general of Poland, who was hanged after being found guilty at the Nuremberg trials. In Germany, there have been—especially from the right wing—long and controversial debates on whether these children should not "foul their own nests" by disclosing and condemning their parents' deeds as Niklas Frank did in his controversial book *Der Vater. Eine Abrechnung*.[8]

Thus, using some very vivid examples from these interviews, I attempt to shed light onto these two opposing poles—the *Nestbeschmutzer* accusations on the one hand and the danger of historical revisionism on the other—that constitute the two main focal points for postwar German society.

Niklas Frank's Interview

Niklas Frank, son of the General Governor of Poland Hans Frank, was born in 1939 as the youngest of four children. Although he was raised in extraordinarily luxurious circumstances in the Castle Wawel in Cracow, he lacked intimacy and love from his parents. His mother sometimes took him "shopping" in the ghetto of Cracow where she "took away" (i.e. stole) furs and jewelry from the imprisoned Jewish population. Frank reports these incidents in his books and says that from an early age he was aware of the fact that something was wrong with the situation in Poland. Later, after the war, Niklas Frank lived in West Germany, studied German, sociology and history and started his research on his family and the Third Reich. Frank currently works as a journalist and author; with his books and eyewitness accounts, he has become a prominent voice in the media.

His interview was chosen for the purpose of this chapter because his open and very harsh way of settling accounts with his parents' deeds is quite unusual. In taking a closer look at some passages from the Kestenberg interview, we are able to analyze reactions of the German majority toward the second generation speaking out openly. At the same time, the psychological patterns found in the pepetrators' childrens' narratives clarify why Judith Kestenberg included interviews with this group of people in her archive.

The Second Generation and German Society

First, it is important to stress that the majority of people in Germany accepted the unhealthy legacy of silence from their families. Not only did their mothers and fathers hush their deeds and gloss over the facts with commonplace, everyday phrases, but now the second generation widely copied this behavior. This way of keeping silent was, and maybe still is, widely accepted in German society. Thus, people like Niklas Frank became very controversial figures due to their openness. They have been called *Nestbeschmutzer* and have been accused of treason. Niklas Frank does not actually refer to the term *Nestbeschmutzer* but it can be inferred from his explanation why his books did not sell well:

NF Frank is here a name like Müller or Mayer. They didn't know that I was THE Frank's son.
JK But then you wrote the book?
NF Yes, then they knew.
JK Did you have some difficulties?
NF I don't think the high echelon was too pleased, but actually, I can't say that I had difficulties. Once I heard that I was called the swine of the nation. The swine of the nation. And 4 of 5 letters were negative. Against me. . . . There were some phone calls that they are going to hang me, but it never bothered me, surprisingly so.
JK I did not understand what you said about hanging.
NF I used to get phone calls and letters that I should be hanged like my father.
JK Were they Nazis?
NF Probably they were Nazis. Two things which amazed me when the book came out and before that the series. The one thing was that most journalists from other papers were against me. And the second thing was that the meanest letters came from women, from German women.[9]

This is his explanation of how society treats *Nestbeschmutzers*. It is interesting that he stresses that the letters from women were meaner than those from men. He does not continue or offer an explanation, but he seems to follow a certain dichotomy of traditional gender concepts that would attribute softness, likability, and empathy primarily to women. The fact that women do not necessarily act according to these attributes is something that has by now been repeatedly proven, for example in studies on female Schutzstaffel guards.[10] Moreover, researchers have been able to show that while gender stereotypes influence the perception of deeds by female perpetrators, they are also used to maintain classic gender roles.[11]

Another thing that is interesting is Niklas Frank's reaction toward the *Nestbeschmutzer* accusation. There is most certainly an element of pride in his narration, especially when you hear the German audiotapes of the interview. He likes to portray himself as the enlightener who is rejected by society as the "swine of the nation."

Acting as an enlightener or some kind of prophet is also a strategy that he uses when he reflects on German xenophobia, a topic which had become very relevant at the time of his interview in the re-united Germany of the 1990s with cases of arson attacks on the shelters of asylum seekers and the growing power of neofascism.

JK What do you think about the murders of the Turks?
NF Well, for me, it is clear that we Germans are walking down the same path again.
JK Back to Nazism?
NF No, in a different form, but again to kill and murder. I don't know why it appears that we cannot lead a normal life. I am really afraid that we are starting all over again. . . . I don't trust us, I really don't trust us.
JK Do you want to work against it?
NF I think only the other countries can counteract it. I contribute in a small way through my articles and also through my book. I appear on talk shows and lecture tours, I always argue with Germans and always admit that I am afraid of them and somehow . . . well, one can explain it, we have never admitted our guilt, it was always dug under and suppressed and like a festering sore, it burst out open here and there.

What is really fascinating in this excerpt is that he starts by saying "us" and "we" ("we Germans," "I don't trust us") and then switches to "them" ("I argue with Germans," "I am afraid of them"). So although the German nation may be divided over the question of identity, in this case the individual of the second generation also does not know which group he wants to belong to. This is even more remarkable in the light of one of his utterances, which will be analyzed more closely below, in which he imagines himself being a concentration camp inmate and a victim of the Nazis. Another way of interpreting this passage is that he is not actually speaking about two groups but rather condemning all Germans—when speaking about collective guilt—although making a clear distinction between himself and the German collective. In this way, on the one hand he appears as self-critical and as accepting collective guilt, while on the other hand he distances himself from this guilt.

Attitude toward Parents and Own Parenting

It is, thus far, evident how Niklas Frank derives self-esteem and pride from his role as a truth-teller and how this shapes his identity. He naturally takes a very interesting approach in depicting his parents. Throughout his innumerable interviews on TV, radio, and in newspapers, as well as in his professional life as a journalist, he has portrayed his father and mother as evil. Frank often describes his mother as a witch or as the bad queen of Poland in both his various interviews and his books.[12] In his interview for the Kestenberg archive conducted by Judith Kestenberg herself in 1993 in her heavily accented German, this topic of his evil parents comes up early:

NF I knew already then that my father was evil.
JK How did you discover that?
NF Already in 1945 and 1946, there were many pictures published from the concentration camps and I know that shocked me. . . . And somehow I knew that my father was in a way responsible for that and that's where it comes from.[13]

When his father was hanged after being found guilty at the Nuremberg trials, Frank recalls masturbating during the radio report of the trial. This is probably one of the most disturbing scenes both in his book and in this interview. His imaginings about his father's cruelty led him to even picture himself as one of the concentration camp victims.

NF I assume, and that is my interpretation, it is my rage against him in person. That's the one thing and then it is surely a puberty rebellion against him, which I never had because he was dead already. I had never, in my life, a father over me. Even in Poland, I never saw him. He also took no notice of me. That may be the second thing. And the third thing, which I am certain of . . . I always imagined myself being one of the victims, his KZ [concentration camp] victims.
JK You had a masochistic fantasy?[14]

Judith Kestenberg's reaction to Frank's narrative underlines the point made earlier that the interviewers were primarily interested in psychological aspects. The interviews were not intended to become oral history documents in an archive used for research and publication. In Frank's case it is easy to describe his fantasy as a form of overcompensation and (over-) identification with the victims. It could potentially also be seen as part of a perpetrator–victim inversion. This point of stressing one's own suffering rather than the victims' is a point that is more obvious in the ensuing interview with Frau Z.

However, it is not only his attitude toward his parents that is interesting here, but that his own childhood had major repercussions on the way he behaved as a father. His intense dealing with the past and with working through his family's guilt clearly had a serious impact on his ideas on education or moral upbringing of his daughter. While it is difficult to generalize, perpetrators' families—the third generation as compared to the second generation—were often confronted with either a stubborn silence and unspoken secrets or were forced to deal with the legacy of the Holocaust too early in their development. At least in the case of Niklas Frank's daughter Franziska, this strategy of teaching a "let something like the Holocaust never happen again!"-position leads to, in my opinion, rather traumatizing events for a three-year-old child.

JK And your daughter was aware of something going on at the age of three?

NF But I played a very mean game with my daughter in order to make her aware of what moves me so. We had very nice neighbors across, an old couple. He with white hair, she a little plump, delighted people. I stood by the window with Franziska and we looked over to them, there was a little garden in front of her house and I said to her: "now Franziska, imagine that a truck pulls up and people jump off it carrying guns, they broke down the door of the Birkis—that was their name—and they dragged the old Birkis out and beat them. Try to imagine that, beat them all the time and then have to climb into the truck. What do we do, should we interfere, what do we do?" And then Franziska started to cry and I cried along with her.[15]

To those who work with survivors and survivors' testimonies, this passage is reminiscent of Holocaust survivors who lead their children through hell from their need for empathy or understanding. The movie *Pizza at Auschwitz* by the Israeli filmmaker and survivor Danny Chanoch depicts a similar situation when his wish to stay overnight at Auschwitz in his old barrack pushes his children, Miri and Sagi, beyond what they can bear. Danny Chanoch states that he does not understand his children's problems because he is of the opinion that they do not really have any. This is the moment when his daughter, luckily an adult with children of her own and not a three-year-old like Niklas Frank's daughter, shouts at him that she cannot take it anymore and that it is unfair to treat her like she does not understand or does not know anything just because she herself was not in a concentration camp. These similar communicative processes within families of both survivors and perpetrators might have been one of the reasons why Judith Kestenberg decided to include the interviews with non-Jewish German second-generation children. However, from a historical and not a psychological perspective, her decision to do so remains controversial.

Frau Z's interview

For a second close reading, I have chosen an interview with the daughter of a Schutzstaffel officer. Frau Z was born in 1941 as one of nine children and the interview was recorded in 1991 in West Germany by EK.[16] Frau Z's father volunteered for the Schutzstaffel during the war; he later influenced his daughter even more strongly by being a nervous wreck and an alcoholic after the war. Due to financial problems, Frau Z left school after sixth grade and started to work first in a private household and later in the health sector. She spent seven years as a nun in a Protestant order. After she left the order, she studied therapeutic pedagogy and music therapy and worked with disabled children, with alcoholics, and in a kindergarten. Frau Z married in 1978 at the age of thirty-eight when her son was already two years old. She stopped working and started therapy in order to come to terms with her past and her loneliness and isolation from her family and her father. At the time of the interview she had two children, aged eleven and six.[17]

Transmission by Language

When explaining some of the specific narrative patterns that can be found in her interview, it is again important to keep in mind that this is a therapeutic interview, not planned and conducted by historians, and that Frau Z is not a survivor but part of German majority society—a society that among Frau Z's parents' generation comprised primarily bystanders and perpetrators.

In analyzing Frau Z's narrative, I concentrate on the retention of Nazi gender concepts, racial stereotypes, and words that Frau Z takes from Nazi ideology as well as her inversion of the victims and perpetrators. As discussed in Viktor Klemperer's brilliant work on the language of the Third Reich, National Socialist propaganda was transmitted implicitly or even explicitly through the use of certain terms.[18] A lack of distance from specific words or phrases and the nonexistence of problematization noted in interviews conducted decades after the war are possible indicators of the spread of Nazi ideology and values. Although during the past few decades politicians, the media, and linguists have tried to cleanse the language of terms and euphemisms that were characteristic of what Klemperer termed *lingua tertii imperii* (language of the Third Reich, or LTI), there are still sporadic outbreaks when a news report uses the term *entartet* (degenerate) or words of extinction and mass murder such as *ausrotten* (to eradicate) *an der Wurzel* (to destroy root and branch).[19]

In Frau Z's interview there are also some slips of the tongue or unreflective adaptions of National Socialist terminology. Similar findings on transmission in language in oral testimonies were made by Dan Bar-On in his book *Legacy of Silence*.[20] This kind of intergenerational linguistic transmission[21] can easily be found in highly ideological topics such as social Darwinism and racial hygiene.[22] For researchers it may be possible to handle these expressions. However, those using oral history sources in, for example, teaching, may present a serious dilemma:[23] although authenticity is the most important criterion for historical sources[24] and teachers should not compromise the sources or work with just tiny bits and pieces, teachers also want the texts they are using for educational purposes to speak in a politically correct language. Deconstructing the complexity of language in oral testimony in general is a rather extreme challenge for history classes in high schools or at college. Although this is an important issue, it is out of the scope of the current chapter.

One aspect that has to be discussed concerning language in the interviews is the fact that it is rather common for German interviewees in their accounts to use Nazi, specifically Holocaust, terminology to describe their postwar lives. One example from the Kestenberg archive for this phenomenon is another interviewee whose account I will not discuss in detail here. Due to its similarity to Frau Z's narration, however, I will quote a passage to emphasize my point. In his interview, DH talks about the *Viehtransporte* (cattle transport trains on which homeless families in Germany were relocated in 1946), and he refers to the relocation site as a *Lager* (camp) and recalls that this was where he was freed from lice—clearly a very bad memory for him. These are descriptions of scenes that, for most readers, would evoke images of the Holocaust and concentration camps and not of the German majority population after the war. Another aspect is that the medial representation of the Shoah has been shaped by the images of movies such as Lanzman's *Shoah* or Spielberg's *Schindler's List* so that cattle cars have become an iconic figure for the deportations and mass murder of the Jewish people.

The above shown use of Holocaust terminology for non-Jewish German families was also raised by Kobi Kabalek in his interviews with the third generation in Germany.[25] In one interview, he shows a young German university student mixing up *Pflichtjahr* (a year's compulsory community service) with *Zwangsarbeit* (forced labor) when talking about the year of *Arbeitsdienst* (labor service) that his grandmother had to complete, as every young woman had to do during National Socialism. Kabalek argues very convincingly that this mistake was influenced by the dominant discourse about forced labor in Germany at the beginning of the millennium. The slight hint at this young student's tendency to portray his own family members as victims of the Hitler regime cannot, however, be ignored. It is thus evident that this perpetrator–victim inversion that Gabriele Rosenthal found in non-Jewish German families in 1998 is clearly a common theme.[26] Similar findings were later published about the third generation of German families and their way of speaking about National Socialism and their grandparents by Harald Welzer and his colleagues in their study *Opa war kein Nazi* (Grandpa was not a Nazi). He explained "the reversed order of the roles of perpetrators and victims" as a structure that usually accompanies discussions about the German people being victims of the war.[27] This victimization of the "ordinary Germans" has also been a central point of the criticism surrounding the Gedächtnis der Nation [Memory of the Nation],[28] an online archive comprising hundreds of video snippets that the founders wanted to be a collection of the stories of the German people that was supposed to become as large and influential as the USC Shoah Foundation's Visual History Archive. This did not in fact happen—not least because of the heavy criticism by academics.[29] Here, the term *Zeitzeuge* (witness) was used for survivors as well as for just about anybody who had experienced a historical event. Thus, the "testimonies" of the "witnesses" of the World Cup in Germany in 2006 can be found on the same platform as the accounts of former concentration camp inmates.

In Germany, there was much discussion about the perpetrator-victim inversion, especially after Jörg Friedrich's 2002 publication of his book *Der Brand* (the fire) in which he called the 1944 and 1945 Allied air raids on German cities such as Dresden a *"Bomben-Holocaust."*[30] Such revisionist interpretations of history are quite popular among radical right-wing parties in Germany, but unfortunately they can also be heard among the regulars in the pub. Wolfgang Benz once referred to the accusation of Hitler and the conceptualization of a whole nation as being seduced and misled as "the lifelong lie of the German people."[31] Or as Völter and Dasberg put it, "an innocent populace that had followed Nazism unsuspectedly."[32] After the war the Germans pitied themselves for what had been done to them both during and after the war and saw the rebuilding of their country as sufficient atonement. And from this successful rebuilding, they derived pride, legitimacy, and meaning.[33] I am quite convinced that Frau Z did not intend a revisionist interpretation, especially when examining her reasons for giving her testimony to the Kestenberg archive, but the fact that she is unaware of how to appropriately express her point of view is problematic.

Attitude toward Parents

In order to discover how interviewees of the second generation interpret National Socialism, it is useful to examine the way in which they reflect on the guilt of their fathers—and sometimes, as in Niklas Frank's case, the mothers too. Frau Z talks at length about her father with the interviewer: "He was a very sensitive man, apolitical, but on the other hand also a very sensitive father. He was sensitive and, knowing from very deep within that there had been terrible injustice, he had to say, 'I was a good soldier, at least I tried to stay human.'"[34]

Meik Zülsdorf-Kersting found similar strategies of victimization and exculpation among high school students when they talked about soldiers in the German Wehrmacht.[35] The myth of the morally clean soldier, the clean Wehrmacht with soldiers who were able to "maintain a sense of justice in the midst of injustice"[36] is something that German society wanted to believe in for a long time and that only started to change in collective memory when the exhibition *A War of Extermination: Crimes of the Wehrmacht* travelled around Germany in the mid and late 1990s.

Frau Z continues by stating that her father "perished emotionally" due to all the terrible things he 'had to' see in Russia.[37] Many researchers have pointed out that the destruction of all the fathers' perspectives on life—career, beliefs, and friendships, to name a few—also killed all positive attitudes and the potential for any father–child relationship for the second generation. Already in 1987, Peter Sichrovsky indicated that children in the postwar years did not see their fathers as heroes in uniforms but rather as victims of a lost war. They did not attribute guilt to them; instead of seeing them as protagonists and active perpetrators of war, they saw them as victims of the war. The children defended their fathers and tried to "sweep everything under the carpet until the amount of dirt under it was so high that you stumbled over the carpet."[38] It is quite obvious that Frau Z excuses her father as a victim. The "tall, blond, prototypical Aryan," as she describes him early on in her interview, who volunteered for the Schutzstaffel[39] and who fought first in the Netherlands and later in the Soviet Union, becomes someone you pity as a victim of the system—a completely depersonalized system with no perpetrators except Hitler.[40]

Frau Z's feelings of being a victim of the war do not only surface when she talks about her father, but also when she tells her own life story. After the war, her father was unemployed and the family was very poor and had to move to state-subsidized social welfare houses. She describes the poverty at length and the language she uses is very telling. She refers to the area as a ghetto: "What was really painful for us kids was the point that we were in this ghetto and were totally isolated."[41] Like the so-called *"Bomben-Holocaust,"* the use of the term "ghetto" is also a way of reversing the role of perpetrators by making the Germans the victims of the war. As Rosenthal stated, "By putting one's own suffering on a parallel with the suffering of Nazi victims, one can avoid confronting the perpetrator aspect of one's family past."[42] A little later, Frau Z calls this area of the city a *Lager*: "and we had to live in the *Lager* [camp]."[43] Thus, the decision to use the words "ghetto" and *"lager"*—terms usually used in survivors' narratives—supports my thesis of a perpetrator–victim inversion narrative.

Frau Z continues by mentioning that her family did not have enough money to buy food to eat or to pay the electricity bill: "We didn't have anything to eat and all around us there were the refugees a hundred times better off than us."[44] This idea of a social hierarchy where, in her mind, the local population should be better off than immigrants or refugees is crucial for understanding why she suffers from the family's poverty so badly and keeps mentioning it: "But we were local people and we were on the lowest level of living standard."[45] If we agree with Birgit Rommelsbacher that homogenizing, polarizing, and hierarchizing groups of human beings is a racist act, then there is blatant racism in her words.[46]

Some studies have proven that it is usually women, especially daughters with their fathers, who seem to have a greater readiness to embark on confrontational situations and discussions.[47] This does not, interestingly, seem to be the case in Frau Z's family at all as she states: "All these important conversations after the war, he just had them with my brothers. His sons were the important ones for him, his contact people."[48] Rather, remarks made by Ute Benz in her study "Maikäfer flieg" seem to apply: the father is seen as a loser and weak personalities need special protection that hinders the socialization of the children.[49] It is clear that for Frau Z there is a legacy of silence that is enhanced by traditional gender roles: she has no first-hand information of her father's life or his feelings about the war. The very traditional gender concept, upheld by the Nazis, remains dominant even after the war: a woman should stay in the house and does not have an opinion on politics, and only the men talk about "important" things.

A look at Frau Z's descriptions of her mother will allow a greater examination of how ingrained National Socialist gender concepts are on her consciousness and how she produces gendered narrations in her interview. Frau Z starts talking about her mother by referring to her siblings, thus totally reducing the female figure to her role as a mother: "I already had 4 siblings; I was the 5th, yes. And later on there were 4 more."[50] It is well known that during the time of National Socialism women were expected to provide the Führer with many future soldiers.[51] The Party therefore implemented a wide range of government programs to encourage high birth rates. There were ideologically inspired incentives such as the *Mutterkreuz*, a special medal that women received for each subsequent birth after their fourth child on and that reached gold status with the eighth child. But there were also financial incentives such as a loan of a thousand Reichsmarks (RM) when a couple got married. With the average worker earning a monthly salary of 190 RM in 1938, a thousand RM was enough to start a family and buy the furniture for an apartment. For every child born into the family, the outstanding debt was reduced by 250 RM so that after your fourth child the family did not have to pay anything back; subsequently this procedure was nicknamed *abkindern* (the paying-off-debt children). Of course, at a time when racial ideology dominated all politics, these incentives were available only for those of Aryan blood.

This racial ideology with its deep-rooted anti-Semitism still seems to be lodged in Frau Z's thinking as late as the 1990s. She relates a very strange episode that is unfortunately not taken further either by the interviewer or by Frau Z herself. She tells a story about how after the war her mother once borrowed money from a Jewish woman: "It was humiliating for my mother, as her husband was with the Waffen-SS [Schutzstaffel]. It was a difficult decision."[52] In my opinion, these words have a clear anti-Semitic undercurrent, and this is in the years following the war. Although just prior to making this statement Frau Z denied her mother's anti-Semitism,[53] if humiliation was the feeling that her mother suffered when borrowing money from a Jewish neighbor, it is obvious that she had at least latent anti-Semitic attitudes. It is possible, however, that this is Frau Z's interpretation of the situation, and her empathy with her mother's undeniably difficult situation led her to remember it as a humiliating and difficult decision.

Another element of her interview that can be ascribed to her National Socialist upbringing is the fact that she bemoans her family's postwar treatment as asocial due to their large number of kids: "It was really hurtful, it was as if everyone had the right to contact us with their feet. . . . We were stamped on—and then I realized that someone who has many children is antisocial."[54] This must have felt like the complete reverse of everything she had been taught: a couple of years before her mother had received the gold medal for motherhood and now they were being treated like social pariahs.

Frau Z's further observations about her mother are very interesting, although it is hard to assess whether these are the results of wishful thinking rather than actual reality: "Well, she studied music and she was a good pianist and what concerned her political attitudes, she for sure didn't share my father's political attitude. . . . My mother later studied to be an organist to play in the church. And that is what tells us that in her innermost self, she didn't share the ideology and the political opinion that my father had."[55]

Reading this part of the interview, people could end up with some strange idea that being both a musician and a Nazi simultaneously was somehow not possible and that especially people who went to church regularly did not share the Party's ideology. This, of course, is not true at all. There were many Christians such as the Deutsche Christen, a deeply anti-Semitic, Protestant community established in 1932, which more than one third of all Protestant reverends joined. Claiming alleged resistance narratives due to a clerical background or religious attachment of the grandparents is a common strategy that has been proven by Welzer, Moller, and Tschuggnall.[56] This might stem from the fact that the interviews with family members of perpetrators show a high level of psychological pressure and a great need for legitimization. It is, therefore, difficult to assume the same level of reliability or authenticity as with other sources or interviews with survivors. I would call this part of Frau Z's narration a strange passing on of family history in which she idealizes members as resistant to the regime that they clearly supported.

Conclusion

The points that I discussed using mainly interviews of two non-Jewish German children of Nazi perpetrators were first the question of whether perpetrators stay perpetrators also in their children's narratives or whether the interviewees use a certain perpetrator–victim inversion to exculpate their parents—usually their fathers. I looked particularly at the use of language and argued that on the societal level it is common for Holocaust terminology to be used to rewrite history and show the suffering of ordinary Germans who were part of a war that nobody seems to have wanted. German TV has recently broadcast a few movies, such as *Unsere Mütter, unsere Väter* (Our mothers, our fathers) or *Schicksalsjahre* (Fateful years), in which German people, especially women, are shown as victims of a depersonalized war conceived by Hitler that led to terrible suffering in the destitute years after the war. This is not just a new fashion in entertainment but something we should keep an eye on because, in my opinion, this is a way of dealing with history and national identity that could take the country on a very wrong path again.

Second, I discussed the difference between those who wanted to know and worked toward knowledge versus those who chose not to ask or suppress thoughts. Individual witnesses can decide which path to take; as has been shown in this chapter, their personal choices have repercussions for the third generation, too. The chosen interviews from the Kestenberg archive highlight the two extremes: going public versus keeping the legacy of silence or even inversing the roles of perpetrators and victims. The death threats made against Niklas Frank show how societal and individual levels can interact and also shape interviews that then influence public memory. Of course, the sample is, as I already stated in the introduction, much too small to make any generalizations. However, looking at extreme examples on the edge can help sharpen the view for the majority of less obvious narratives in the center.

Third, I pointed at the historical context of the interviews that shaped the interviewees' narratives. In the 1990s, for example, the attacks on the Turks and other foreigners in Germany were a huge topic in the media. Also in the 1990s there was a public debate on forced labor, which found some resonance in the language used in German non-Jewish interviews. This again shows us that oral history can provide much insight into the time and social context in which the interview was conducted.

Finally, by examining Frau Z's interview, the legacy of the language of the Third Reich becomes most apparent. This emphasizes the aforementioned points of exculpation and perpetrator–victim inversion but also broadens the level of analysis to racial and gender stereotypes that remain in use.

Interviews such as Niklas Frank's can provide material for much reflection on the controversy of how to deal with the past. Other interviews, however, that lack a similar depth of reflection and distance, may be rather dangerous and could lead the readers to very wrong conclusions. I therefore believe that the uncommented online publication of such sources would be a risky endeavor. Parts of the interviews could then easily be used out of context by Holocaust deniers. That would definitely be the opposite of what Judith Kestenberg wanted to achieve—namely, that something like the Shoah can never happen again as included in the consent form about the rights of using these testimonies that all of her survivors and witnesses had to sign.[57] Any publication of the sources must therefore be aware of the different contexts and controversies that can lie in the narrative; an annotated printed version, for example, could provide starting points for interpretation.

Moreover, although their interviews are part of the Kestenberg archive, it should be heeded that neither Frau Z nor Niklas Frank are survivors in the original meaning of the word and that this term should be reserved for real survivors. Suffering from similar psychological consequences caused by a legacy of silence in the family might provide an interesting field of research for psychoanalysts. However, as historians we have to carefully distinguish between the groups in order not to reverse history.

And finally, extreme care is always necessary when analyzing the narratives of perpetrators and their descendants. Listening to or reading testimonies can be a very productive way to learn about the past, especially the way people perceived their realities and how they recall them later. However, language has the power to suppress, to cover up and to hurt. And language sometimes expresses suppressed thoughts: a specific choice of words can reveal hidden truths. It is important to be aware that words that stem from the language of the Third Reich—whether used consciously or unconsciously—may have a dangerously suggestive effect.

Author

Christina Isabel Brüning started her career as a teacher of college and high school students. She subsequently worked as a research assistant at the Freie Universität in Berlin and is now a lecturer in history and history didactics at the University of Education, Freiburg, Germany. From 2015–2017 she had a research fellowship at the Center for Jewish Studies Berlin-Brandenburg. Her main research fields are National Socialism and neo-Nazism, oral history and survivors' testimonies, and gender studies.

Notes

1. All interviews quoted in this chapter were held at the Oral History Division, Hebrew University of Jerusalem; depositions can be found at the Jewish Historical Institute, Jerusalem.
2. My method follows the case study approach of Schneider, Stillke, and Leineweber, *Das Erbe der Napola*, esp. p. 10.
3. The German word *Vergangenheitsbewältigung* (overcoming or managing the past) is a very problematic term because it suggests that one can win the battle and defeat the past.
4. Halbwachs, *Das kollektive Gedächtnis*; Welzer, *Das kommunikative Gedächtnis*; Welzer, Moller, and Tschuggnall, *"Opa war kein Nazi."*
5. Bothe and Brüning, *Geschlecht und Erinnerung.*
6. PRO ASYL, "Fakten, Zahlen und Argumente."
7. For the major debates and topics that express Germany coming to terms with its Nazi past, see Niven, *Facing the Nazi Past*; and Moses, *German Intellectuals and the Nazi Past.*
8. Frank, *Der Vater.*
9. Testimony of NF (257) 35-10, 46 (German transcript), 1993. Interview conducted by Judith Kestenberg on October 1, 1993, originally in German; transcript is in English (translation by Judith Kestenberg).
10. Dublon-Knebel, "'Erinnern kann.'"

11. As Habbo Knoch pointed out, "Vielfach wird das Skandalon der Beteiligung von Frauen, insbesondere eigener Gewalttätigkeit, zum Leitmotiv der Analyse gemacht, was vor allem dadurch erklärbar wird, dass Gewalt zunächst einmal als 'männlich' gesehen wird. Das belegt die lange Dauer von Geschlechterstereotypen der 'eigentlichen' Frau und gewaltgehemmten Mütterlichkeit selbst in Kreisen der Frauenforschung." [In a lot of cases, the scandal that women were involved, especially concerning violence, is the starting point for the analysis. This can be explained by the fact that violence is primarily seen as something masculine. This shows the long continuity of gender stereotypes of the 'real' woman and non-violent motherhood even within the gender studies. These kind of attributions have been activated again and again as a consequence of pre-research reception of single cases after 1945, such as the one of Ilse Koch, the wife of the commander of Buchenwald: Scandalising their implicit sadism as a deviation of the norm also served to reconstruct gender roles.] (Knoch, "Völkische Verantwortung," 35).
12. Frank, *Meine deutsche Mutter*.
13. Testimony of NF, (257) 35-10.
14. Ibid., 28–29 (German version).
15. Ibid., 48–49 (German version).
16. Testimony of Frau Z, (257) 26-70, 1991.
17. Information taken from the Kestenberg's catalogue on the interview with Z.
18. Klemperer, *LTI*.
19. Of course we have to keep in mind that LTI words have not necessarily been coined by the Nazis: in many cases there was a specific and widespread use that has not been there before, as Klemperer correctly pointed out. Compare also Volmert, "Politische Rhetorik"; and idem., "Utz Mass."
20. Bar-On, *Die Last des Schweigens*, 274.
21. The different types of transmission of Nazi history within family narrations can be found in the study by Welzer et al., *Opa war kein Nazi*, esp. pp. 81–88.
22. Massing, "Auswirkungen anhaltender," 57.
23. Heimannsberg and Schmidt, "Einführung," 10.
24. Brüning, "Umgang mit Textquellen."
25. Kabalek, "Spuren vergangener Geschichte/n," 129f.
26. Rosenthal, "National Socialism," 308.
27. Welzer in his study *Opa war kein Nazi* called this way of passing on family history the *"Opferdiskurs des deutschen Volkes"* [the German people as victims].
28. www.gedaechtnis-der-nation.de
29. Nägel, "'Die Nation spricht?'"
30. Friedrich, *Der Brand*.
31. Benz, "Schweigen," 177.
32. Völter and Dasberg, "Similarities and Differences," 22.
33. Benz, "Schweigen,"178.

34. Testimony of Frau Z, (257) 26-70; all translations from the original German transcript by CB.
35. Zülsdorf-Kersting, *Sechzig Jahre danach*.
36. Rosenthal, "Similarities and Differences," 19.
37. "Was wohl auch die Ursache war, warum er seelisch so zugrund ging. Ja, seelisch ist er zugrunde gegangen" [This might have been the cause why he deteriorated emotionally. Yes, he deteriorated emotionally] (testimony of Frau Z, (257) 26-70, 4). Especially that repetition shows how important it is for her to make her father's emotional situation clear to the interviewer.
38. Sichrovsky, *Schuldig geboren*, esp. 17, 25.
39. Earlier in the interview she says that he did not have to join the army because he worked in a strategically important enterprise. However, he was an early member of the Nazi Party and volunteered for the Schutzstaffel against his company's will.
40. "*Viele Taten, wenig Täter*" [many deeds, few perpetrators] is a very common motive for the media depiction of the Third Reich on German TV. In postwar West Germany, dealings with the past in a multiperspective and differentiated way was seldom seen in the media.
41. Testimony of Frau Z, (257) 26-70, 5.
42. Rosenthal and Bar-On, "A Biographical Case Study."
43. Testimony of Frau Z, (257) 26-70, 5.
44. Ibid.
45. Ibid.
46. Rommelspacher, "Was ist eigentlich Rassismus?"
47. Greven and von Wrochen, "Wehrmacht und Vernichtungskrieg," 19.
48. Testimony of Frau Z, (257) 26-70, 5, translation by CB.
49. Benz, "Maikäfer flieg!"
50. "Ich war die fünfte, ja. Und später kamen noch 4 Geschwister" [I was the fifth, yes. And then later 4 more siblings were born.]. Testimony of Frau Z, (257) 26-70, 1.
51. Frevert, "Frauen."
52. "Es war für meine Mutter demütigend, wo ihr Mann doch bei der Waffen-SS war. Das war ein schwerer Gang" testimony of Frau Z, (257) 26-70, 4.
53. "Und hat, was so die politische Einstellung angeht, wohl sicher nicht die politischen Einstellungen mit meinem Vater geteilt . . . Und daran kann man auch ablesen, dass die im Innersten nicht diese Ideologie geteilt hat" [And concerning her political attitudes, she surely did not share them with my father . . . And this shows you that in her inner self she did not share this ideology.] testimony of Frau Z, (257) 26-70, 2.
54. "Es war wirklich so verletzend, es war so, wie wenn jeder das Recht hat, uns mit Füßen zu treten. Niemand, der noch die Würde in uns gesehen hat (-weint-). Wir waren abgestempelt, das habe ich dann ja auch begriffen— wer viele Kinder hat, ist asozial" [testimony of Frau Z, (257) 26-70, 8.
55. "Und ich denke auch, meine Mutter hat dann später nochmal den Organistendienst gelernt. Also an der Orgel gelernt, um in der Kirche zu spielen. Und daran kann man auch ablesen, dass sie im Innersten nicht

diese Ideologie geteilt hat und die politische Meinung auch, die mein Vater hatte" testimony of Frau Z, (257) 26-70, 2.
56. Welzer, Moller, and Tschuggnall, *Opa war kein Nazi*, 44.
57. "Da durch meine Teilnahme, das Erreichen des entgültige [sic] Ziels dieser Forschung,die Wiederholung eines Holocausts zu vermeiden, fördert, befreie ich Ihre Organisation und deren Representanten (sic) und Rechtsnachfolgern von jeglichen Ansprüchen an der Veröffentlichung, Verlagsrechte, oder jegliche Anwendung des von mir gestellten Materials" [As by my participation, the ultimate goal of this research ist to prevent another Holocaust, I will not make any claims to your organization or any of your representatives and heirs concerning publication, property rights or the use of the by my provided material], (Jerome Riker International Study of Organized Persecution of Children, Dr. Judith S. Kestenberg, Consent Form).

References

Bar-On, Dan. *Die Last des Schweigens. Gespräche mit Kindern von Nazi-Tätern* [Legacy of Silence: Encounters with Children of the Third Reich xxx]. Frankfurt am Main: Campus Verlag, 1993.
Benz, Wolfgang. "Schweigen, Verweigern, Bewältigen. Vom Umgang mit nationalsozialistischer Vergangenheit (=Nachwort)" [Remaining silent, Denying, Overcoming]. In *Schweigen die Täter reden die Enkel* [When the perpetrators remain silent, the grandchildren will speak], edited by Claudia Brunner and Uwe von Seltmann, 175–190. Frankfurt am Main: Fischer, 2004.
Benz, Ute. "'Maikäfer flieg! Dein Vater ist im Krieg.' Aspekte der Heimkehr aus familiärer Sicht." ["Cockchafer fly away! Your father went to war." Aspects of homecoming from the families' perspectives]. In *Heimkehr 1948* [Homecoming], edited by Annette Kaminsky, 176–191. Munich: C.H. Beck, 1998.
Bergmann, Martin S., Jucovy E. Milton, and Judith S. Kestenberg, (eds.). *Kinder der Opfer. Kinder der Täter. Psychoanalyse und Holocaust* [Children of the Victims. Children of the Perpetrators. Psychoanalysis and Holocaust]. Frankfurt am Main: Fischer, 1995.
Bothe, Alina, and Christina Brüning: "Introduction." In *Geschlecht und Erinnerung im digitalen Zeitalter—neue Perspektiven auf ZeitzeugInnenarchive* [Gender and Remembrance in the Digital Age. New Perspectives on Testimonies and Archives], edited by Alina Bothe, and Christina Brüning, 1–37. Berlin: Lit. Verlag, 2015.
Brüning, Christina. "Umgang mit Textquellen im Geschichtsunterricht" [Using historical Sources in the History Classroom]. In *Handbuch Praxis des Geschichtsunterrichts. Band 2* [Manual of applied History Teaching], edited by Michele Barricelli, and Martin Lücke, 92–107. Schwalbach im Taunus: Wochenschau-Verlag, 2012.
Dublon-Knebel, Irith. "'Erinnern kann ich mich nur an eine Frau Danz . . . ' Die Aufseherin Luise Danz in der Erinnerung ihrer Opfer" [I can only remember a certain Misses Danz…]. In *Genozid und Geschlecht. Jüdische Frauen im*

nationalsozialistischen Lagersystem [Genocide and Gender. Jewish Women in the Nationalsocalist Lagersystem], edited by Gisela Bock, 66–84. Frankfurt am Main: Campus, 2005.

Frank, Niklas. *Der Vater. Eine Abrechnung* [The Father. A Revenge], 6th ed. Munich: Goldmann, 2005.

———. *Meine deutsche Mutter*. Munich: C. Bertelsmann Verlag, 2005.

Friedrich, Jörg. *Der Brand. Deutschland im Bombenkrieg 1940–1945* [The Fire. Germany in the War of Bombs form 1949 until 1945], 9th ed. Munich: Propyläen, 2003.

Frevert, Ute. "Frauen." In *Enzyklopädie des Nationalsozialismus* [Women, entry in the Encyclopedia of National Socialsm]., edited by Wolfgang Benz, Hermann Graml, and Hermann Weiß, 220–234. Munich: dtv, 2001.

Greven, Michael Th., and Oliver von Wrochen. "Wehrmacht und Vernichtungskrieg zwischen Gesellschaftspolitik, Wissenschaft und individueller Verarbeitung der Geschichte" [Wehrmacht and destruction war between politics, science and individual coming to terms with history]. In *Der Krieg in der Nachkriegszeit. Der Zweite Weltkrieg in Politik und Gesellschaft der Bundesrepublik* [The Was in the Postwar era. The Second World War in Politics and Society of West-Germany], edited by Michael Th. Greven and Oliver von Wrochem, 9–22. Opladen: Leske + Budrich, 2000.

Halbwachs, Maurice. *Das kollektive Gedächtnis* [Collective Memory]. Frankfurt am Main: Fischer, 1991.

Heimannsberg, Barbara, and Christoph J. Schmidt. "Einführung. Zur Symptomatik der Nazi-Erbschaft" [Introduction. On the Symptomatology of the Nazi heritage]. In *Das kollektive Schweigen. Nazivergangenheit und gebrochene Identität in der Psychotherapie* [Collective Silence. Nazi Past and scattered Identitites in Psychotherapy], edited by Barbara Heimannsberg and Christoph J. Schmidt, 7–10. Heidelberg: Roland Asanger Verlag, 1988.

Heye, Uwe-Karsten , and Thomas Kirchner, and Miguel Alexandre, team workX for ZDF.

Hofmann, Nico, and Philipp Kadelbach, and Stefan Kolditz. *Unsere Mütter, unsere Väter*. http://www.zdf.de/unsere-muetter-unsere-vaeter/unsere-muetter-unsere-vaeter-26223848.html

Kabalek, Kobi. "Spuren vergangener Geschichte/n: Die ‚NS-Zeit' in Interviews mit jungen Deutschen aus der ehemaligen DDR" [Traces of histories. The NS-Era in Interviews with young Germans from the former GDR]. In *Erinnerungen nach der Wende: Oral History und (post)sozialistische Gesellschaften* [Remembrance after Reunification. Oral History and (post)socialist Societies], edited by Julia Obertreis and Anke Stephan, 121–132. Essen: Klartext, 2009.

Klemperer, Viktor. *LTI. Notizbuch eines Philologen* [The Language of the Third Reich: A Philologist's Notebook]. Berlin: Aufbau Verlag, 1947.

Knoch, Habbo. "Völkische Verantwortung und nationale Kameradschaft. Geschlechterverhältnisse in der nationalsozialistischen Aufwertungsdiktatur" [Ethnic Responsibility and National Comradeship. Gender relations in the National Socialist Revaluation Dictatorship]. In *Macht und Gesellschaft. Männer und Frauen in der NS-Zeit. Eine Perspektive für ein künftiges* [Power and Society. Men and Women during the NS], edited by Archiv der Münchner

Arbeiterbewegung e.V. et al., 33–45. Munich: NS-Dokumentationszentrum, 2004.
Lanzman, Claude *Shoah,* France 1985.
Mass, Utz. "Sprache im Nationalsozialismus" [Language during National Socialism]. In *Sprache im Faschismus,* [Language during Fascism] edited by Konrad Ehlich, 162–197. Frankfurt am Main: Suhrkamp, 1995.
Massing, Almuth. "Auswirkungen anhaltender nationalsozialistischer Weltanschauungen in Familienschicksalen" [Consequences of ongoing National Socialist Believes on Family Destinies]. In *Das kollektive Schweigen. Nazivergangenheit und gebrochene Identität in der Psychotherapie* [Collective Silence. Nazi Past and scattered Identitites in Psychotherapy], edited by Barbara Heimannsberg and Christoph J. Schmidt, 55–67. Heidelberg: Roland Asanger Verlag, 1988.
Moses, Dirk A. *German Intellectuals and the Nazi Past.* Cambridge: Cambridge University Press, 2007.
Nägel, Verena. "Die Nation spricht? Ein kritischer Blick auf das Projekt Unsere Geschichte. Das Gedächtnis der Nation" [It's the Nation speaking? A critical review of the Project "Our History. The Memory of the Nation"]. In *Geschlecht und Erinnerung im digitalen Zeitalter—neue Perspektiven auf Zeitzeug-Innenarchive* [Gender and Remembrance in the Digital Age. New Perspectives on Testimonies and Archives], edited by Alina Bothe and Christina Brüning, 295–315. Berlin: Lit. Verlag, 2015.
Niven, Bill. *Facing the Nazi Past: United Germany and the Legacy of the Third Reich.* London: Routledge, 2002.
PRO ASYL. "Fakten, Zahlen und Argumente" [Facts, Data and Arguments]. http://www.proasyl.de/de/themen/zahlen-und-fakten/
Rommelspacher, Birgit. "Was ist eigentlich Rassismus?" [What is Racism?]. In *Rassismuskritik. Bd1 Rassismustheorie und -forschung* [Racism Criticism and Research]., edited by Claus Mecheril and Paul Melter, 25–38. Schwalbach im Taunus: Wochenschau Verlag, 2011.
Rosenthal, Gabriele, and Dan Bar-On. "A Biographical Case Study of a Victimizer's Daughter." *Journal of Narrative and Life History* 2, no. 2 (1992): 105–127.
Rosenthal, Gabriele. "National Socialism and Anti-Semitism in Intergenerational Dialogue." In *The Holocaust in Three Generations. Families of Victims and Perpetrators of the Nazi Regime,* edited by Gabriele Rosenthal, 305–314. Opladen: Budrich, 2010.
———. "Similarities and Differences in Family Dialogue." In *The Holocaust in Three Generations. Families of Victims and Perpetrators of the Nazi Regime,* edited by Gabriele Rosenthal, 13–19. Opladen: Budrich, 2010.
Schicksalsjahre. http://xt.zdf.de/schicksalsjahre/
Schneider, Christian, Cordelia Stillke, and Bernd Leineweber. *Das Erbe der Napola. Versuch einer Generationengeschichte des Nationalsozialismus* [The Napola Heritage. Essay on a History of Generations of National Socialism]. Hamburg: HIS, 1996.
Sichrovsky, Peter. *Schuldig geboren. Kinder aus Nazifamilien* [Born Guilty. Children from Nazi families]. Cologne: Kiepenheuer und Witsch, 1987.
Spielberg, Steven. *Schindler's List,* USA 1993.

Volmert, Johannes. "Politische Rhetorik des Nationalsozialismus" [Political Rhetoric of National Socialism]. In *Sprache im Faschismus*, edited by Konrad Ehlich, 137–161. Frankfurt am Main: Suhrkamp, 1995.

Völter, Bettina, and Michal Dasberg. "Similarities and Differences in Public Discourse about the Shoah in Israel and West and East Germany." In *The Holocaust in Three Generations. Families of Victims and Perpetrators of the Nazi Regime*, edited by Gabriele Rosenthal, 21–25. Opladen: Budrich, 2010.

Welzer, Harald. *Das kommunikative Gedächtnis. Eine Theorie der Erinnerung.* Munich: Beck, 2002.

Welzer, Harald, Sabine Moller, and Karoline Tschuggnall. *"Opa war kein Nazi." Nationalsozialismus und Holocaust im Familiengedächtnis* ['Grandpa wasn't a Nazi'. National Socialism and Holocaust in Family Memories]. Frankfurt am Main: Fischer, 2002.

Zimmermann, Moshe, and Miri Chanoch, and Danny Chanoch. *Pizza at Auschwitz*, Documentary, Israel 2008.

Zülsdorf-Kersting, Meik. *Sechzig Jahre danach. Jugendliche und der Holocaust. Eine Studie zur geschichtskulturellen Sozialisation* [60 years later. Adolescents and the Holocaust. A Study on historical and cultural Socialisation]. Berlin: Lit. Verlag, 2007.

Internet Sources

www.gedaechtnis-der-nation.de

PART FIVE

PERSONAL REFLECTIONS

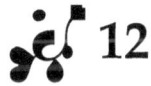 12

Always Moving Forward
Andrew Griffel

A friend, a noted Holocaust scholar, would often say to me, "Andy, you've been screwed by Jewish history twice." The first was being born in Poland in the midst of the Holocaust, hidden by a Polish Catholic family from my day of birth to the age of three, and, at age three, taken back by my Jewish parents. The second was my wife Anita being killed in a terrorist attack in 1985 at Ras Burka, Sinai. Anita saved our six-year-old daughter Tali from also being killed by shielding her from the terrorist's bullets with her own body.

Cracow, Poland 2002

One beautiful, sunny day in the charming medieval city of Cracow, I was running shoulder to shoulder with my daughter Tali, then twenty-three years old. I was very mindful that we were running through one of the oldest cities in Europe, its pre–World War II buildings still intact due to the Nazi's use of this beautiful city as the location for their Gestapo headquarters. My hair was as white as my T-shirt, Tali's long brown hair was flowing freely behind her head, and we both were basking in the cool breeze of the clear, crisp autumn morning. I was exhilarating in the father–daughter bond that Tali and I were sharing at that moment, very much aware that both of us were alive because our mothers, each in her own way, had miraculously saved our lives.

We had just left Cracow's Old City and were running through the streets of the once-Jewish district, Kazimierz, where my father's family had lived until they were deported to Auschwitz-Birkenau. Suddenly and most uncharacteristically for my usual reserved self, I heard myself repeatedly shouting out at the top of my lungs, "Damn you, Hitler, you didn't win! You didn't win!" There I was, running with Tali by my side through Cracow's once-Jewish district, feeling healthy in mind and body and very much alive!

Though my parents survived the Holocaust, my mother never stopped claiming, "Hitler won!" She stated emphatically that the never-ending, unbearable pain and anguish suffered by my parents and other survivors was clear evidence of Hitler's ultimate victory. Personally, I always shrugged off these assertions, busy trying to lead a productive life as a non-victim that included making aliyah to Israel and serving in the Israeli Army at the mature age of thirty-five.

Radom, Poland 1992

"Impossible," says the young Polish archivist at the Radom city registry. "You cannot be who you think you are. No Jewish baby born in Radom in October 1942 could have survived the liquidation of the ghetto. No Jewish baby could have lived undetected by the Nazis or their many Polish informers." The young archivist, in his mid thirties, was intelligent, very pleasant, and trying to be helpful. However, as far as he was concerned, I did not exist. It took me a long time and the help of Irena, a young Polish history student who was serving as my translator, to convince him. He took out the old records, amazingly still undamaged after the war: Yes, there was a leather factory called Elgold owned by Israel Werchaizer located at 9 Czarna Street, at that time on the remote outskirts of the city. Yes, Israel Werchaizer and his wife, Leah, gave birth to Pola Sura Perl and twelve other children. No, there was no record of Sura Perl marrying Henryk Griffel and no record of the birth of a son.

I asked the archivist to look in the Radom telephone directory for Jan and Alexandra Szczepanski, the names of my Polish parents during the first three years of my life. He chuckled and said that the name Szczepanski is one of the most common names in Poland—like Smith or Jones in America, added Irena, the history student translator. I cajoled and pleaded. He reluctantly agreed to go through the list of a dozen Szczepanskis in the Radom directory and started making calls. First on the list, no answer; second, never heard of the Elgold factory or Israel and Leah Werchaizer; and so on through about ten Szczepanskis. Then, on perhaps the eleventh call, a woman answered. Her parents Jan and Alexandra had died five years ago and she, Helena, was living in their apartment. Yes, her father was a chemical engineer in a leather factory—Elgold sounded familiar. Yes, her parents took in a Jewish newborn, born in secret at the factory to the factory owner's daughter. She herself was then two years old. The infant's name? Andrzej-Marek. When asked what happened to him, she replied that his biological parents came and took him away at the end of the war. Would she agree to meet this fifty-year-old American man who is claiming that he was born in secret in a leather factory in Radom in 1942 and immediately handed over to a young Polish couple, the husband having worked in a leather factory? "Come now quickly," she said to the archivist. "I have pictures. We will be able to check it out."

We rush over to the woman's apartment. As she opens the door, I instinctively reach into my coat pocket and take out an old, crumpled picture of me as a three-month-old baby that my mother had given me a long time ago. Helena, opening the door with one hand, was holding a baby picture in the other. We show each other the pictures: they are identical!

As we enter her apartment, I notice a familiar wooden crucifix on the wall. Helena tells me that her parents hung it in each apartment where they had lived. She has an envelope of pictures and shows me photos of me with my Jewish parents, photos sent to her mother a few years after they abducted me, and a letter from my father that I never knew he had written. The letter, very formal in tone, written after my Jewish parents had taken me back, thanked Helena's parents for taking such good care of me. It was dated September 30, 1945, in Cracow, where my parents had made a brief stopover while escaping with me from Poland into Czechoslovakia, occupied by the Allied Expeditionary Force.

Helena tells me that her parents took care of me at great risk to themselves. Harboring a Jewish child was punishable by death, but they did it because it was "the right thing to do" and because of her father's great affection for my grandfather, his employer, and my mother, who was the manager of the factory. Helena continues to tell me that her family—including me—had to move many times in order to protect themselves and me lest someone get suspicious and report them to the Nazis. Her parents did not baptize me although they themselves were devout Catholics. Now crying, Helena recalls that her parents loved me very much and that her mother had breastfed me so she has always considered herself my "milk-sister." They were distraught when I was taken away, never certain that I had survived, although her mother had had an abiding faith that I was still alive.

Helena is visibly shaken by the unexpected appearance of her long lost "milk-brother" about whom her parents had often spoken. She tells me that she never comes home to her apartment in the middle of the workday (she is a water engineer) but that today she had forgotten an important document for a meeting later that afternoon so she had returned to her apartment to get it. As she entered the apartment, the phone was ringing, and it was the young archivist calling on my behalf.

We then go to visit the graves of Alexandra and Jan where we light a memorial candle for each of them. Helena and I stand together in a moment of silence; my arm is wrapped around her.

I then continue to 9 Czarna Street. My grandfather's factory complex is still standing, fully intact, a beautiful and majestic red brick factory, four stories high with a huge chimney reaching into the sky. My heart is aching as I approach the place where I was born in secret fifty years ago. I try to imagine what it was like for my mother to give birth in her family's factory with Gestapo officers one floor down closely supervising the Polish workers preparing the leather used to make boots for Nazi soldiers. I make my way to the main office where I introduce myself to the director of the factory, a young mustached Polish man, born after the war, friendly but wary and a little suspicious. He tells me that the factory manufactures pollution control equipment that segregates industrial waste; at least my grandfather's factory has good karma, I say to myself. The young director, appointed just six months before, knows that the factory was built by Israel Werchaizer in the 1930s and that it was one of the most state-of-the-art leather factories in Poland at the time. I am proud of my grandfather. The director says that until 1967 the factory continued to operate as a leather tannery, and he points to the tall chimney originally built especially for the tanning process. In 1967 the Polish government decided to convert the factory into a manufacturer of pollution control equipment.

As he shows me around the complex, the director introduces me to a sixty-eight-year-old worker who, he says, knows the whole story of my birth. The worker tells me that he was a teenager in 1942 and lived in a small village not far from the factory. He remembers the story vividly: "it is legendary," he says. The Nazis had taken over the leather factory, needing the leather to make boots for their soldiers. "A young Jewish woman was smuggled into the factory from the ghetto about two miles away. She gave birth, and then she and the baby disappeared. How was it," he asks rhetorically, "that the two hundred or so Polish workers laboring in the factory under Nazi scrutiny did not hand her and the baby over to the Nazis? Why instead did they stand guard and protect her during the ordeal? It was a miracle," says the old worker, "that not one worker nor any of the Poles living in the village near the factory betrayed her. Your grandfather was a fair and decent man and treated everyone with respect, no matter who they were," exclaims the sixty-eight-year-old worker. "Everyone loved him and his daughter, your mother, their Jewish employers."

The worker cannot believe that I—that baby born in the factory under such dire circumstances—am standing here before him. He has to touch me, he says. He leads me about thirty yards away to where my grandfather's house once stood. It was a huge house, he tells me, big enough for my grandfather's large family with thirteen children. He also shows me where the stables once stood with stalls for many horses. All these buildings had been burned down. "He was a very pious man," says the worker about my grandfather. "Very successful, very wealthy, very generous, and charitable."

He then speaks of the many atrocities he witnessed as a young man, particularly when the Gestapo dragged my grandfather and his sons into the factory courtyard and shot each one in the head, including one son who was crippled and confined to a wheelchair. There are tears in his eyes as he says he will never forget this. I recall that my mother gave testimony about witnessing this murder of her father and brothers.

At the time that I was conceived, January 1942, my mother, Sura Perl Werchaizer Griffel, and father, Henryk Griffel, were imprisoned in the Radom Ghetto. Radom was, at the time, an important industrial center located in central Poland about sixty miles south of Warsaw. The Nazis occupied Radom in September 1939 and began liquidating the ghetto and transporting its Jewish inhabitants to concentration camps in August 1942.

My father came from a very religious, wealthy, and aristocratic Jewish family for whom preserving the family's bloodline was extremely important and having a son was critical. This desire seemed to override all dangers of bringing a Jewish baby into the world during the darkest days of the Holocaust. The dangers by the time of my conception were unimaginable; my parents became more and more traumatized each day from their ghetto imprisonment, and my mother's mind and body absorbed all the terror she was experiencing, making her womb a very unsafe and unhealthy place for a fetus.

Jewish law clearly states that a law does not have to be followed if one's life is in danger. Having an abortion during that time would surely have been permitted since my mother's pregnancy endangered not one but two lives—hers and mine. I have always wondered why my parents decided to have a child in the midst of the Holocaust. Whenever I asked my mother how they could have allowed themselves to make a baby during that cataclysmic time, her response was that I was an affirmation of life at a time of destruction. There are many conflicting theories and opinions as to whether an embryo is considered a living being, and there is really no way to know what it must have been like to grow inside the womb of a mother besieged by constant terror, knowing that the Nazis were stabbing pregnant women in their stomach and murdering newborn babies. Neither years of therapy nor regressive hypnosis have helped me remember what I may have experienced during those nine months. Today, psychologists and neuroscientists would say that, as a fetus, I absorbed all the traumas that my mother experienced during her pregnancy.

My father was very exacting about following the letter of Jewish law, even when living in the Radom Ghetto. After my mother became pregnant, he was confronted with a dilemma: If the fetus were a boy, should my father find a way to circumcise his infant son amid the annihilation happening around them? The Nazis were examining boys' penises to see if they had been circumcised; discovery meant instant death. My father decided to ask the Belzer Rebbe, one of the most revered rabbis in Poland. He managed to smuggle a small piece of paper with his *sheilah* (official religious query) written in Yiddish to the Belzer Rebbe who was in hiding in another city: "If the newborn baby is a boy, do we circumcise him when he is eight days old?" The Rebbe's cryptic official *teshuvah* (response), likewise scrawled in Yiddish on a very small, crumpled and torn piece of paper and smuggled to my father from his hiding place said, "Wait until the *geulah* [salvation] to circumcise him." My father believed that the Belzer Rebbe's *teshuvah* was a genuine *nevuah* (a holy prophecy): the baby will be a boy, all three of us will survive the Holocaust, and afterward he will circumcise me. My father carried the Belzer Rebbe's *teshuvah* in his pocket until his dying day.

September 1945

The Russian army is sweeping west into Poland. It is approaching the outskirts of Radom, advancing rapidly toward the city. My Jewish parents, who have been hiding in the basement of a Polish family in Warsaw since Polish partisans smuggled them to there two years earlier, decide to risk going back to Radom to reclaim their now three-year-old son. Many years later, my mother told me that I immediately ran to her the first time I saw her when they came to take me back. My mother claimed that I had known instinctively that she was my *real* mother. The biological blood tie was overpowering, she asserted.

My Jewish parents are afraid that my Polish parents might change their minds at the last minute about giving me back to them. A Jewish neighbor, also a recent survivor, alerts my mother that she saw my Polish mother putting on my coat and warns my Jewish mother that my Polish parents are planning to run away with me. My Jewish mother told me, again many years later, that the neighbor's warning had confirmed their worst fears. She and my father had to act quickly to take me away from my Polish parents. Later she also told me that Alexandra, my Polish mother, had not wanted to give me back. The Jewish neighbor diverts Alexandra's attention for a moment, and my Jewish mother pulls me outside where my Jewish father is waiting with a horse and cart. I have been kidnapped! Soon after, my Jewish mother bumps into my Polish mother in the street. My Polish mother tells my Jewish mother, "If I had known you were going to do this, neither of us would have had him." My Jewish mother saw this as Solomonic proof that my Polish mother did not really care about me.

The following day we hide in the back of a truck full of empty oil barrels and make our way 160 miles south to Cracow and then 250 miles west into Allied-occupied Prague. Eventually we make our way to the Stuttgart Displaced Persons (DP) camp, also under the jurisdiction of the victorious Allied Expeditionary Force.

Two Mothers

Who was my mother? From the first day of my life my Polish parents raised me as if I were their own child. My Jewish parents, my biological parents, were total strangers to me when they returned to reclaim me. But I grew up believing my Jewish mother's story that the moment I saw her I knew her as my true mother and I ran to her and held on to her. There is nothing stronger than the biological blood bond between mother and child, said my Jewish mother, and I accepted this obvious law of nature. When I visited Poland in the hope of recapturing those first three years, I learned from my milk-sister, Helena, that our mother, Alexandra, had loved me very much and that she never fully recovered from losing me.

Hela Spus, the woman who, together with her husband, had hidden my parents in Warsaw, told me a completely different story when I visited her in Gdansk in 1995. Hela would periodically travel to Radom to "check up on me" and, on one of her visits, my Polish parents had given her the photo of me at three months that I later showed Helena when we met in 1992. My mother had written Hela a letter from Cracow a few days after my parents had reclaimed me, and she had told Hela that I had adamantly refused to go with them. It seems, Hela continued, that I had been desperately clinging to my Polish mother and that Alexandra had been forced to push me away toward my Jewish mother. Hela's version of my mother's Solomonic story was that Alexandra had only been stating the obvious that if she had not taken me in at birth and raised me as her own child, the Nazis would certainly have killed me.

Thus, only fifty years later, did I learn the truth: that when my Jewish parents suddenly appeared after three years, I refused to go with them. My Jewish biological parents were strangers to me when they came to get me and remained strangers to me afterward. They did not tell me what was happening at the time. There were no explanations, no feelings expressed, no crying out. So for fifty years those first three years, such important and formative years, had remained a total mystery to me. It was almost as if I had been born in 1945.

My father was not a Zionist. He was grateful to the United States for taking us in after the Holocaust and believed that this was our new home, our country, where we belonged. I was raised in a very orthodox Hasidic home yet educated in fundamentalist, *mitnagdim* [who were opponents of the Hasidic way] yeshivas—two vastly different approaches to Judaism. I also attended the Conservative Movement's Camp Ramah for many years that added yet another dimension, at times conflicting, to my Jewish identity. When I started college I managed to throw off what I considered the heavy yoke of compulsory religious observance that had been forced on me at home and in the yeshivas my father had made me attend. However, I used my knowledge of the Bible and Talmud to teach at afternoon religious schools, which helped me pay my way through college and law school. This inadvertently kept me connected to my Jewish heritage, as did my American born roommates in college who all had a strong sense of their own Jewishness, grounded in the Conservative Movement of the Jewish Theological Seminary.

Therapists have told me that my real trauma began at the age of three when my Jewish parents, having survived the Holocaust, returned to Radom and abruptly took me away from my Polish parents, the only parents I had ever known. My parents did not talk about what we had experienced; we lived our lives in an uneasy silence. Yet, internally and unconsciously, I experienced myself through the mirror image of how my parents were silently experiencing themselves: as victims. This was before post-traumatic stress disorder (PTSD) became a recognized psychological condition and before the neurobiological phenomenon of mirror neurons was discovered, showing how we internalize the emotions of others, especially our parents.

In addition, my parents did not talk about what had happened to them, and I was raised in near denial and total silence—not only about my first three years, but also about the aftermath of the trauma that we all endured as Holocaust survivors. And, my father seemed determined to squeeze every drop of Christianity out of me: first, having me circumcised at the age of five, then sending me to Orthodox fundamentalist yeshivas, and, finally, compelling me to abide by very strict Orthodox observances at home. I grew up fearing that God would strike me down for any transgressions, however minor.

Jerusalem 1968–1984

After graduating from law school in June 1968, I postponed launching my legal career as a civil rights lawyer in Washington, DC in order to spend a year in Israel. I felt privileged to be living at that time in history when Israel was a reality, particularly after so many millions of Jews, including most members of both sides of my family, had perished in the Holocaust and after the threat to Israel's existence in the 1967 Six-Day War. It seemed somehow natural, if not inevitable, that I would become involved in Israel's ongoing task of nation building during this exciting and promising time in Jewish history.

Anita and I met in Jerusalem in the late summer of 1968, married the following year in Jerusalem and, after living in New York for the next two years to help my mother and sister relocate after my father died, we made aliyah at the end of 1971. Anita started her doctoral studies at Hebrew University, and I worked as a lawyer and publisher. In retrospect, it seemed settling in Israel became part of my almost obsessive effort to purge myself of the stigma of victimhood under which I had grown up when living with my Holocaust traumatized parents. It was my singular act of defiance and an attempt to discover and demonstrate my own strength, the most dramatic expression of which was becoming an Israeli soldier at the age of thirty-five. I learned to shoot an M-16 rifle and an Uzi machine gun, crawl in full army gear through mud in the pouring rain, and stand guard for ten hours straight in total isolation in the middle of the barren Sinai Desert. I eventually became a military judge on a special appeals tribunal set up by the Israeli Supreme Court to adjudicate complaints from Palestinians in the West Bank against arbitrary rulings and treatment. Serving in the Israeli Army was the culmination of my long journey to escape from the feelings of victimhood my parents had instilled in me from the day they took me back from the Polish family who had raised me for the first three years of my life. Having been educated in the heroic myths of Jewish history, I was especially thrilled to spend part of my basic training in Modiin, home of the heroic Maccabees.

Washington, DC, 1984–1985

In mid-1984, I was offered a job I could not refuse and moved back to the United States to become the director of the international trade division of the prestigious economic consulting firm Robert R. Nathan Associates in Washington, DC. Anita and Tali stayed in Israel, and I visited them often. Then, a few minutes after midnight on October 6, 1985, my birthday, I was awakened by a phone call that would change my life forever. A friend, calling me from Jerusalem, had just heard on the early morning Israeli news that Anita and six other Israelis had been shot and killed by an Egyptian soldier at a campsite in Sinai on a beach off the Gulf of Aqaba called Ras Burka. There was no word whether our daughter Tali, who had been with Anita, had also been killed. As I struggled to make the mental shift from total shock to crisis-action mode, knowing I had to get myself to Israel immediately, I kept calling Israel trying desperately to find out whether Tali was still alive.

I was the first person off the plane at Ben-Gurion Airport, the first through customs, and, running quickly, the first to get to the waiting area outside. There was Tali, in the arms of a close friend, a big smile radiating across her face on seeing me. When I saw her, something immediately clicked deep inside me, a strong feeling, a primal instinct perhaps, that I would find the wisdom and strength to help my daughter overcome the horror that she had just experienced.

2008–2014

To this very day, I do not how I managed to help Tali deal with what she experienced. I do not know where I found the inner strength and sense of certainty that I actually knew what I was doing. Where did this confidence come from? In no other spheres of life had I ever experienced such certainty. From the moment I knew that Tali had survived the Ras Burka massacre, I vowed to do everything in my power to ensure that she would never perceive herself as a victim.

During the years that I was raising Tali as a single parent, I believed that my own past had prepared me for this challenge—all I had gone though as a hidden child and as a child survivor of the Holocaust and then having been raised from the age of three by my Jewish parents who, as survivors, were themselves severely traumatized by their own Holocaust experiences.

Most importantly, I was determined that what happened to me starting at age three would not happen to her: the total suppression of my thoughts and feelings by my parents. I knew what shutting down did to one's psyche and spirit and how difficult, if not impossible, it is to overcome the consequences of such pervasive silence. I would often think of the telling line "silence like a cancer grows" in the Simon and Garfunkel song "The Sound of Silence." In some almost mystical way the demons that I lived with for so many years—PTSD in today's lexicon—gave me the capacity to help Tali with her own trauma. I stayed focused and committed to ensuring, as much as I could, that Tali would discover and draw on her own inner strengths to lead a successful and fulfilling life on her own terms.

I felt an exhilarating sense of joy when I saw Tali holding her one-day-old baby in the hospital maternity ward. Then, unexpectedly, I was bombarded by a succession of vivid images: I imagined my mother secretly giving birth to me in the attic of her father's leather factory while Nazis were supervising the Polish workers below; I envisioned Alexandra, my Polish foster mother, holding me just hours after I was born; then I remembered Anita embracing Tali close to her body when we saw her for the first time several days after she was born.

Today, Tali lives in Israel where she was born, happily married to a wonderful man, enjoying being a mother to three beautiful children, and engaged in professional work of her own choosing. Raising Tali, I drew constructively on my own trauma as a Holocaust child survivor to ensure, as much as possible, that she would overcome her trauma and reach this triumphant point in her life. Since then, I have been struggling with a formidable new challenge: trying to integrate the various pieces of my diverse and, at times, paradoxical experiences so I can move on to the next stage of my journey in a fulfilling and life-affirming way.

Author

Andrew Griffel has extensive experience as an international lawyer, strategic policy advisor and organizational consultant to multi-national corporations, financial institutions and Bi-national R & D Foundations and was the CEO of an international development agency working in Africa, Latin America, Asia and The Former Soviet Union. For many years he worked to foster economic cooperation between Jews and Palestinians within Israel as well as in the West Bank and Gaza. While living in Israel, he served as a Military Judge in the Israeli Army. He currently advises companies on business-nonprofit partnerships, institution building and restructuring, board leadership training and corporate responsibility.

 # Index

abandonment, 22, 24–5, 64, 73, 208, 214,
Adin, Jurek, 54
adjustment and resilience (Rachel and Rosa), 180–82
Agamben, Giorgio, 122
age, 17–26, 28, 49–52, 62, 64, 66, 68–70, 72, 74, 84, 89, 102, 105, 111, 123–26, 128, 129, 130–133, 135–37, 138, 139, 140, 142–43, 150, 154–57, 160, 163, 171, 173, 175–76, 187, 189, 191, 193, 200–1, 204, 209, 216–18, 227, 231–32, 249–50, 256–58
Aktion, 52
American Gathering of Jewish Holocaust Survivors (Philadelphia), 2
anti-Semitism, 83–84, 125, 133–34, 144, 155, 158, 161, 164–65, 203, 225, 237
   1968 campaign, Poland, 184
   Poland, during the war, 188, 192–93
   prewar Poland, 189, 193, 195
anxiety, 16–17, 20–23, 25, 28, 92, 182, 200–1, 203
   annihilation anxiety, 182
   mutilation anxiety, 21, 23–24
   separation, 21, 25
   shame anxiety, 21, 23–24
attachment, 16–18, 24, 27, 29–30, 126, 134, 176, 180–81, 194, 203, 218, 238
attitudes
   towards perpetrators, 150, 153, 155–56, 158–59, 161, 163–65
   towards Polish society, 45

Auerbach, Rachel, 4, 46
Avengers, the, 150–51

Balta (Transnistria), 126–27
Barnet, Rozalia, 51
Bauer, Yehuda, 7
Becker, David, 202
Benz, Wolfgang, 234
Berger, Alan, 132
boycotts, 153, 156–57, 159, 163
Bram, Milka, 52
Bruner, Jerome, 8
Bucci, Wilma, 29
Bukovina, 125, 139, 143
boycotts, 153, 155, 157, 159, 163
bystanders, 195, 202, 217–19, 232

Caruth, Cathy, 88, 128
case studies (Rachel and Rosa), 175–80
CDR (Child Development Research), 25, 19–20, 170, 183
   CDR *Code Book*, 19–20, 22, 26, 28, 172
central theme, 175
child bearing, 17
children
   hidden. *See* hiding
   war children, definition, 1, 5
child survivors of the Holocaust, 1–4, 6, 15–17, 23, 49–50, 56–57, 62–63, 68–70, 73–74, 83, 86, 102, 107, 111, 115, 122–25, 129, 132, 135, 137, 138, 139, 142, 143, 152–55, 162–65, 202, 219, 259
   definition, 1, 5
Christensen, Pia, 45

Central Jewish Historical Commission (CJHC), 7, 43, 45–46, 55
coding child survivor narratives, 172
cognitive development, 17, 43, 48–49, 129, 143
Cohen, Boaz, 44–45, 123
compensation, 2
content analysis, narrative, 7, 16, 26, 28, 225
content (variable), 16, 28
Czechoslovakia, 154, 157–58, 162, 251
Częstochowa, 195
Czernowitz, 125

Demjanjuk, Ivan, 151
deportation, 48–52, 64, 72, 125, 140, 142, 233, 249
depression, 16, 17, 20–26, 28, 68, 129, 139, 203, 219
  self-accusation, 22–24
  separation, 25
diaries, 44
Din assassins, 151
displaced persons, 201, 255
dissociation, 128, 138
Durst, Nathan, 123, 138
Dwork, Debórah, 2, 132, 136

education, National Socialist, 204–5, 215, 218, 225
Eliach, Yaffe, 2, 43
emigration, 66, 194–95
encampment, 15
Engel, Susan, 47–48
Erős, Ferenc, 83, 90

Families, family, 53, 63, 124. *See also* parents, parenting
  abuse within, 129
  biological, 65, 123–27, 131, 134–36, 142, 144, 250, 255–56, 258–59
  dysfunctional, 73–74, 125–26, 129–30, 135–37, 139, 144, 208–210
  foster, 64–67, 72, 75, 123, 125–26, 131–36, 142, 250–51, 254–57, 259
  losses, 160
  new, 72
  new siblings, 72
  reconstituted, 62–76, 135–36
  reunions, 64–67, 75, 113, 249, 254
Family-of-origin relationships, 62–76, 87, 133, 150, 155, 163–65, 200, 202, 205, 209–10, 212, 214, 216–18, 225–26, 229–30, 234
Fogelman, Eva, 3, 9, 85, 132
France, 154, 160–61
Frank, Hans, 226–27
Frank, Niklas, 226–31, 239
Freitag, Pearl, 54
Freud, Sigmund, 142–43
Frymet, Dwojra, 52
Furnschein, Syda, 54

Gedächtnis der Nation [Memory of the Nation], 234
gender, 154–55, 205, 217, 224, 226, 228, 232, 236, 239
generation, 217–18, 225, 227, 230–34
genocide, 15, 150, 152, 163–64
Germans, 114, 150–52, 156–62, 202, 226, 229, 232–34, 238
  children, 200
Germany, 2, 123, 151–53, 155–58, 160, 210
  East, 226
  West, 226–27, 231
ghettos
  children escaping from, 190, 193–94
  Częstochowa, 195
  deportations from, 196
  Kraków (Cracow), 227
  Litzmannstadt (Łódź), 188, 191
  Moghilev, 136–39, 142
  Polish perception of, 187, 189–91
  Radom, 250, 253, 254
  Warsaw, 189–90, 193
Gottschalk-Gleser (Scales), 28

Index • 263

grief, 17, 73
Grüss, Noe, 47
guilt, shame, 3, 5, 22, 83, 131, 135, 171, 175
　German, 202–3, 210–11, 217–18, 224, 226, 229–30, 234–35
Gushee, David, 195

Hamburg Firestorm Project, 204
Hartman, Geoffrey, 57
Hartup, Willard, 48
hatred, hate, 152–53, 155, 159–61, 163–65
Hidden Child Foundation, 43
hidden children, 2, 17, 27, 3, 54, 64, 73, 131–35, 193, 249, 258
　Jewish identity, 193–94
　postwar Poland, 194
　wartime fate, 187, 193
hiding, 1, 15, 18, 25–26, 50–51, 64–65, 68–69, 71–72, 125, 127–28, 132–34, 136, 145n5, 155, 157–60, 173, 176, 182, 193, 254–55
Hirsch, Marianne, 137
Hochberg-Marianska, Maria, 47
Hochspiegel, Sondek, 51
Hoffman, Halina, 50
Hoffman, Jerzy, 50, 52
Holland; 154, 157
Holocaust, 1–4, 6–8, 10n3, 15–16, 22–25, 27, 43–44, 63, 73, 75, 82–85, 88, 90–91, 92nn5–6, 99, 100–6, 108–111, 113–14, 116–17, 122–27, 129, 130–32, 134–42, 144, 170, 174, 179–80, 189–90, 192, 195, 224, 226, 249–54
　denial of, 239
Horváth, Rita, 45, 123
humiliation, 21, 23, 237
Hungary, 6, 81–93, 93n6, 105, 154, 156

identity, 17, 81–82, 89, 106, 109, 123–24, 129, 132–33, 135, 137, 143–44, 193–94, 216, 256
inadequacy, 21, 217

information, gathering, 51–52, 56
intergenerational transmission, 16, 26, 126, 136, 232
International Study of Organized Persecution of Children (ISOPC), 2, 15–16, 19, 170–72
　Code Book, 172
intolerance, 150, 153, 155, 163–65
interviews, 6, 7, 8, 15
　narrative content analysis, 16, 18, 23
　qualitative, 6, 7, 8, 15, 16
　quantitative, 15, 16
Israel, 129, 157, 161, 194–95, 257–59

James, Allison, 45
Jewish Central Historical Commission, 45

Kahn, Charlotte, 85
Kangisser-Cohen, Sharon, 9, 187
Kaplan, Ann E., 128
Katowice, 126, 135
Keningsberg, Edward, 50, 53
Kessler, Zofia, 55
Kestenberg Archive of Testimony of Child Holocaust Survivors, 2, 4–6, 8, 43, 57, 63, 86–87, 100–1, 104–5, 115–17, 124–26, 152–53, 164–65, 187–89, 192, 196, 200, 224–25, 233–34, 239
　Hungarian interviews, 81–93
Kestenberg, Judith, 2, 17, 43, 47, 85, 105–7, 129–30, 138, 141, 153, 163, 171, 225, 227, 229–31, 239
Kestenberg, Milton, 2, 141, 153, 171, 225
Kindertransport, 65, 173
Klarsfeld, Serge, 151
Kovner, Abba, 150–51
Kraft, Robert, 46–47

Langer, Lawrence, 192
Lehrer, Erica, 192–93
Levi, Primo, 122
Likert-scale, 19–20, 27

Lodz (Łódź),188, 190–91. *See also* Litzmannstadt
Lvov, 194

Majzlisz, Hieronim, 54
Maskit, 29
Matecka, Karolina, 49–50
maternal adjustment, 7, 22, 25, 29
memory, 1, 2, 4, 6–8, 20–25, 28–29, 44, 46, 48, 54, 56–57, 67–70, 74–76, 84, 99–117, 119n29, 123–29, 131–43, 157, 171, 173, 175–77, 180, 187, 193, 200, 202, 212, 215–16, 233, 235, 239
  autobiographical, 4, 15
  body, 107–8, 119n29
  cognitive, 131, 135, 136, 143
  core, 46–47
  culture of, 102–4, 201, 202, 218
  declarative, 18
  evoked, 8, 18, 28, 105, 110, 112
  kinesthetic, 3, 18
  multidirectional, 115, 140–41
  narrative, 47, 57, 99, 137, 139
  nonverbal, 107, 126, 171
  olfactory, 18
  postwar, 105
  performative, 99, 102
  postmemory, 109, 126–27, 135–38
  prewar, 17–18, 20–25, 28, 47, 53, 105, 137
  procedural, 15, 18
  received, 105–6, 112
  reconstructed, 110
  relational, 53–54
  screen memory, 138–39, 141–43, 215
  sensory, 28
  shame-memory, 24
  somatic, 46, 126–28, 131, 135, 138, 143
  visual, 142–43
Mészáros, Judit, 83
Michlic, Joanna, 45, 55, 126, 189
mixed-method (research design), 15, 26, 29

Moghilev (Transnistria), 136–39, 142
Müller, Beate, 45, 46, 54, 123

narrative content analysis; *See* content analysis
National Socialism, effects of, 200–7, 210, 212, 214, 216, 218–19, 224–25, 233–34
Nazis, 43, 114, 126, 154–56, 158–59, 162, 203, 216, 224, 228, 232, 251–55
  ideology, 226, 232, 236–37
Nestbeschmutzer, 226–28
Netherlands; *See* Holland
nonverbal, 23, 28–29, 50, 107, 126, 171

Ofer, Dalia, 8, 10
Oneg Shabbat; *See* Ringelblum Archive, 44
oral history, 4
organized child persecution, 16
outcome, 16, 18, 25, 102, 136

parenting, 6, 17, 20–25, 29, 49, 52, 73–74, 174, 200, 202, 215, 229
  postwar, 20–23, 25, 27, 74–76, 174
parents, 2–3, 5–7, 16–17, 21–23, 49–50, 52–57, 62–70, 72–76, 83, 86, 103–4, 106–7, 109, 111–115, 124–26, 130–31, 134, 136–38, 140, 143, 155–57, 160–61, 234, 250–51, 253–59. *See also* families
  abusive, 73–74
  biological, 26, 64, 65, 67, 69–73, 124–25, 133–34, 174, 250, 255–56
  competence, 7, 20, 22–23, 27, 29, 53
  dead, 51, 54, 68–69, 130, 160, 190
  foster parents, 21, 26, 64, 72, 134, 136, 174, 178, 250–51, 254–56
  Nazi perpetrators, 5–6, 200, 202–3, 205–7, 210–11, 214–219, 225–27, 229–30, 232, 238
  new parents, stepparents, 67–70, 72, 76
paternal adjustment, 20

perpetrators, 230, 232, 238
  children of, 22–27, 231, 238–39
perpetrator-victim inversion, 231, 233–35, 238–39
persecution, 1, 2, 4–5, 9, 15–17, 19–24, 26, 43, 47, 82, 107, 124, 130, 138, 145n6, 155–56, 163–64, 170–72, 174–75, 177, 187–90, 192, 202
  state-sponsored, 15
persecutory trauma, 23, 26
Pető, Katalin, 90
Poland, 43, 44–45, 55, 113–14, 123–26, 132, 134–35, 143, 154–55, 157, 159, 161, 227
  Poles, 154, 159–61, 189–96, 227, 230, 249, 251, 254, 255
Polenjugendverwahrlager der Sicherheitspolizei in Litzmannstadt, 188
Polish-Jewish relations
  prewar Poland, 189, 192–93
  postwar Poland, 191–95
Portelli, Alessandro, 8
post-traumatic stress disorder (PTSD), 5–6, 16, 17, 102, 201, 203, 215, 259
postwar adjustment
  immediate, 174, 208
  long-term, 174–75, 233, 234
postwar reality, 1, 6, 17, 20–22, 47, 62–63, 66, 68–69, 73, 75, 122–23, 134–35, 140, 208, 209–10, 236
Poznań, 189
prewar background variables, 172–73
process, variable, 16, 30
Psychiatric Content Analysis and Diagnosis (PCAD), 19–20, 28
psychological collapse, 52, 134
psychological processing, 15
psychological symptoms, 20–23, 64, 68, 203, 206, 217. *See also:* depression, anxiety

quality of life, 17, 20–22, 28, 175
Quindeau, Ilka, 85

reactions, 1, 44, 56, 65, 85, 196, 227–28
  adults', 29, 50, 52–53, 209–210, 226, 230
  emotional, 50, 52, 55, 114, 126, 156, 200, 210, 217
  recurrent theme, 175
referential activity, 29
reflective functioning, 24, 29
relational world, 17–18, 48
religious affiliation, religiosity, 47, 150, 154, 159, 161, 163–65, 256
reparations, 2
repercussions, 5, 21, 200, 230
resilience, 6, 17, 23, 62, 75, 170–82, 203, 206, 258
respondent demographics, 172
revenge, 6, 150–56, 161, 163–65
  concrete, 150
  fantasizing about revenge, 162–65
  symbolic revenge, 151–55, 163–65
revisionism, historical, 226–27, 234
Riker, Jerome; *See* International Study of Organized Persecution of Children
Ringelblum Archive (Oneg Shabbat), 44
Romania, 124–25, 139, 143
Rubin, Zick, 48
rupture, 16, 62–63, 75

Scheeringa, H. S., 49, 57
secrets, 68–70
secondary silencing, 193–94
Sendler, Irena, 187
sensorimotor, 15, 119n29
separation, 22, 25, 27, 30, 54–55, 64–67, 71, 112, 126, 132, 135–36, 145, 174, 180, 203
Shoah. *See* Holocaust
siblings, 52–53, 67, 69, 76, 111, 130, 132, 155, 160, 172, 177, 207, 236
  new siblings, 67, 72
Siekerka, Wladyslaw, 53
Steiner, Mania, 50
Steinlauf, Michael, 196

suicide, threatened, 209–10
surrogate figure, 17

testimonies, 43–45, 69, 82, 84–85, 102, 115–17, 123–26, 134, 137, 231, 239, 253. *See also* Kestenberg Archive
Transnistria, 125, 126, 138, 140
transposition, 106–108, 111–12
  defined, 106
trauma, 1, 4–6, 15–17, 22, 43, 67–68, 75, 83–85, 87–88, 90, 102–3, 112–13, 124, 128, 135–36, 139, 141, 201–7, 210, 213, 215–19, 225, 230, 254, 256–59
  transposition of, 181
  trauma psychology, 15

Ukrainians, 154, 159, 161
unmentalized states, 23, 26

Vilna Ghetto, 150
Virág, Teréz, 81, 84

Vikár, György, 82–83
Vygotsky, Lev, 56

War Child Project, 200, 207, 212
war children, 201
  German, 200–3, 206–7, 214–18, 224
war, effects on children, 49, 200, 202–3, 207–8, 210–13, 217
  Soviet children, 49
wartime experiences, 74–75, 173, 203, 205, 207–18, 234
Warsaw, 47, 126, 131–33, 189–91, 194
Warsaw Ghetto uprising, 191
Weinman, Henryk, 55
Weinreb, Zygmunt, 51
Wiesenthal, Simon, 151
World Federation of Jewish Holocaust Child Survivors, 43

Yad Vashem, 4, 7

Zeanah, C. H., 49, 57

www.ingramcontent.com/pod-product-compliance
Lightning Source LLC
Chambersburg PA
CBHW072148100526
44589CB00015B/2133